UNBELIEF:
THE DEADLY SIN

Taking Back what the Enemy Has Stolen

Theresa Ann Reyna

WESTBOW
PRESS

A DIVISION OF THOMAS NELSON

WestBow Press books may be ordered through booksellers or by contacting:

WestBow Press
A Division of Thomas Nelson
1663 Liberty Drive
Bloomington, IN 47403
www.westbowpress.com
1-(866) 928-1240

ISBN: 978-1-4497-5231-6 (sc)
ISBN: 978-1-4497-5232-3 (hc)
ISBN: 978-1-4497-5230-9 (e)

Library of Congress Control Number: 2012908400

Printed in the United States of America

WestBow Press rev. date: 5/21/2012

DEDICATION

ALL GLORY GOES TO my Lord and Savior, Jesus Christ—the *Author* and *Finisher* of our faith. I dedicate this book to You, Lord Jesus. May this book bring You the glory and honor that You deserve.

To

The *Remnant*—the *Joshua Generation* that God is preparing in the wilderness. You are about to come forth out of the desert to shake and rock the nations of this world with mighty signs and wonders. Be strong in the Lord and in the power of His might in this final hour. Take hold of your Inheritance in Christ, and go forth and take your "promised land"—for the glory of His name!

To

My husband Ron, my children: April, Sarah, and James, and to my grandchildren: Alicia, Amber, Anabel, Nathaniel, Savannah, and my spiritual granddaughter, Destiny. You have been called with a holy calling. May you realize and take hold of your calling and destiny in Christ. You are part of the *Gideon army* that the Lord is raising up. His promises are for *you*! Take back what the enemy has stolen from you! I bless you in the name of Jesus!

CONTENTS

INTRODUCTION

RECENTLY, AS I PONDERED on the sin of unbelief and its effect on us, the Lord spoke the word "insidious" to me. Although I'd heard this word before, I couldn't remember its meaning. According to the <u>American Heritage Dictionary</u>, *insidious* means: "Working or spreading harmfully in a subtle or stealthy manner. Intended to entrap; wily; treacherous. Sly; beguiling. Lying in wait for."

Unbelief has had a devastating effect, not only in my life, but in the lives of many of God's children. The Church has been bound by this sin for centuries, but the Lord is about to come with one last shaking, to remove this sin from the hearts of His people. The Bible says:

> ...whose voice then shook the earth; but now He has promised, saying, "Yet once more I shake not only the earth, but also heaven." Now this, "Yet once more," indicates the removal of those things that are being shaken, as of things that are made, that the things which cannot be shaken may remain.
> -Hebrews 12:26-27

In order to bring forth His kingdom in power and might to this generation, the Church will be shaken up in this final hour like she has never before experienced. Everything that is not of God will fall to the ground: the works of the flesh, man-made ministries, idolatry, and everything that is built on sand. We will be *shaken* as all sin and unbelief is exposed in our lives. God is about to come with a purifying fire so hot that we will either surrender our sin and lives completely to Christ, or we will run away in fear and lose our inheritance in Christ; the choice will be ours. There is no *middle ground*, no *grey area* in the kingdom of God, and this is the hour when all compromise and unbelief in our hearts will be exposed.

This sin of unbelief is not only deadly, but it is a *subtle* sin. The enemy of our souls does not usually come to us in obvious ways, but as a snake—quietly—waiting to entrap us when we least expect it. He is sly and treacherous, and he desires not only entrap us with this sin, but to *destroy* us. As we study the root beginning of this sin, we will see not only how this sin entered in, but also how many are still bound today. Isaiah 29:13-14 says:

> Therefore the Lord said: "Inasmuch as these people draw near with their mouths and honor Me with their lips, but they have removed their hearts far from Me, and their fear toward Me is taught by the commandment of men, therefore, behold, I will again do a marvelous work among this people, a marvelous work and a wonder…

Unbelief is a heart issue, and the day of exposure and judgment is coming soon; it will begin in the Body of Christ. Not only will the Lord expose the deep, hidden unbelief that is in our hearts, but the motives and intents buried in our hearts will also be revealed as the probing eyes of Jesus look deep into our souls. No more will the Lord tolerate a lukewarm, compromising Church, where the fear of Him has been greatly quenched because of the "doctrines of men," and not the truth of His Word. God desires a burning, red-hot, passionate relationship with His people, and He will do whatever it takes to bring us back to His heart of love. God is about to do a marvelous work in the midst of His people, and many, many souls will run back to Him in deep repentance.

Many in the Church have been wandering in the desert of doubt and fear, but the Lord is saying: "You have dwelt long enough at this mountain. Turn and take your journey…" (Deut. 1:6-7). For too long the Church has been stagnant in her faith journey, and the Lord is telling us to press forward for all that He has promised to give us in His Word. No more will He tolerate our fears, unbelief, and blatant sins. He is drawing a line of demarcation between the holy and the profane. God's purifying fires will come and expose those who are merely hearers of His Word, and not obedient *doers* of His commands.

God is looking for true, honest hearts that will surrender all. He needs warriors who will go forth into this dark and dying world, and who will give everything to win the lost. He is looking for faith-filled, true believers in this hour, who will not tolerate compromise or unbelief in their own hearts, and who will speak the truth in love to others. Unbelief, as we will see, was the first sin committed in the garden of Eden, and it is a root in the hearts of every one of us.

As our hearts are broken open; we will see how this sin has kept us in bondage for many years, just as it did the children of Israel in the wilderness for 40 years. It is time for us to trust the Lord implicitly, and to enter our "promised land," which is the very fullness of Christ in us. (See Colossians 1:27.)

God's desire is to grant us total restoration in this hour so that we can begin to walk in our inheritance and bring in a harvest of souls in this last great outpouring of His Spirit, but how can He use us if we are walking in disobedience and unbelief? So many who are working in church ministries believe that they are pleasing the Lord, but they have not surrendered to the will of Christ. They are walking in their own will and way, and their works are works of the flesh.

Jesus says:

> Not everyone who says to Me, "Lord, Lord," shall enter the kingdom of heaven, but He who does the will of My Father in heaven. Many will say to Me in that day, "Lord, Lord, have we not prophesied in Your name, cast out demons in Your name, and done many wonders in Your name?" And then I will declare to them, "I never knew you; depart from Me, you who practice lawlessness!" Therefore whoever hears these sayings of Mine, and does them, I will liken him to a wise man who built his house on a rock.
>
> -Matthew 7:21-23

Many read this Word from Jesus, but they do not truly believe it or apply it to their lives. God is looking for surrendered souls who will pick up their cross and follow Him, but many are doing works in the Church that have not been ordained by Him. This has been a generation striving in their own works and will, and God is about to come with His fire and explosive presence and burn up all that is not of Him. Those who are willing and obedient will begin to enter into and experience the tranquility and peace of God's rest. They will cease from their own works and will do only what they see the Father doing. They will wear the mantle of Joshua, and go forth to take the land by force. They will walk in miracles, signs, and wonders in a measure this world has never seen. I believe that *we* can be this "generation" *if* we embrace our cross fully, and repent of the sin of disobedience and unbelief that has kept us bound for so long. We need His presence and power as we never have before if we are to walk in holiness and bring in this final harvest.

We have doubted His love in our trials, and have not truly believed that He knows what is best for us. Families have been split through divorce, death, and devastating circumstances; many of us have felt abandoned and unloved deep in our hearts. Many have continued to serve God outwardly, but God spoke this word to me, saying:

> *"Unbelief has plagued the hearts of My people from the beginning of time. There is no sin that hurts Me more than unbelief. It is like a cancer in the soul that eats away the spiritual life of My children. It destroys their relationship with Me more than any other sin. Unbelief tears away at the very fiber of My children's spiritual being. It is like the marrow in a bone that if destroyed, brings only sickness and death. Unbelief is a ravaging disease, and if it is not detected it can be a silent killer, as a cancer, or high blood pressure, or an infectious disease.*
>
> *Unbelief must be exposed—cut out—and it must be dealt with now quickly or many will perish in their unbelief! Many of My children do not believe My Word, My promises, the sufficiency of My grace or in the power of My blood and My cross. They do not truly believe that I love them. They read My Word; I speak to them, but so very little is penetrating their souls. My children's hearts have grown hard their ears dull but I have a plan to soften them and open their ears to My voice in this final hour!"*

This is a journey from doubt to faith—from unbelief to radical faith! My earnest prayer is that everyone who reads this book will be set free from this "insidious" sin, and come to know the deep love of the heavenly Father as they are restored fully to His heart. I pray that the eyes of our hearts would be opened to receive all that He desires to pour into us in this hour! May it be so!

Chapter 1: The Deadly Sin of Unbelief

Unbelief is *sin*. All sin, any sin—no matter how small—contains a seed that will eventually bring forth death. James 1:13-15, tells us that when one is tempted he can be drawn away by his own evil desire, and that "when desire has conceived, it gives birth to sin; and sin, when it is full-grown, brings forth death."

Satan is the mastermind behind the lie that tells us that the Old Covenant truths and the law are not relevant in this hour. Many believe this lie and do not believe God's truth in the New Covenant that says: "*All* scripture is given by inspiration of God, and is profitable for doctrine, for reproof, for correction, for instruction in righteousness" (2 Timothy 3:16, emphasis added). Some believe that we should only learn from the New Testament, but God's truth and righteousness is revealed in both Testaments of the Bible for our growth and learning. The lessons we learn from the children of Israel are set for us in the Word as an example of what to avoid in our lives and the consequences of unbelief and disobedience; they were written for our admonition. (See 1 Corinthians 10:1-11.) We can learn much from the journey of the children of Israel, and as we journey with them my prayer is that each one of us will find ourselves in them. Many say: "If I had been there, *I* would have believed God after witnessing all the signs and wonders that they saw!" It is easy to say this, but if we were in their shoes would we truly have believed God?

I ask that you dismiss all your preconceived ideas and open your hearts as we explore the Scriptures together, for I believe that each one of us will begin to see areas of unbelief and darkness in our hearts. The Holy Spirit will pinpoint hidden areas deep within our souls that we have not seen before as His Word brings light and understanding to us. I believe with all my heart that this sin lurks deep in the souls of a multitude of Christians. As "the love of money is a root of all kinds of evil," so, too, is unbelief a root of a multitude of sins (1 Tim. 6:10).

Unbelief's First Entry

As we begin this journey, we see that everything was blissful when the Lord created Adam and Eve. The garden of Eden was a garden of delight with unbroken communion and intimacy with their Creator God. God walked with them and talked with them, and their hearts were filled with love and joy. God gave them dominion and authority over all the earth, and over every creeping thing: over the birds of the air, and over the fish in the sea. They walked in perfect obedience with the Lord. They were to fill the earth and subdue it as they ruled and reigned with their Creator; their authority and dominion was to spread over the whole earth. (See Genesis 1:26, 28-30, 2:9.) Freedom and love ruled their lives as they lived in joyous abandonment to the Lord. They were pure in spirit, and their "spirit-man" (the part that is connected to the spirit of God) ruled and controlled their lives. They were in a body made suitable for earth, but they were ruled and governed by their spirit-man first and foremost. Though they lived in a body of flesh, their flesh did not rule their lives—their spirit-man did. God gave them *natural* senses to function on the earth, but their *spiritual* senses ruled over them. Their mind, will, and emotions were fully controlled by the Spirit of God. They did not even know the meaning of fear and shame—until sin entered in.

In Genesis 3:1-8, we see that when Eve was knew not to eat from the tree of the knowledge of good and evil that was in the midst of the garden. Yet the devil, that sly snake, tempted her as he subtlety spoke these words to her, "Has God indeed said, 'You shall not eat of every tree of the Garden'?... Then the serpent said to the woman, 'You will *not* surely die. For God knows that in the day you eat of it your eyes will be opened and you will be like God, knowing good and evil.'" It was a lie that she wouldn't die—for soon she would find out that the "wages of sin is death," but it was true that her eyes would be opened and that she would know good and evil. (See Romans 6:23.)

She *chose* to believe the lie that she wouldn't die and that God was holding something back from her that was good. She *doubted* the perfect

2

love of God and took the bait that Satan offered her. Little did she realize the pain and heartache that would come: spiritual death for all mankind—a death so devastating that it would take the shed blood of God's only begotten Son to bring us back into fellowship with Him. God's desire was to spare us this "knowledge of good and evil," but because of His love in giving us a free will, He allowed us to *choose*, even when the results would be devastating.

When Adam and Eve ate of this tree they died spiritually, and eventually they would die physically. Their spirit-man died, and they would walk and be ruled by their natural reasoning and their own will, and they would live in deep emotional pain. Their lives were now lived independently; no more were they fully dependent on the Lord. They felt shame, grief, turmoil, and a fear and insecurity that they had never known. Sin had set its destructive course in their lives, and this seed of sin would now be passed down to all mankind.

Because of their disobedience, the power and authority that God gave them was handed over to Satan; these powerful keys were forfeited. (See Luke 4:5-6.) God sent them out of the garden of Eden and placed cherubim at the east of the garden, and a flaming sword which turned every way to guard the tree of life. (See Genesis 3:22-24.) You see, if they would have eaten from the tree of life *after* they had sinned, they would have forever lived in that unholy state. God in His mercy protected them and us from eternal destruction, for He had a plan that would redeem us from this deadly curse of sin and restore us back into fellowship with the Father.

Many do not believe the truth of God's Word that says, "…whoever commits sin is a slave of sin." (See John 8:34.) God's Word that tells us that sin will destroy us and send us to an eternal hell. God chastises us in order to free us from sin, but many do not believe that God has His best interest in mind for them when they suffer; they do not believe that God desires to bless them. Satan takes the truth and twists it to his advantage, and he will use seeds of doubt to turn our hearts from our loving Father. He will use past rejections and wounds as an entrance into our hearts in order to cause us to doubt the perfect love of Jesus. God knows what is best for us, even when we don't understand at the time why we have to suffer in so many areas of our lives. It is *our choice* whether to believe the lies of Satan or the truth of God's Word.

A POWERLESS CHURCH

Now He did not do many mighty works there because of their unbelief.

Matthew 13:58

And Jesus rebuked the demon, and it came out of him; for the child was cured from that very hour. Then the disciples came to Jesus privately and said, "Why could we not cast it out?" So Jesus said to them, "Because of your unbelief..."

Matthew 17:18-20

Later He appeared to the eleven as they sat at the table; and He rebuked their unbelief and hardness of heart, because they did not believe those who had seen Him after He had risen.

Mark 16:14

UNBELIEF SHUTS THE POWER of God out of our hearts and lives. So many in the church have a "form of godliness," but they deny its power. They go to church, and may even be involved in many ministries within the church, but there is no true power in their lives to transform them on the *inside*. They are doing their own works, and not the works of the Father. They do not believe that God can heal their diseases, or set the drug addict free. They believe that they have to live life of their own strength. They are often prayerless, Wordless, and therefore powerless—powerless because of unbelief. (See 2 Timothy 3:5, Matthew 13:58, 17:20.)

Unbelief will bind us, even more than the graveclothes that bound Lazarus when Jesus resurrected him and he came out of the tomb. He walked out of his tomb of sin, but he was still bound—head and foot with graveclothes, and his face was wrapped with a cloth. Jesus said, "Loose him, and let him go" (John 11:43-44). In the same manner, many in the Church have had a born-again experience and have come out of their graves, but the graveclothes of unbelief still have them bound and tightly wrapped. This is why, especially in our nation, we see so few miracles in our churches, for most have not truly repented of their sin. Many have not yet learned how to embrace their cross in order to be freed from the strongholds that still bind their souls.

God's desire is to use those in the five-fold ministry—apostles, prophets, evangelists, pastors, and teachers—and those who understand

His ways to teach His children the *whole* truth, and set the multitudes in the Church free who are yet bound. (See Ephesians 4:11-13.) I believe this is the season of deliverance for multitudes, for the Lord is about to raise up a Remnant who will be filled with the power and glory of the risen Savior, who know who they are in Christ, and who can release God's children from their graveclothes. Deception will be exposed, and God's truth will come forth in power!

An example is the story of Zacharias. This powerful story tells of the angelic visitation that he experienced as he was burning incense to the Lord in the temple. He loved the Lord and was a man of prayer, but when the angel told him that his wife Elizabeth would bear him a son who would be named John and about John's high call, doubt and unbelief immediately entered in, as he thought of his advanced age and his wife's barren womb. "The angel answered him and said, 'I am Gabriel, who stands in the presence of God, and was sent to speak to you and bring you these glad tidings. But behold, you will be mute and not able to speak until the day these things take place, because you did not believe my words which will be fulfilled in their own time.'" (See Luke 1:11-20.)

I believe this is why most churches in our nation, and in many nations around the world, have been struck mute and have not seen the multitudes coming into the kingdom of God. Many pastors and preachers are speaking out truth, but it has not been in Christ's *true* and *living faith*. The words that have been coming forth have been filled with unbelief. God has struck us mute—we speak words of faith, but God knows that in our hearts there is still a root of unbelief. I believe God has been working in a *Remnant* of His children, pulling up and burning all unbelief out of their hearts, and they will speak His Word in the power of the Holy Spirit. They are a company of believers who have yielded fully to Jesus, and they are daily embracing their cross as Christ is being formed within them.

Luke 1:57 says, "Now Elizabeth's full time came for her to be delivered, and she brought forth a son." At this point, Zacharias was still mute, but when they asked the mother what her son's name would be, she said "John," and her relatives disapproved because there was no one in the family named John. "So they made signs to his father—what he would have him called. And he asked for a writing tablet, and wrote, saying, 'His name is John.'... Immediately his mouth was opened and his tongue loosed, and he spoke, praising God" (vv. 60-64). He was then filled with the Holy Spirit and began to prophesy.

Just like Zacharias' tongue was loosed when he *wrote in faith* concerning his son, so, too, as the Church embraces the cross of Christ and truly begins to believe His spoken promises, her tongue will be loosed, and she will proclaim the glories of God to the nations near and far. A *Prophetic Church*, filled with people who walk in the truth of what He's revealing to them, is about to rise and uproot this demonic curse that has kept it bound for so long. No more will the Church be weak and powerless! Zachariah had a deep heart change, and so will multitudes in the true Church be changed on the *inside*, and go forth in the power, anointing, and strength of the Holy Spirit.

The Church has been powerless for so long because she has lacked a true *vision* from the Lord—personally and corporately. Proverbs 29:18 (KJV) states, "Where there is no vision, the people perish." This has been a major problem in many churches in this hour. Only as we spend time with the Lord, listening to His voice and receiving revelation from His heart, will we be able to rise up and out of the grave of unbelief and doubt. We need a vision—direct from heaven—to burn in our souls, so that we can come alive spiritually and be released from our lukewarmness and lethargy. Many have grown cold and live a life of compromise because they do not believe that God has a *personal plan* and *destiny* for their lives. Many in the Church live off of someone else's vision or passion, but that will never satisfy the hunger deep within them for a personal encounter with Jesus.

After Jesus was raised from the dead, Thomas needed a personal encounter with Him. Hearing what the other disciples experienced was not sufficient for him. It did not satisfy his soul hunger for a deep, personal touch from Jesus, and neither will it be enough for us. Each of us needs a personal encounter and revelation of God's love, or we will perish spiritually. We will live a barren and empty life, not believing that God has destined each person for a divine purpose that only we can accomplish through Him. No one else can take the place of you or me, for in the sight of God we are indispensable. If we do not embrace God's vision for our lives, souls will be lost, lives will be left barren and impoverished, and we will never find the deep fulfillment and satisfaction that comes from doing the will of the Father on earth. The loss that we will suffer will be immeasurable if we do not believe the truth of our value in Christ.

God's desire is to use each one of His children in this hour, for the harvest will be larger than we could ever imagine. We need to be like the disciples of old, for when they caught so many fish that the net was breaking, "they signaled to their partners in the other boat to come and help them. And they came and filled both the boats, so that they began to sink" (Luke 5:6-7).

As God reveals to us how valuable our lives are to Him, and we receive and believe His vision for our lives, we will then be able to lock hands with others and work as one to bring in this final great harvest of souls. So many in the Church do not have the slightest idea of what God desires to do in and through them, but as we will see, it will take much breaking, emptying, and a filling with God's glory before the Church will come to see and believe the purpose for which she has been birthed. As the Church embraces her destiny, and the vision of God burns in her heart, she will begin to rise up into the place and position of authority and power where God desires her to walk.

FALSE FREEDOM

> *For certain men have crept in unnoticed, who long ago were marked out for this condemnation, ungodly men, who turn the grace of our God into lewdness and deny the only Lord God and our Lord Jesus Christ.*
>
> Jude 4

> *Therefore if the Son makes you free, you shall be free indeed.*
>
> John 8:36

UNBELIEF HAS ROBBED A multitude of souls in the Church from the true freedom that Christ has for them. There are many who long to be free, but they have believed the lie that worldly pleasures, relationships, church ministries, marriage, children, and even religion would satisfy them and fill the void in their souls. Instead of being satisfied, what they have found is only emptiness and a gnawing ache deep within their hearts. These *false freedoms* can never fill that deepest place in our souls; they are only a shallow cover-up for what will truly satisfy us, and that is a deep, intimate relationship with Christ, and His perfect will for our lives.

Our adversary uses many tactics to distract us and keep us from the fullness that Christ has for us by taking us on detours that only lead to dead-ends. You, see, it is *sin* that make us miserable, *not* our circumstances. Sin keeps us from that satisfying love relationship with Christ that we long for so deeply. The Lord desires to free us completely from the sin and strongholds that bind us, and only through the blood that He shed on

Calvary can we ever be set free *internally*. Only in Christ will we find the peace, love, and joy that our hearts so long and hunger for. We can only be freed from the chains of our sin as we confess them and allow godly sorrow to work deep in our hearts. Sin is an internal issue, when our minds don't line up with the heart of God and our will doesn't surrender to His will. Internal issues give root to the sins of the flesh. Sin has separated us from our loving Father in heaven, and that brings our greatest sorrow and misery. If our hearts are clean our lives will be clean.

Unbelief has robbed us and tells us that we have to wait until we get to heaven to be free from sin and the strongholds that keep us from a liberating love relationship with Jesus. Believing this lie causes us to keep sinning and embracing the very darkness that Christ came to set us free from.

Christ desires to impart to us His very own life and holiness so that we can live a life of abundant joy through the grace that He desires to pour into us. We must believe as Paul did when he said:

> ...and be found in Him, not having my own righteousness, which is from the law, but that which is through faith in Christ, the righteousness which is from God by faith; that I may *know* Him and the power of His resurrection, and the fellowship of His sufferings, being conformed to His death.
> -Philippians 3:9-10, emphasis added

Jesus wants us to *know* Him, deeply and intimately, and His desire is to lavish His love upon us. Many do not want to "know" Christ in the "fellowship of His sufferings," but they want His power—to walk in signs and wonders. Multitudes believe that worldly success is God's stamp of approval on their lives, but this is not necessarily true. God is looking for submission to His will, whether the path is joyous or darkened with grief. His desire is that we embrace our cross daily and follow Him, even when it leads to a path of suffering. His idea of success and freedom is so different than ours; success in His eyes comes as we allow His fire to transform us into the image of His Son. (See Romans 12:9.) Most of the time His design and will for our lives is not what *we* would consider "good." We want sunshine, not rain—pleasure, not grief—but His purpose is to make us holy, even when it brings great pain and suffering. Jesus would say: "'For My thoughts are not your thoughts, nor are your ways My ways.' says the

Lord. 'For as the heavens are higher than the earth, so are My ways higher than your ways, and My thoughts than your thoughts'" (Isa. 55:8-9).

As we come to know Him in His sufferings, we can then be empowered to carry His message of repentance and holiness to this generation. Yes, God's greatest desire is that we know Him intimately, but it must be in *truth*. He wants to empower us, but there is *order* in God's kingdom—death must come before His resurrection power. How can God give His power and authority to those who walk in bitterness and unbelief, to those who do not apply the Word of God to their lives? If God would give them this power it would eventually destroy them, because they would not have a solid foundation of holiness and purity to stand on, and this faulty foundation would soon crumble beneath their feet. One of the deadliest and most destructive things in our lives is to be a *hearer* of the Word and not a *doer* of it. In order to be free, we must believe what God's Word tells us, and then simply do it!

Many have been deceived. They believe that they are safe and on their way to an eternal heaven because they had once prayed a "sinner's prayer," regardless of the lifestyle they continue to lead. Speaking about false teachers who tell people this lie, Peter states:

> For when they speak great swelling words of emptiness, they allure through the lusts of the flesh, through lewdness, the ones who have actually escaped from those who live in error. While they promise them liberty, they themselves are slaves of corruption; for by whom a person is overcome, by him also he is brought into bondage.
>
> -2 Peter 2:18-19

There are deceivers in the body of Christ who are wolves dressed in sheep's clothing; they preach and teach that God's grace covers us even when we are not living a life of holiness. They deceive millions into believing that there is no need to embrace their cross, or die to the sin that binds them. They believe and teach that when we sin it is only necessary to say "I'm sorry," with no true godly sorrow or heart change. In deception they teach that since we are in the "age of grace," we are no longer bound with the Law. They negate the commandments of God and make light of them, thinking that God will overlook their sin. Jesus says in Matthew 5:17-19:

Do not think that I came to destroy the Law or the Prophets, I did not come to destroy but to fulfill. For assuredly, I say to you, till heaven and earth pass away, one jot or one tittle will by no means pass from the Law till all is fulfilled. Whoever therefore breaks one of the least of these commandments, and teaches men so, shall be called least in the kingdom of heaven; but whoever does and teaches them, he shall be called great in the kingdom of heaven.

Those who believe these lies are deceived. They believe that everyone has to sin a little because no one's perfect. Their mind-set will not allow the Word of God to penetrate their hearts and break them open with godly sorrow so that the Spirit can make the deep internal changes that He desires to make inside of them. (See 2 Corinthians 7:10.)

In the book of Jeremiah, it says, "An astonishing and horrible thing has been committed in the land: The prophets prophesy falsely, and the priests rule by their own power; and My people love to have it so. But what will you do in the end" (Jer. 5: 30-31). Many in *this* generation have not received the whole truth of God's Word but have chosen rather to believe only parts of the "Gospel,"—those parts that make them feel good, because they "love to have it so." Sin will be exposed in this hour, and the truth that the power of the cross is able to eradicate the sin that binds us.

In Christ, sin and iniquity can be rooted out of our souls (our mind, will, and emotions), and even from our flesh. *If* we believe the Word and allow the Spirit to work in us, God will set us completely free and we will experience the abundant life that He has promised us. Unbelief would tell us: "You'll never be free from that sin or stronghold." If we do not believe that the blood of Jesus and His cross paid the price to free us, not only from the penalty of our sin, but also from the *power* of sin, we will forever stay bound in our sin and unbelief. Only as we completely embrace the truth of God's Word will we be made ready for our eternal home in heaven. God's grace empowers us to live a holy life, for without holiness no one will see the Lord. (See Hebrews 12:14.)

God's desire is to expose the lies of Satan in the Church, and release a multitude of captive souls that are sitting in pews still bound in their sin. One of the greatest harvests of souls will be in the Church, because many have been inoculated against the truth through a "false gospel" that has told them that all they have to do is *believe* that Jesus died for their sins—with no true heart-felt repentance. These false prophets have given them false comfort and a false hope. They have not told them of their need for repentance, and that surrender to the lordship of Christ is necessary.

There has been little heart change in many of God's children because of the preaching of this light and false gospel, and unbelief is rampant in the Church.

Roots of rebellion, disobedience, self-will, lust, fornication, adultery, fear, hate, bitterness, unforgiveness, gossip, pride, dissention, greed, self-pity, envy, selfish ambitions, idolatry, and a multitude of other sins still bind the hearts of many in the Church. Many who call themselves Christians are still bound with these sins because they have never truly repented of them. They just say: 'Well, I'm under the blood. God knows my heart and how weak I am." Yes, God does know our hearts, and that is why He sent His Son to die the most horrible, excruciating death for us, and He sent us His Holy Spirit so that we could be free from all of our besetting sins. We walk in unbelief by believing the lie that our sins are all covered when we are not *confessing* and *repenting* of these sins before the Lord. (See 1 John 1:9.)

God's Word tells us,

> But in accordance with your hardness and your impenitent heart you are treasuring up for yourself wrath in the day of wrath and revelation of the righteous judgment of God, who "will render to each one according to his deeds": eternal life to those who by patient continuance in doing good seek for glory, honor, and immortality; but to those who are self-seeking and do not obey the truth, but obey unrighteousness — indignation and wrath, tribulation and anguish, on every soul of man who does evil...but glory, honor, and peace to everyone who works what is good.
>
> -Romans 2:5-10

We must never take sin lightly:

> Shall we continue in sin that grace may abound? Certainly not! How shall we who died to sin live any longer in it? Or do you not know that as many of us as were baptized into Christ Jesus were baptized into His death?...Likewise you also, reckon yourselves to be dead indeed to sin, but alive to God in Christ Jesus our Lord. Therefore do not let sin reign in your mortal body, that you should obey it in its lusts... For

sin shall not have dominion over you, for you are not under
the law but under grace.

-Romans 6:1-3, 11-12, 14

The path of grace will lead to holiness, faith, love, and peace; it will
free us from sin and not bind us. The grace of God was never meant to be
a license to sin, but a love call to surrender all—spirit, soul, and body—to
our loving Creator in order to release us from sin and transform us into the
image of His dear Son. God's grace is meant to bring us to a place of deep
repentance, "Or do you despise the riches of His goodness, forbearance,
and longsuffering, not knowing that the goodness of God leads you to
repentance?" (Rom. 2:4).

The Lord is coming with a strong fire to expose sin and hypocrisy in
His Church and to expose the lies of the enemy that has kept His people
bound in sin for so long; this day is fast approaching.

Judgment will begin in the house of the Lord, and these fires of true
repentance will bring forth a glorious freedom and a revival in the Church
that will spread to every nation on the face of this earth.

Jesus tells us in Mark 9:23, "'If you can believe, all things are possible
to him who believes.'" In verse 24, a father seeking healing for his child
who had a mute spirit said with tears, "Lord I believe, help my unbelief." In
this hour we must come to the Lord Jesus in deep sorrow and repentance
and ask Jesus not just to *help* our unbelief, but to *burn it out of us*, to do
whatever is necessary to eradicate this darkest sin from our hearts and
lives—whatever the cost!

Darkest times are just ahead of us, and if we do not allow Jesus to deal
with this sin and cut it out of our lives, we will be ensnared by a wily devil
that will come to us in our weakness, doubts, and fears, and our lives will
be shattered. We must deal with this sin *now*, for in the coming storms it
may be too late! The snare of unbelief must be broken, or we may be caught
in the trap of the enemy in the days ahead. We must cry out to God to
expose our sin while it is yet day, for truly the night is fast approaching!

THE LORD'S REBUKE!

THIS IS THE DAY and hour when the Lord will rebuke our unbelief and
hardness of heart as He did the disciples of old.

We have many churches, His Word, and we've seen miracles, signs,
and wonders. We have spiritual books galore, and Christian teachings

from the radio, television, and many spiritual teachers. Here in America we have innumerable Bibles, Christian concerts, conferences, and freedom to preach even on the streets, and yet the majority of Christians, especially in our nation, walk in unbelief. We walk in *indifference* to His Word and to His will for our lives.

The Word says, "Beware brethren, lest there be in any of you an evil heart of unbelief in departing from the living God" (Heb. 3:12). Unbelief is evil in God's sight, even deadly. It can even be the cause of eternal separation from God. We must open our hearts and allow God's fire to purify us fully, for "To the pure all things are pure, but to those who are defiled and unbelieving nothing is pure; but even their mind and conscience are defiled" (Tit. 1:15).

The book of Revelation shows us just how damning this sin of unbelief is, "But the cowardly, *unbelieving*, abominable, murderers, sexually immoral, sorcerers, idolaters, and all liars shall have their part in the lake which burns with fire and brimstone, which is the second death" (Revelation 21:8, emphasis added). Here we see that the unbelieving are put in the same category as the murderers, sexually immoral, and idolaters! We must never make light of this sin that has brought so many souls into an eternal hell!

There is nothing wrong with honestly seeking the truth, for all of us suffer from doubts, but we must take all of our doubts and fears to the Lord. We all desire to have a deeper revelation of His love, and to know the purpose for which we were born. Thomas, the disciple, wanted a personal encounter with the living Christ, and Jesus did not disappoint him. Neither will He disappoint us. What is so damning in our lives is when we allow willful ignorance to dull our hearts spiritually. We must never allow our doubts to keep us from God's presence.

We must fight indifference and spiritual lethargy with all the grace that our loving Lord will give us. If our hearts begin to doubt God's love, and we become cold and callous, we must not make excuses for this—let's "fight the good fight of faith," and press on to the high calling that we have in Christ. (See 1 Timothy 6:12.)

God has given us everything that we need:

> ...as His divine power has given to us all things that pertain to life and godliness, through the knowledge of Him who called us by glory and virtue, by which have been given to us exceeding great and precious promises, that through these

you may be partakers of the divine nature, having escaped the corruption that is in the world through lust.

-2 Peter 1:3-4

I have experienced much unbelief in my own soul, but there is hope in repentance as we return to the Lord with our whole heart. "In returning and rest you shall be saved; in quietness and confidence shall be your strength" (Is. 30:15).

Not only is there hope for us, but I see a new move of the Spirit coming—I see a "New Breed" of believers rising up from the ash heap.

As we journey with God's children in the wilderness, we will see the pitfalls and dangers of not submitting to the loving discipline of our heavenly Father, and the blessings of those who believed fully the promises of God.

THE WILDERNESS JOURNEY – LOST INHERITANCE

WHEN THE CHILDREN OF Israel left Egypt and began their wilderness journey, Moses spoke to them and said, "It is eleven days' journey from Horeb by way of Mount Seir to Kadesh Barnea" (Deut. 1:2). God spoke to them at Horeb and said:

> You have dwelt long enough at this mountain. Turn and take your journey, and go to the mountains of the Amorites... as far as the great river, the River Euphrates. See, I have set the land before you; go in and possess the land which the Lord swore to your fathers—to Abraham, Isaac, and Jacob—to give to them and their descendants after them.

-Deuteronomy 1:6-8

This is the same Word that the Lord is giving to us today. His desire is to fulfill His covenant promises to each one of us. Even as God called His children so long ago to go to the mountains of their enemies, the Amorites, so is God telling us to go and face *our* enemies, to tear down the gates of hell, release our loved ones, and free souls from the captivity of Satan. Will we believe His promises and enter in, or will we doubt and lose our inheritance as God's people did in the wilderness?

God's children wandered in that desert for 40 years, and the majority of them never entered into the "promised land," or overcame their enemies.

Deuteronomy 8:2 says, "And you shall remember that the Lord your God led you all the way these forty years in the wilderness, to humble you and test you, to know what was in your heart, whether you would keep His commandments or not."

God's desire was to test and train them in the desert and bring them to a place of absolute trust and obedience to His will. He humbled them and allowed them to hunger, and then fed them with manna that they might know "that man shall not live by bread alone; but man lives by every word that proceeds from the mouth of the Lord" (Deut. 8:3).

When we are in a dry, arid place *spiritually*, what is in our hearts will be exposed. We will see the bitterness, unbelief, and poverty of spirit that is truly there. Pride will so often fill our hearts when things are going well for us. God humbles us and shows us our desperate weakness so we will run to Him and eat and drink at His banqueting table. In the easy times we feel self-sufficient, but when the storms come and the wind and waves beat upon us, it is then that we run to our God for shelter and warmth.

God longed to make the children of Israel into mighty warriors, but they needed the wilderness experience so that they could be emptied of self in order to be filled with His life. His desire was to free them from fear as they focused on Him, rather than the giants that were before them. God's desire was to empty them, and show them the way of the cross, so that they might begin to learn His *ways*. God had a *new pattern* for their lives, but first their old ways and mind-sets had to be changed. One of His major purposes was to make them so dependent on Him that they would come out of the wilderness "leaning upon" their Beloved, a place of total dependence for everything they needed. (See Song of Solomon 8:5.)

How He longed to remove all the unbelief and doubts from their hearts, and to reveal His love and mercy to them. How He longed to make them His children of faith! Old habits and patterns die hard, and most of them were unwilling to change because of the pain that would be involved in the process.

Israel's inheritance included:
- They were the *Lord's* inheritance (Deut. 9:26).
- Land promised to Abraham's seed (Gen. 15:17-18).
- Limits defined (Gen. 15:18-21).
- Limits fulfilled (1 Kings 4:21, 24).
- Blessed by the Lord (Deut. 15:4).
- Eternal possessions (Is. 60:21).

There is a spiritual inheritance in Christ for each one of us that is just as real as the physical land that the Lord told them to go into and possess. What is this inheritance? These are just a few of them, according to <u>Strong's Exhaustive Concordance of the Bible</u>.

Our inheritance in Christ is:
- His kingdom (Mt. 25:34).
- Eternal life (Mt. 19:29).
- God's promises (Heb. 6:12).
- Blessing (1 Pet. 3:9).
- All things (Rev. 21:7).
- Glory (Prov. 3:35).

There were many blessings or curses tied with obedience or disobedience listed in the 28th chapter of Deuteronomy. We would do well to read these, and believe that if we do obey the Lord's commands blessings will truly follow, but if we deliberately disobey His commands the Lord will discipline us, even severely at times. Do we really believe God's Word, or do we ignore His Word that says, "Jesus Christ is the same yesterday, today, and forever"? (See Hebrews 13:8.)

Because they journeyed in the wilderness in unbelief and rebellion, the Bible reveals that "With most of them God was not well pleased, for their bodies were scattered in the wilderness" (1 Cor. 10:5.) The Bible says:

> These things became our examples, to the intent that we should not lust after evil things as they also lusted. And do not become idolaters as were some of them....Nor let us commit sexual immorality, as some of them did, and in one day twenty-three thousand fell; nor let us tempt Christ, as some of them also tempted, and were destroyed by serpents; nor complain, as some of them also complained, and were destroyed by the destroyer. Now all these things happened to them as examples, and they were written for our admonition, upon whom the end of the ages has come. Therefore let him who thinks he stands take heed lest he fall.
>
> -1 Corinthians 10:6-12

When Moses sent men to spy out the land, they returned and brought a false bad report to the people, God's people believed their evil report and not the good report that Joshua and Caleb gave. This was one of the main reasons why the wilderness children missed out on their inheritance. They were made to wander 40 years in the desert for their unbelief. Those who brought the evil report "died by the plague before the Lord." (See Numbers 14:36-37.)

The Word says, that "Death and life are in the power of the tongue" (Prov. 18:21). When we speak evil of a person or a situation instead of believing what the Lord has promised us in His Word, we are on very dangerous ground. God does not look upon this lightly; we must repent before Him and ask Him to cleanse our hearts, "For out of the abundance of the heart his mouth speaks" (Luke 6:45). In chapter 4 we'll study in greater depth the deadly effect that the tongue can have in our lives when it is not controlled by the Holy Spirit, and how it can even rob us of our inheritance in Christ.

God's children fell before their enemies because they would not listen and obey the voice of the Lord. Their hearts were hard. (See Deuteronomy 1:42-45.) They rebelled against the Lord and were hardened by the deceitfulness of sin. God was angry with them for 40 years, and because of their rebellion, most of them died in the wilderness; they did not see the land that God swore to their fathers. (See Numbers 14:22-23, 29.)

Let's apply this to our own lives. How do we respond when we are brought into fiery trials or when our hearts feel dry and empty? Do we praise the Lord, and speak the truth of His promises over our lives? When we suffer lack as they did in the desert, do we trust Jesus then to meet all of our needs according to His riches in glory? We must search our own hearts in our times of affliction and repent for our unbelief and rebellion for which we so often make excuses.

We must believe God's Word and apply it to our lives, for it says,

> But fornication and all uncleanness or covetousness, let it not even be named among you, as is fitting for saints; neither filthiness, nor foolish talking, nor coarse jesting, which are not fitting, but rather giving of thanks. For this you know, that no fornicator, unclean person, nor covetous man, who is an idolater, has any inheritance on the kingdom of Christ and God.
>
> -Ephesians 5:3-5

God's Word tells us to let no one deceive us with empty words, for because of these things the wrath of God comes upon the sons of disobedience (v. 6). We must not be partakers with them in sin. When grief takes hold of our hearts we must run quickly to Jesus for comfort.

The Israelites were very much like Esau, who sold his birthright for one morsel of food. And many of God's children today are negating their birthright because of sin and unbelief. The Word says that Esau was profane and a fornicator, and that even afterward when he wanted to inherit the blessing, "he was rejected, for he found no place for repentance," though he sought it diligently and tearfully. (See Hebrews 12:16-17.) Many, like Esau, are refusing to give up their "pet sins," and are willfully disobeying the commands of the Lord, thinking that there will be no consequences for their rebellion. We *are* in the day of grace, but we must listen to His Word warning us not to take unbelief and sin lightly.

If we reject His discipline, if we despise our inheritance as the children of Israel and Esau did, how can we expect to receive the blessings that the Lord so longs to give us? We must repent for our rebellion, complaining, and willfulness, for only then will we begin to receive the inheritance in Christ that He has in store for us.

There is a time coming when God will no longer strive with man—and I believe that time is fast approaching. (See Genesis 6:3.) We must earnestly seek Him with our whole mind, will, and heart; we must not be slack, but diligent to enter into our "promised land."

As we have read, these things have been written for us, to warn us so that we will not lose our inheritance as they did. We must not become sluggish, but imitate those who through faith and patience inherit the promises. (See Hebrews 6:12.)

Numbers 18:20 says: "You shall have no inheritance in their land, nor shall you have any portion among them; I am your portion and your inheritance among the children of Israel." Even as the Lord spoke these words to Aaron, so He speaks them to us in this hour. Do we hunger to have the Lord as our inheritance? What more do we need? He is our life, our joy, our all in all!

Praise be to the Father "...who has qualified us to be partakers of the inheritance of the saints in the light. He has delivered us from the power of darkness and conveyed us into the kingdom of the Son of His love" (Col. 1:12-13). He calls each of us "...to an inheritance incorruptible and undefiled and that does not fade away, reserved in heaven" (1 Pet. 1:4).

Chapter 2: How Unbelief Enters In

When we enter into this world, we are like a sponge that absorbs all the sounds, sights, and smells around us. We are like a rootless tree looking for something, or someone, to latch onto. Our identity is unformed, and we are looking and longing to find warmth and comfort. As our mother nurtures us, and as those around us hold us close and speak loving words to us, our character begins to form and our self-image begins to take root inside our souls.

Even if we initially received love, the bumps and bruises in life will take its toll on us through rejections, painful words, abuse, failures, lack of love and nurturing, painful losses, betrayal, and many other experiences in life. These wounds are used as an entrance, even a doorway, for the lies of the enemy to enter in, for he sees our vulnerability and will take advantage of our weaknesses when we least expect it.

Through a myriad of dysfunctions, personality disorders, generational curses, and rebellion, the sin of unbelief will begin to take root. This sin will bring forth a harvest of death in our lives if we do not deal ruthlessly with it. As we continue to study God's children in their wilderness journey, we will see a clearer picture of how unbelief entered in and why they never entered into the promises of God.

God's Wounded Children

In spite of all the miracles, signs, and wonders that God performed, God's children still would not believe His words, nor would they obey

His commands. They saw the plagues in Egypt and how He miraculously brought them out. God parted the Red Sea and delivered them from their strong enemies. When they were hungry He fed them manna and quail, and in their thirst He gave them to drink out of the flinty rock. So many miracles, and yet unbelief was so deeply rooted in their hearts that no matter what they saw, and no matter how severely God disciplined them, they still fell back into disobedience, time and time again. These roots of unbelief and rebellion were so deep in their souls that only the power of God could ever release them.

Do we ever ponder this, or do we read about their wilderness journey and just automatically believe that we would never have been so rebellious? As we study their journey, my prayer is that we will look deep into our own hearts and see where we do not believe God fully. I believe every one of us has one or more areas where we simply do not trust God fully. I pray that as we open to the Spirit of God, He will point to those areas and make the deep internal changes that are necessary in our hearts, and that the deep roots of unbelief will be pulled up from our hearts.

So how did unbelief enter the hearts of God's children? In the first chapter of Exodus, it reads:

> Therefore they set taskmasters over them to afflict them with their burdens. And they built for Pharaoh supply cities, Pithom, and Raamses …So the Egyptians made the children of Israel serve with rigor. And they made their lives bitter with hard bondage —in mortar, in brick, and in all manner of service in the field. All their service in which they made them serve was with rigor.
>
> -Exodus 1:11, 13-14.

Ponder these Scriptures with me and see where these bruises from Satan entered their hearts, and how unbelief and a myriad of other sins were able to enter in.

Think of their afflictions and about the hard taskmasters that were over them. Their lives were bitter and their bondage was severe. To work with rigor means to work with *strictness* or *severity*. This is not like most of our jobs in current times where we may work at a steady pace in a job that is not physically exhausting. Most of us get breaks or a lunch hour during our work time. Think of God's children as slaves in Egypt, whipped and beaten if they did not make a certain quota of bricks for the building of these cities. Think of their blood, sweat, and tears as they labored under inhumane circumstances. And only God knows how many hours they worked each day.

I believe that God's children at this time felt deserted and abandoned by the Lord. They must have cried out day and night to God and felt like He didn't hear them or even care about their situation. Their hearts became hard and bitter, and I believe unbelief and rebellion began to enter in as they thought that God had abandoned them. They were weary, bruised, and weakened from their hard labor, and their wounds were a perfect entrance for the enemy to come in and say, "God doesn't care about your afflictions; neither does He hear your cries!" They began to believe the enemy's lies.

Not only were they suffering under these unbearable circumstances of labor, but when Moses confronted Pharaoh, the Egyptians stopped supplying the people with straw to make the bricks and made them go and gather the straw themselves without reducing the quota of bricks to be produced each day. (See Exodus 5:6-14.)

At this point the children of Israel rejected Moses and Aaron, and by rejecting them they were rejecting God. In Exodus 1:22 it says, "So Pharaoh commanded all his people, saying, 'Every son who is born you shall cast into the river, and every daughter you shall save alive.'" The hard labor the Israelites endured was severe enough, but many of God's children suffered the loss of their sons as they were thrown into the river, which is a pain beyond description. Only those who have suffered this kind of loss would be able to empathize with them.

When the Israelites were brought out of Egypt, Moses led them into a barren place where God began to test them. They were also humbled in many different ways. God was trying to bring them to a place of absolute trust and abandonment to Him, but they didn't understand the purpose of their desert experience. Many times their souls felt barren and dry, and they looked for refreshment apart from God. This opened them up to demonic influences. There were times of hunger and thirst, and also times of waiting on the Lord as they camped out in this barren desert. God was teaching them discipline and control, to follow Him and not the impulse of their flesh, but like most of us, they did not want to wait for the Lord's answer or for His perfect timing. Because of their unbelief and impatience, they opened up to worshipping the golden calf, and began to party in the flesh, instead of waiting for Moses to come down from the mountain with the Word of the Lord. So few of them were truly willing to wait for God or desired to walk in the commands of the Lord.

I am not making excuses for God's children in the wilderness, but I want you to see the depths of their suffering from the very start. God had great compassion on them, and He earnestly desired to set them free. His patience with them was beyond anything we could ever imagine. He came to them time and time again, longing to reveal Himself to them as their loving heavenly Father.

The Israelites' physical and emotional wounds were deep, but if they would have obeyed the Lord and embraced His promises and the love that He desired to give them, they could have known deep healing in their hearts. If only they would have believed that, "God is not a man, that He should lie, nor a son of man, that He should repent. Has He said, and will He not do? Or has He spoken, and will He not make it good?" (Num. 23:19).

God's desire for His children was that they would fear Him and not man. When He revealed Himself to them from Mount Sinai, they trembled and stood a distance away. They said to Moses, "'You speak with us, and we will hear; but let not God speak to us lest we die'" (Ex.20:18). They did not want to draw near to God; they did not want to die to their sin, "...but Moses drew near in the thick darkness where God was." (See Exodus 20:21.) Fear came from the gap between their sin and His holiness. There is a healthy fear that we need to have of God, for He is a holy God, but listen to His cry in Exodus 19:4: "'You have seen what I have done to the Egyptians, and how I bore you on eagles' wings and brought you to Myself.'" This is the cry of a gentle, loving Father calling out, asking to His children to draw close to Him. Moses heard the cry of God's heart and did not fear to draw near to his King.

They longed in the wilderness to go back to Egypt because it was *familiar* to them; this kept them in unbelief and out of the "promised land." God was trying to make them into a *spiritual* people, but because of the deep internal changes that were required of them, they wanted to stay where they were, in their *physical senses*. They lived by what they saw, heard, touched, tasted, and smelled. Through obedience to God's will, their natural lives could have been transformed into the spiritual, but they were not willing. Their story is like that of an abused woman—one who is beaten and battered. She says she wants out of the situation, but even if she divorces, she is likely to gravitate to a man who is equally abusive because she is *familiar* with this kind of lifestyle. These patterns can only be broken in the power of the Holy Spirit, but many are not willing to pay the cost to have these internal changes made.

Is it any different in the Church in this hour? *Egypt* can represent the *world* in the Bible, just as *Pharaoh* could *Satan*. We can apply this story because we, too, have suffered under the hard labor of sin in our lives. Satan has been a hard taskmaster, but we are familiar and have felt at home with our sin and unbelief. These sinful patterns must be broken, but we must first realize how deeply sin has bound our lives.

Many of us have had bruises and deep wounds from the enemy, and have been bound with unbelief for a long time. When we came to Jesus we rejoiced greatly, for our spirit-man was set free. But many, many of God's children are still captive in their souls to unbelief, rebellion, idolatry, a party spirit, greed, lust, envy, hatred, contentions, fornication, adultery, selfish ambitions, heresies, and fear. Those who practice these things will *not* inherit the kingdom of God. (See Galatians 5:19-21.) Many in the Church still walk in the flesh, and not after the Spirit. Their minds are on the things of this world, and not on the Lord's plan and purpose for their lives. (See Romans 8:5-8.)

Multitudes are in a desert place and are angry at God. They feel as if He has deserted them, not realizing that He is with them, desiring to empty them of the things of this world so that He can fill them with His glory. We cannot have the world and have the blessings of God too. Jesus tells us to come out of the world's system—its customs, belief system and sinful idolatry and activities—and be separate from it. We are *in* the world, but not *of* it. (See 1 John 2:15-16.) God wants us to thirst for Him, not for the things of this world. We must not partake of its lusts, longings, and fleshy desires or we, too, will fall in the wilderness.

MY TESTIMONY

EVE WAS *DECEIVED* BY the wiles of the devil, even though she was not wounded as we are. No sin had opened the door for her vulnerability to the Devil's lies. If she was susceptible, how much more vulnerable does that make us? Truly my life was one of great deception and unbelief because of the bruises of Satan. I was left as one bruised, shattered, and rejected, but as you will see, the Lord Jesus had great mercy and compassion on me.

Through verbal, sexual, physical, and emotional abuse, something died in my soul at a very young age. I suffered deep rejection, betrayal, and loss. These deep bruises opened a door in my heart, and the enemy came in with his lies and deception. A deep root of unbelief began to grow that would have eventually destroyed my life if it wasn't for the grace of God!

I was raised in a dysfunctional home where my father was an alcoholic and very abusive. My mother was a God-fearing woman, and if it wasn't for the love and care that I received from her, only the Lord knows where I would be. I have fond memories of a mother who spent much time with my siblings and me; she took us for walks and on many outings. I still remember all seven of us piling into a taxi for a fun trip to a lake. But in spite of some good memories, I never felt like I fit in anywhere, not in my family, not in school, and ultimately not even in the church. I tried so hard to fit in, but there was always a deep sense of not belonging—a sense of detachment, which I now realize was part of God's blueprint to set me apart for His plan and purpose for my life.

I was raised in a *religious* home, but I was never taught how to have a deep, vital relationship with the living Christ, the relationship with Jesus that brings "abundant life."

Even after my salvation experience with Jesus, I understood in my *head* about the grace of God, and I rejoiced when I repented and asked Christ in, but little did I realize the years of brokenness and suffering that were ahead in order to bring the healing into my *soul* that I so desperately needed. My *spirit* was saved, but my soul (my mind, will, and emotions) was a mess!

Two dreams from the Lord impacted my soul greatly at this time; they showed me the work that the Lord needed to do inside of me. The first one was a dream of being in the basement of the home that I was raised in. I had a broom and I was sweeping the floors and walls vigorously. There was much dirt, and as I swept, suddenly a trapdoor opened and a strong wind came through. The wind powerfully began to remove all of the dirt and debris from the basement. The basement in this dream represented my deep subconscious, where so much of the turmoil, pain, and abuse were buried, for you see I had never dealt with any of the sexual or emotional abuse at this time, it was just too painful. The wind was the Holy Spirit that was coming to remove all the dirt of my past, and it would bring the healing that I so desperately needed and desired.

The second dream also occurred in the early years of my walk with the Lord. I dreamed I was on a large boat. Suddenly a storm with strong winds and a heavy rain began shaking the boat in a most fearful way! I was thrown from the boat, and as I was in the water a large sea serpent came and wrapped itself completely around me, from head to foot. The serpent completely destroyed me, and in the next part of the dream I was lying dead under a tree. All of a sudden, a "Man" in white came and stood in front of me. He bent down and began to remove the poison from my body where I had been bitten by the serpent, and life began to come back into me. These dreams revealed to me the deep work that needed to be done in my heart in order for me to be made whole. I knew my journey would be arduous, but as I allowed Him to remove the poison from my soul, I knew that His life would flood my whole being.

I remember the night when I cried out to the Lord, "Oh Father, I want to be crucified with Jesus." Little did I realize what I was asking for! It was the Spirit of God who birthed that prayer deep in my soul. Shortly after this prayer, my soul entered into a "darkness" that would envelope me for many years. I didn't realize at the time that I would one day cry as Jeremiah did when he said: "He has set me in dark places like the dead of long ago. He has hedged me in so that I cannot get out; He has made my chain heavy" (Lam. 3:6-7), or that "He bowed the heavens also, and came down with darkness under His feet... He made darkness His secret place; His canopy around Him was dark waters and thick clouds of the skies. From the brightness before Him, His thick clouds passed with hailstones and coals of fire" (Ps. 18:9, 11-12).

As a young Christian I didn't understand the ways of the Spirit and that the darkness I entered was actually *His* dark cloud. I could not endure His brightness, so He came to me in a thick, dark cloud, and with the fire of His love He began to expose and consume all of my sin! He is the One who hedged me in and set me in a dark place, not to destroy me, but to reveal to me His love and glory in a way that I never dreamed! The Word says that, "....even the night shall be light about me; indeed, the darkness shall not hide from You, but the night shines as day; the darkness and the light are both alike to you" (Ps. 139:11-12). I found this to be true: The dark night that I was in could not obscure His lovely face; in reality it only caused me to see Him more clearly. I think of a diamond lying on a black velvet cloth—it only shines more brilliantly because of the *dark* background. In the darkness I began to see into the spiritual realm more and more clearly. As my eyes became blinded to the things of this world, His presence and love began to fill my soul in a new and deeper way.

But at that time I did not understand the ways of the Lord; I was a babe in the Lord and because of this, there was much resistance. When the breaking process began, there was great anger and fear that began to surface in my soul. I suffered from many panic attacks, and the anger was so great that at times I raged against God and would scream, "Why are You destroying me?" Little did I realize that He was only taking from me the darkness and sin that I needed to be freed from! You see, we are born with iniquity binding us; it is so much a part of us, even in our DNA, that when these strongholds are cut from us, we feel as if a limb is being severed because of its attachment in our souls. King David said: "Behold, I was brought forth in iniquity, and in sin my mother conceived me" (Ps. 51:5).

In Christ, we receive a new heart: a new nature, spiritual DNA, a new bloodline. But it must be worked into our souls through the renewing of the mind, healing of the emotions and surrender of the will. Sin is such a part of our personality that when God begins His surgery in us, we feel as if we are being destroyed—when in reality we are coming into the life of Christ in us. The Lord showed me that dying to sin is a death as real as any physical death. It is a spiritual surgery that only God can perform in us!

At the time, I didn't realize that I was being "sifted as wheat," just like Peter was so long ago! In the midst of a deep fiery trial, the Lord spoke to me and said, "Satan is demanding to sift you as wheat!" I read Luke 22:31 (NASB), where the Lord said: "'Simon, Simon, behold, Satan has demanded permission to sift you like wheat. But I have prayed for you, that your faith should not fail; and when you have returned to Me, strengthen your brethren.'" I asked the Lord how Satan could demand to sift me, and the Lord replied that it was because many souls would come into the Kingdom through the ministry He was bringing me into. I needed to be sifted so that what was unholy in me would be blown away through the winds of persecution that He would allow to come into my life. After all the suffering and death to my flesh, Jesus knew that I would return to Him and strengthen many souls in their walk with Him. Thank You, Jesus, for never giving up on me!

Years of depression and grief still loomed before me, but I felt in my heart a glimmer of hope and a light and a love that was strangely warming me as the days went by. As I kept my focus on Jesus and on the joy that was set before me, in His grace I could daily embrace my cross. This does not mean that I did not fall, for I fell many times on my journey through this "valley of the shadow of death."

I remember times when I was extremely depressed, and felt great guilt because of my past. Because of this guilt, I punished myself unknowingly by not releasing to the Lord my pain, shame, and grief. Jesus wanted to release me and give me joy, but I walked in deception, even in the Old Covenant, trying to somehow make up for my past sins.

Many are still in this stronghold from Satan. Instead of receiving the freedom that comes from *true* repentance, they still try to make amends and atonement for their sins through self-flagellation and by doing many good works. This will never eradicate sin from our souls, for it is only through the shed blood of Jesus that we can be freed. God revealed this truth to me in the dark valley of suffering that I was walking through.

I have experienced times of great pain as I watched my loved ones come close to death because of demonic strongholds. I have, by the grace of God, held on to His promises for me and for my loved ones through the greatest storms. I have confronted strong devils who told me that they would kill my daughter, but as I spoke the truth of God and said: "She will not die, but will live and proclaim the works of the Lord," the enemy then left. (See Psalm 118:17.)

I have suffered sleepless nights, paralyzed with fear, not knowing if one of my loved ones was lying dead in the streets. There was a time in my life when all I could do was cry, even for hours in a day, but God was with me. Sometimes the darkness in my soul was so great that I did not want to face another day. Thoughts of suicide entered my mind many, many times, even to the point where the enemy told me what I should do to destroy my life. God never failed to love and comfort me as I died daily to all that I held dear. At the time, the Lord had me memorize a Psalm each week. He knew my deep need was for His Word to fully saturate my heart.

When Satan comes to us it is not usually as a roaring lion, but with a sweet voice, and at times even quoting God's Word. In my early years of walking with Jesus, when I did not yet have much of the Word in my heart, the enemy came and said, "'There is no peace,' says the Lord, 'for the wicked'" (Is. 48:22). At first I thought it was the Lord because it was a Scripture I had heard before, and I felt guilt and fear, but then by God's grace I realized that it was the enemy that spoke these words to me. Satan will even use the Word of God to condemn us in our weakness and pain. God comes to us in conviction, *not* condemnation. He brings life through godly sorrow, but the enemy will bring death through condemnation.

Prayer and praise became my greatest lifeline to Jesus, and at times I would spend up to six hours a day praying and crying out to the Lord in my distress. In praise and worship Jesus came and comforted me and revealed His great love to me. He never failed me and never left me alone in my grief. Even when the clouds were darkest, I could feel His gentle touch and hear His soft whisper. I still managed to function outwardly, and most of my loved ones did not realize how deeply I was suffering.

This was my time of trial and purification, and my greatest need was for the renewing of my mind. God showed me that if I did not keep my thoughts "captive to the obedience of Christ" I would never come into the full blessings that He had for my life. I was at the end of my rope! Unbelief entered in because I did not discipline my mind in the Word as I should have been doing. I allowed stray thoughts to enter in, and I entertained them. The Lord showed me that it was like stroking snakes and demons when I entertained these negative thoughts. I had to take full control of my thought life; it was the only answer. It took a while to be freed in my mind, but it was worth the discipline and suffering in order to be liberated from these tormenting thoughts.

In this time of suffering and weakness the enemy came again and again and whispered to me that the Lord didn't truly love me, and many times I was ready to just give up. It is in our times of weakness, pain, and depression that the enemy will come to us with his relentless lies. Even as Eve was tempted to doubt the goodness and love of God, so does the enemy come to us, and because of past hurts and rejections from our parents and loved ones, we believe the lie that if they couldn't love us, then neither can God. Somehow we tie the two together—loved ones and God—at least emotionally, and when they reject us, *emotionally* we believe that God also rejects us.

I never felt that my earthly father loved me, and I have suffered devastating abuse from him through sexual and verbal abuse. Because of this, for a very long time I could not receive the love of my heavenly Father. I could never fully believe that He loved me with a pure, unconditional love. My heart had so many walls built up, and I believed the lie that even God couldn't tear them down. It took many, many years for me to learn how to receive the love of My *true* Father, and I feel that at this point in my life, He is finishing a deep, deep work in my soul. I do not believe there is any greater pain than the feeling of utter rejection from a loved one, especially one you love. I believe this is where millions of souls need the touch of God the Father. Many people desperately need deep healing in their emotions, and as we receive the Lord's love, we can be made whole in this area of our lives.

When we come to Christ and He enters in, our spirit-man comes alive, but that does not mean that our soul, which includes our mind, will, and emotions, are automatically healed. Our minds must be daily renewed in the Word of God, and we must learn to walk in our *wills*, not by our circumstances, or by what we feel. We must "walk by faith, not by sight." (See 2 Corinthians 5:7.) It is only then that we will begin to grow into the "fullness and stature of Christ." It is in the fiery trials of life that His perfect love will cast out all of our fears. It is here that unbelief will be fully consumed, and we will "live by faith in the Son of God!" (Gal. 2:20).

The part of my soul that has been the hardest to heal has been my emotions, for the pain in my heart was so deep that I didn't believe that I could ever be *fully* healed, which is a lie from the pit of hell. I have studied and meditated on the Word for many years, and by God's grace my mind has been greatly renewed and many, many deep wounds have been healed. I have loved the Lord and have learned to obey Him even when I'm hurting, but I have found that even though I have had great encounters with Jesus and have felt His deep love, there is still a part of me that hurts, that feels that others are loved more than me, and this has left me open to great struggles with unbelief. God is healing this deepest place in me, even as I write this book.

I believe that many of you reading this book feel the same way. You love the Lord with all your heart, but there is still a nagging doubt, a deep-seated fear, that someday, something will happen, and you will lose this love. You know the Word; you know that He loves you, and yet there is a fear, coupled with a longing to be loved, and a need for a deeper sense of security in your life. Maybe Satan has robbed you of your identity through sexual or physical abuse. He has had others lie about you and slander your name, and though you know you are a child of God, you still feel as though there is something missing. There is still a sense of insecurity, a loss of identity, and you know it is so deep that only the Lord can restore this broken area in your life. We must admit to the Lord that there is unbelief in our souls, and only by the power of the Spirit will it be removed! God is about to restore our souls fully as this deep root of unbelief is pulled up and out of our souls! I want to share this personal word from the Lord that He gave to me concerning my deep emotional pain. I pray it will encourage you and fill your hearts with hope.

> *"It has been a long, hard journey for you, but you have found your way back to My heart. For so long I have desired to reveal Myself to you, but you have felt unworthy and unloved by Me, child. You say, 'I know God loves me,' and I see deep in your spirit that you believe this, in spite of what you feel in your emotions, but I say, this is the day and hour when I*

*want—I desire earnestly—to reveal Myself to you in your emotions—in your deep heart. You've given up ever realizing the fullness of My love, but you have determined in your heart to serve Me and to obey Me, even if you never experience My love on this earth. This must change now; this must be eradicated in your heart—this sense of rejection, this sense of not being loved deeply and passionately. I must remove this root and come to you in a deeper way. There is a root of anger because of this lack of love in your heart, and child, also indifference. You feel you no longer matter. You feel you will never move forward in this. I know you feel emotionally dead, but I can resurrect your emotions. You will feel **My** emotions now, **My** love, and **My** passion. All I have, child, is a deep, deep love —a love beyond comparison. I know there is nothing in your heart at this point, and all you have to give Me is emptiness, but I say, 'Then give Me your emptiness, and I will fill you to overflowing!'*

"Oh child, you wrestle not against flesh and blood, for it is the enemy that has robbed you of love—of healthy love emotions. Stand firm now, for I am about to resurrect you fully! Trust Me and release all your pent-up emotions. I will help you. I know how to help you. Let go and allow Me to be your all in all. I'm coming. Don't doubt—don't run from Me. I will do it. I will finish this deep work in your soul."

Many do not believe that they have this deep root of unbelief in their hearts, but as we study some of the signs and symptoms of this sin, we may see that because of rejection, unbelief may be what we've been struggling with for many years. It may be that this root has kept us from the "abundant life" that God has promised us. I believe that in many souls these deep roots and wounds have been covered up with many vices and outward activities that have caused hearts to become numb, and at times to even feel *dead* to the love of God. We have put up walls of indifference and have run ourselves ragged with activities, even spiritual ones, to keep from facing what is truly on the inside of us. We fast and pray and attend church, hoping no one will look behind the mask we wear and see our pain and weariness. We have walked in our prisons of fear and doubt for so long that we have grown cynical and do not believe that we will ever again see the light of day! We have learned not to feel too much, whether it be of joy, love, or laughter, for we fear we will be disappointed and that this love is maybe not for us. Those who are willing to be honest with the Lord in this hour will be delivered from their darkness and unbelief, but we must be open and honest with God and allow Him to remove from us our rose-colored glasses. As we take off our "religious masks," God will fill us with His love, glory, and presence.

Some may think that this is far-fetched, and that a child of God could never feel such depths of pain, but the "dark night of the soul" is a real spiritual experience for a multitude of God's children. I believe this is especially true for those who are allowing the Spirit to penetrate their painful wounds and also for those who desire to be free and to walk in holiness.

I want to end this part of my testimony by telling you of the love and comfort that the Lord gave to me during this time of great struggle. God was so faithful to me during this time of darkness, and at times He would pour into me a love from heaven that saturated my whole being. This love was so tangible, so comforting, that it far outweighed the pain that I was suffering. Remember: Jesus will never give you more than you can bear, and He will give you the grace to endure whatever suffering comes your way. His patience and mercy toward me knew no end, and only in eternity will I be able to express fully to Him the depth of love and gratitude that I owe Him! Jesus has filled and satisfied my heart, and yet I hunger and thirst for so much more! It has been worth every tear, every loss, every betrayal, every temptation, and every fiery trial—even the loss of man's approval, position, reputation, and friends. There is nothing in this world that can ever satisfy me, no love that can quench this deepest place within my soul—but *Jesus*. He is all I want—all I will ever need—now and throughout the endless ages! My desire is to love and worship Him passionately and to serve Him endlessly. I want to please Him *alone*, to fulfill the plan and purpose for which I was created, and to finish the course and to hear Him say, "Well done, My good and faithful servant… enter into the joy of your Lord!" (See Matthew 25:23.)

Chapter 3: Unbelief: A Harvest of Unrighteousness

Do you not know that the unrighteous will not inherit the kingdom of God? Do not be deceived. Neither fornicators, nor idolaters, nor adulterers, nor homosexuals, nor sodomites, nor thieves, nor covetous, nor drunkards, nor revilers, nor extortioners will inherit the kingdom of God.

1 Corinthians 6:9

As we examine the fruit that comes forth from unbelief, we need to look deep within and allow the Spirit of God to penetrate our souls with the light of His truth. We will study and examine the deadly harvest of sin that comes forth from the soil in the hearts of those who are bound with unbelief.

Evil deeds and acts, as well as negative words, are corrupt seeds. When fully grown, evil seeds will yield a *harvest of sin*. What we sow is going to grow, and eventually this harvest, whether good or evil, will come forth in our lives. "Do not be deceived, God is not mocked; for whatever a man sows, that he will also reap. For he who sows to his flesh will of the flesh reap corruption, but he who sows to the Spirit will of the Spirit reap everlasting life" (Galatians 6:7-8).

Even sins that our forefathers never repented of can go through the bloodline and wreak havoc in future generations. Do you ever wonder why King David, who loved the Lord with all of his heart, fell into adultery with Bathsheba, and put Uriah in the front line of battle so that he would be killed? There was more than one reason why David fell so hard, but I would like to expound on one of them.

Rahab was the great-great-grandmother of David. She hid the Israelite spies when they were scoping out the land promised to them. She placed a scarlet cord in her window when Joshua and his men took Jericho, and by doing so, she and her family were saved. She was a harlot, but because of her faith, the Lord saved her. The iniquitous seeds of harlotry in her were passed down from generation to generation, and because this sin was never fully eradicated from the bloodline, David had a *propensity* for lust in his heart. This sin was as a seed lying dormant, and when the temptation came through his "eye-gate," David gave in and was caught in the snare that Satan had set for him. This iniquitous sin of not only lust, but murder, was also passed down into two of his sons. (See 2 Samuel, chapters 11 and 13.)

Seeds have a coating of protection over them, and when each seed has the right condition, the "seed coat" begins to fall away and it begins to germinate. Germination is the awakening of the seed from the dormant stage. In David's life the conditions were right (because of disobedience) for this iniquitous seed to sprout. (See 2 Samuel 11:1-2.) It began to bring forth sin and darkness in his heart that would eventually even spread to his children. That evil seed had been dormant in the heart of King David, and it only needed the right condition to come forth. Satan laid the trap for David, and he took the bait.

God's Word says that we were brought forth in iniquity and that in sin our mothers conceived us. God desires *truth* in the inward parts. (See Psalm 51:5-6.) This was true not only for King David but for us as well. God wants to go deep into the soil of our souls in this hour, and as the "Master Gardener," He desires to pull up every sinful root, just as any gardener would pull up the destructive weeds that would try to take over a garden. Our heavenly Father longs to cut and prune every unfruitful branch from our lives, even though to us it may look destructive at the time.

Even in the natural—when the vinedresser prunes a tree he sometimes lops off even more than seems necessary, so that he can have a more fruitful tree. Sometimes, in the wisdom of our God, He will take even some things that are *good* in our lives, in order to give us His *best*. (See John 15:1-2.)

In the "parable of the sower," we see that some seed fell on stony places. Although the seed initially sprouted, they quickly withered because they had no depth of earth to take root. God wants to plant good seeds in the hearts of His children, but the stones of unbelief, and a myriad of other sins, keep the good seed from taking any root in their hearts. As soon as fiery trials come, these young sprouts wither away because of discouragement and rebellion. Unbelief, like thorns, spring up and choke them.

The root of unbelief will bring forth a crop of unrighteousness, and unless it is dealt with ruthlessly, it will destroy the whole harvest—our whole heart. It is more deadly than any poisonous weed known to man.

Even though the children of Israel experienced in the wilderness how the Lord carried them everywhere they went, yet, for all that, they *did not believe* the Lord their God. (See Deuteronomy 1:31-32.) God wanted to take the unfruitful and even deadly seeds from their hearts as they wandered in the desert for so many years.

Here are some of the deadly weeds that must be pulled out of our souls in order to bring forth a harvest of righteousness.

Deception is one of *the* most deadly weeds that any child of God can walk in, for if caught in this trap, only the Lord will be able to remove the blinders from our hearts and show us where we are deceived. We will feel that our hearts are right with God and yet we'll be completely out of His will. We may be doing many good works, but they will not be the works of God. Jesus only did what He saw the Father doing, and the Word tells us that only those who do the Father's will shall enter into the kingdom of heaven. (See John 5:19-21, 30, Matthew 7:21-23.)

I remember a time when I couldn't understand why I was not moving forward in the things of God. I loved the Lord with my whole heart (or so I thought), and yet I was not entering into the ministry that He had placed in my heart. Some time ago, at a conference, a brother ministered on the "spirit of Jezebel," and said that not only does she bind a soul with lust, but also with *compromise.* That day, as I wept great tears, the Lord confronted me and said, "Tonight you must make a choice—will you step over that line and give Me *everything* in your life—no matter what the cost?" It was a life-changing event for me as I abandoned *all* before Him. My life has never been the same.

Deception blinds us to things in our souls, but as the Spirit of God shines His light into us He will reveal the deep hidden sins. Deuteronomy 11:16 says, "Take heed to yourselves, lest your hearts be deceived, and you turn aside and serve other gods and worship them."

Idolatry came forth in Israelites' hearts and lives because of disobedience and rebellion. This idolatrous spirit manifested itself as they worshipped and danced before the golden calf. (See Exodus 32:4, 19-25.) Many in the Church see no connection between themselves and God's people worshipping the calf in the wilderness. We cannot see that "going our own way" and "doing our own thing" is actually rebellion and idolatry in the sight of God. Many in the Church have a "party spirit" and enjoy worldly music and festivities that are just as evil in the sight of God. Many have grown tired of "waiting on God," and have gone into ministries that are of the "flesh," even *"Ishmael"* ministries—ministries that, like Ishmael, were birthed from the flesh and not from God's promise or intention. We have tried to comfort our wounded hearts and spirits with worldly entertainment, over indulging in food, so-called "Christian entertainment," worldly television programs, shopping, and even serving the Lord in areas that are not His will for our lives. Are we any different in this hour than they were? We must examine our hearts and ask the Lord to reveal to us the many ways that we avoid His scrutiny in our lives. Are we laying down our wills daily before the Lord—or are we running from God by doing what others say are "good Christian works"?

Negative talk is another evil outgrowth from this harvest. Be careful what you say, little tongue, for in it you hold the power of death or life. (See Proverbs 18:21.)

The children of Israel cried out: "Where can we go up? Our brethren have discouraged our hearts, *saying,* 'The people are greater and taller than we; the cities are great and fortified up to heaven; moreover we have seen the sons of the Anakim there'" (Deut. 1:28, emphasis added). We must never underestimate the power of words; for they are a creative force that comes forth from us that will set in motion either darkness and death or life and health to the hearer. Has anyone ever spoken negative words to you and you literally felt that someone punched you in the pit of your stomach? You could actually *feel* the darkness that was coming forth from that person. "He who speaks truth declares righteousness, but a false witness, deceit. There is one who speaks like the piercings of the sword, but the tongue of the wise promotes health" (Prov. 12:17-18).

Lack of intimacy with God is a dangerous sign and symptom that shows that we do not truly believe that He loves us passionately. We stay at arm's length and do not allow Him to come near to us. We'll serve Him and praise Him, but when it comes to deep heartfelt worship, our hearts close up and there is no true intimacy with Christ. When we begin to worship, deep-seated fears surface from the unhealed wounds within us, and the walls of protection rise. The fear of truth and the fear of exposure keep many souls from drawing close to Jesus in a deep, heart-to-heart, love relationship. The knowledge of the truth will set us free, but for some the cost is too great. They do not want to let go of their idolatry and "pet" sins, though they would never admit it. God's children in the desert "… stood afar off, but Moses drew near the thick darkness where God was" (Exod. 20:21).

Another example is from Matthew 26:58, when Peter followed Jesus *at a distance* to the high priests' courtyard. Peter loved Jesus, and I believe he longed to be close and intimate with Him, but fear of suffering and death kept him from walking close to His Savior at this time. Only God's perfect love can set us free from the *fear* of intimacy. (See 1 John 4:18.)

Hardened hearts caused the wilderness children to rebel against the commands of the Lord. Their hearts were so filled with unbelief that they believed that the Lord hated them, and that He brought them out of the land of Egypt to deliver them into the hand of the enemy and to destroy them. (See Deuteronomy 1:26-27.)

Before we judge them, we need to examine our own hearts. Was there ever a time of deep, emotional pain or fiery trial when we felt abandoned by God? Have we ever felt overwhelmed with grief and spoken out rashly against God or doubted His love for us? I want us to bring it home, where we live, because if we are not honest with ourselves and others, we will deceive ourselves and not believe that we, too, have at times walked in unbelief, and have not believed in our Savior's undying love for us.

There have been times when I felt as if I was being literally destroyed in the fiery trials that I found myself in. We must confess to God, to ourselves, and to others that we have sinned in not believing that our heavenly Father loves us and that we have had deep roots of unbelief in our hearts and lives, just like the children of Israel did. Admitting this sin and repenting of it before God and others will set us free.

Indifference was seen in the Israelites' hearts at Meribah because of their contention. They tempted the Lord, saying, "Is the Lord among us or not?" (Exod. 17:7). They became indifferent to His presence, and the fear of the Lord departed from their hearts. This can come to any of us in times of discouragement, for when we grow weary in waiting and see no changes in our lives or in our loved ones our hearts can grow callous. This deadly sin can bring hardness to our hearts, and only the fire of God can burn it away. Unbelief will cause us to remove from our lives all restraints. We will run into this world and do our "own thing," and sin will no longer make us blush.

It is a dangerous sign when our passion and zeal for Christ begins to die; only *true* repentance will keep our hearts soft and pliable in the hands of the "Potter."

A **lack of trust** was seen in God's children when Pharaoh changed his mind and began to pursue them in the wilderness. (See Exodus 14:9-12.) They were terrified and cried out to the Lord. They had seen many signs and wonders in Egypt, but this was a *new* and *different* crisis. Haven't we seen miracles in our own lives and in the lives of our loved ones, even the miracle of our salvation, and yet when a new crisis comes, we quickly forget how many times He has delivered us? Without a deep and genuine trust in the goodness of God, we will never move into our "promised land" and partake of all the blessings that He has for us.

Complaining and murmuring is a major symptom of unbelief. "Now when they came to Marah, they could not drink the waters of Marah, for they were bitter. Therefore the name of it was called Marah. And the people complained against Moses, saying, 'What shall we drink?'" (Exod. 15:23). "And the people spoke against God and against Moses: 'Why have you brought us up out of Egypt to die in the wilderness? For there is no food and no water, and our soul loathes this worthless bread'" (Num. 21:4-6). God does not take it lightly when we murmur and complain. So much of the time we justify our complaining because we don't feel well or are weary and tired, but there is never an excuse to be unthankful when we consider all that the Lord has done for us. When we think of the cross, and the ultimate sacrifice that Christ made for us, our "light affliction" is *nothing* in comparison. When we drink of the bitter cup that the Lord gives to us out of love—not to hurt us, but to refine us and bring us to a place of repentance—we, too, at times, murmur about our lot in life. Many times we do not see the hand of the Lord in our suffering, and we rebuke the enemy that we believe is bombarding us so mercilessly. We will never grow into the full stature of Christ until we begin to learn the ways of the Lord. The children of Israel saw His *acts*, but Moses, Caleb, and Joshua learned the *ways* of the Lord. God's desire is that we come to a place where we will truly know Him. (See Psalm 103:7, 81:13.)

A root of **bitterness** and **hate** can spring up and cause trouble—and by this many can "become defiled" because our deep wounds have not been dealt with and healed. (See Hebrews 12:15.)

"So Moses cried out to the Lord, saying, 'What shall I do with this people? They are almost ready to stone me!'" (Exodus 17:4). This bitterness, if not dealt with, can even turn into a murderous spirit, as we can see from this Scripture. Bitterness and hate can go deep into a soul, and many do not even realize that this root is in them. Having no water to drink, and in anguish and thirst, this wilderness company cried out in bitterness of soul. Whether it is a physical, "soulish," or spiritual thirst, when we are hungering for and craving satisfaction, and that need is not met, these unholy, sinful reactions can surface in our lives. God will lead us into a dry, desert place in order to bring *up* what we try to hide deep in our souls. When we're in a boiling pot of suffering, what is deep within us will come to the surface.

Because I did not deal with the bitterness and unforgiveness against my father, the Lord showed me that I had a "spirit of murder." Many times in prayer this hatred would surface, and out of my mouth would come forth words of hate against my father for what he did to me. Poison filled my soul as I vented the hate that I had toward my father. This kept me from the love, joy, and peace that I so longed for. As I repented deeply for my sin, the Lord was then able to begin the deep work of healing and deliverance in my soul that I so desperately needed. Apart from God's grace I would never have seen this deep sin inside my soul, and it would have destroyed my life completely.

Fear, I believe, is one of the most deadly offspring from this root of unbelief. When the Israelites saw how strong their enemies were, and that the giants had fortifies cities, they lost sight of the bigness of their God. Their focus was on themselves, and they knew that they could never overcome them. It was true, in their own strength they couldn't face such an enemy, but if they had kept the enormity of their God in view, they would never have come to this place of discouragement. (See Numbers 13:28-29, 32.) We are in danger of making the same mistake if we do not keep our focus on Jesus. Jesus, for the joy that was set before Him, endured the cross. Jesus focused on the prize, and so must we. (See Hebrews 12:2.)

Rejection—they rejected God and others. "Then the Lord said to Moses: 'How long will these people reject Me? And how long will they not believe Me, with all the signs that I have performed among them?'" (Num. 14:11). Can you hear the cry of the Lord in this Scripture? His heart's longing and desire was that they would be brought to a place of trusting and believing Him. God asks each one of us these same questions in this hour. He has performed many signs and wonders; He has given us His written Word, and yet many times we, too, reject God with our unbelief and negative talk. We refuse to believe what His Word tells us, and we listen to the lies of Satan. Instead, we live in our own thoughts and feelings. God feels our rejection of Him deeply in His heart and weeps profusely. Let's bring Him joy in this hour and walk in faith and trust—no matter what circumstances or fiery trials we find ourselves in.

Pride and **jealousy**—along with **rebellion against God's authority**—was not only a problem back in the days of Moses, but it is a major issue in the Body of Christ today. Numbers 16:3 says, "They gathered against Moses and Aaron, and said to them, 'You take too much upon yourselves, for all the congregation is holy, every one of them, and the Lord is among them. Why then do you exalt yourselves above the assembly of the Lord?'" Here we see that Korah, the son of Levi, gathered with 250 leaders of the congregation and confronted Moses, God's chosen leader, and Aaron, God's chosen priest for the congregation. There was no fear of God in their hearts; they were not rebelling against Moses only, but they were also coming against the Lord. Truly they found out that "It is a fearful thing to fall into the hands of the living God" when "the earth opened its mouth and swallowed them up, with their households and all the men of Korah, with all their goods... And a fire came out from the Lord and consumed the two hundred and fifty men who were offering incense" (Heb. 10:31, Num. 16:32, 35).

David, before he became king, would not lift a finger against King Saul, God's appointed authority and his father-in-law, even when Saul was trying to kill him. Many in this hour would justify David if he would have lifted up his hand against the king, but David knew better and placed Saul, and his life, in the hands of the Lord. We must also learn the hard lesson of submission to God's appointed authority—even when we are under leadership that may hurt or undermine us. We must never gossip or come against even *ungodly* "kings," but pray for them and say nothing that will hurt their reputation or destroy them. If God is telling you to leave a church or fellowship, leave—but make sure that it is God that is telling you to leave or you may be missing the greatest growth opportunity and inner change in your heart that God desires to make in you! But this may be a test, and if you fail the test, you may never be raised up as David was or be brought into the inheritance that God has for you. The key is to act in obedience.

Lust and **greed** are destructive weeds, and if they are not dealt with powerfully—through the blood of the cross of Jesus—they can lead us to eternal destruction. We read in the Word that the Israelites "lusted exceedingly in the wilderness, and tested God in the desert" (Ps. 106:14). They complained before the Lord and desired meat; the Lord sent gave them quail to eat, but "while the meat was still between their teeth, before it was chewed, the wrath of the Lord was aroused against the people, and the Lord struck the people with a very great plague ... they buried the people who had yielded to craving" (Num. 11:33-34).

God *will* meet all of our needs, but we must not lust as unbelievers do or try to meet our needs apart from the Lord. God knows our need, and He knows how to meet them. When Jesus was tempted by Satan in the wilderness to turn the stones into bread, He did not give in to the temptations of the evil one. Jesus trusted His heavenly Father to care for Him; He placed His whole life in the hands of His Father. The Lord will always give us grace in our time of need *if* we turn to Him and surrender every lust in our souls to Him. We must "...not lust after evil things as they also lusted" (1 Cor. 10:6).

Achan sinned exceedingly against the Lord. When he saw among the spoils of battle a beautiful Babylonian garment, two hundred shekels of silver and a wedge of gold weighing 50 shekels—he coveted them—and took them. He hid them in the earth in the midst of his tent, with the silver under it. (See Joshua 7:20-22.) This was blatant disobedience, for they were not to take any of the accursed goods from their enemy. When Achan's actions were discovered, Joshua and all Israel with him, took him and all his goods and stoned him, and burned the items in a fire. He had been warned. In Joshua 6:18 it says, "And you, by all means abstain from the accursed things, lest you become accursed when you take of the accursed things, and make the camp of Israel a curse, and trouble it."

Joshua gave them this command when they took Jericho; it was a command from the Lord. This was such serious rebellion that if this cancer of greed was not dealt with fully, Israel would have been under a curse, and this sin would have eventually spread throughout all of Israel—destroying them. They would have lost their inheritance and everything that God had planned for their lives and their future.

Impatience must be rooted out fully from the soil of our hearts. Psalm 106:13 says that they did not *wait* for the Lord's counsel. This sin can be catastrophic in our lives, for if we do not wait on the Lord for His will, His timing, and His purpose to come forth in our lives, we will fall into the deadly trap of doing our own will and birthing a fleshy ministry that will one day burn up. We can completely miss the will of God in our impatience. God's delays are meant to be used as a purifying fire in our lives. These delays are meant to draw us to Him as we cry out to Him and seek His face earnestly. During these very times of delay we are to be emptied of our own will and desires. It is during this time of waiting that the Lord desires to break our wills and make them one with His.

During delays, the fire is heated "seven times hotter," and the sin that is buried within us will come to the surface. Some of these sins will be the very ones that we're studying: bitterness, anger, lust, greed, fear, rejection, pride, rebellion, indifference, hardness of heart, and idolatry. As we wait on the Lord we must allow this fire to do its perfect work in us. Delay is *not* denial.

When King Saul was supposed to wait for Samuel to offer the burnt offering before the Lord, he waited seven days, according to the time set by Samuel, but when Samuel didn't come at the appointed time, the people began to scatter. Saul had them bring him the burnt offering and he offered it himself, which was not in accordance with the law of God. As soon as he was done presenting the offering, Samuel came, and Saul's excuse was, "When I saw that the people were scattered from me, and that you did not come within the days *appointed*, and that the Philistines gathered together at Michmash, then I said 'The Philistines will now come down on me at Gilgal, and I have not made supplications to the Lord.' Therefore *I felt compelled*, and offered a burnt offering" (1 Sam. 13:8-14, emphasis added.) Saul felt compelled; this man was led by his flesh, *not* by God's Spirit. He disobeyed the commands of the Lord, flunked the test, and lost the inheritance that God had for him. Out of fear, and because of disobedience and impatience, he lost it all. Let this be a warning to us the next time we get impatient, when our answers are delayed in our time of testing. God's desire in such delays is to develop the fruit of long-suffering in our lives, "But let patience have its perfect work, that you may be perfect and complete, lacking nothing" (Jas. 1:4).

Discouragement comes into our lives when we refuse to be still and wait upon the Lord. When we are impatient, discouragement will most assuredly come forth. When we don't see the answer coming, and we wait and wait, it is then that we experience the truth of Proverbs 13:12, which says, "Hope deferred makes the heart sick, but when the desire comes, it is a tree of life." This happened to the wilderness children time and time again, when they did not see the fulfillment of God's promises in their lives. God wanted to *prepare* them for their inheritance, but they refused to bend to His preparation process—they wanted it now. Discouragement manifested itself in their complaining, murmuring, rebellion, and anger, and instead of repenting of these sins, they hardened their hearts and never received what the Lord so longed to give them.

I remember a time in my life when I felt greatly discouraged because of the *long wait* in the fiery trials that I was in. The Lord showed me in a dream that I was to receive a beautiful necklace, which symbolized the blessings that He had promised me. In this dream there was no joy in receiving this priceless gift. When I awoke there was heaviness in my heart as I went to my "secret place" to spend time with Jesus. As I sat at the table, I felt something in my hand. I opened it to find a small green branch. As I looked at it, I wondered where this branch came from—there were no plants or flowers in my house. As I opened up a devotional and read the Scripture from Proverbs 13:12, I wept as God reassured me that He had not forgotten me or the promises that He had spoken to me so long ago. He showed me that when these promises come to pass they will be like a tree of life to me—restoring joy, love, and laughter once again.

We do not hope as the world does, for worldly hopes are based on a system which is built on "sinking sand." Our hope is based on the eternal covenant that God made with us through the shed blood of His Son Jesus. Jesus is the solid Rock that we stand on, and His promises are "Yes, and in Him Amen, to the glory of God through us" (2 Cor. 1:20). "This hope we have as an anchor of the soul, both sure and steadfast, and which enters the Presence behind the veil" (Heb. 6:19). "Now hope does not disappoint, because the love of God has been poured out in our hearts by the Holy Spirit who was given to us" (Rom. 5:5). God will *not* disappoint us.

When we speak a promise to a loved one, how would we feel if they looked at us in mistrust and unbelief and started weeping because they feared we would not keep our word? We would feel hurt and grieved! How much more does our loving Father in heaven weep when we do not believe the promises that He has given us in His holy Word. We may fail a loved one in our weakness and sin, but God will *never* fail us! I pray that we will wait in hope for what we do not see, and persevere till we receive our inheritance in Christ, as we hold fast the confidence and the rejoicing of this hope firm to the end. (See Romans 8:25, Hebrews 3:6.)

We take sin so lightly in our generation, when in reality, it is more deadly than any cancer known to man! Sin mist be cut out of our souls, or we, too, will be destroyed by it. God spoke to Cain and said, "If you do well, will you not be accepted? And if you do not do well, sin lies at the door. And its desire is for you, but you should rule over it" (Gen. 4:7). We must rule over sin. Christ's blood alone can cleanse us from all of our iniquity and sin, but we must receive Jesus, and allow His blood to cleanse us. (See 1 John 1:7.) "For the wages of sin is death, but the gift of God is eternal life in Christ Jesus our Lord" (Rom. 6:23).

May our hope in Christ purify us fully as He removes every unholy and ungodly root from our souls, and as all unbelief is forever eradicated from our hearts. (See 1 John 3:3.)

CHAPTER 4: THE BIBLICAL PATHWAY TO FREEDOM

"PRAY, PRAY, PRAY THAT multitudes will repent and come to the foot of the cross. There is no other remedy for the soul—no other sacrifice that can be made for the soul of man. Tell them, child, tell them quickly—they must repent; this is the first step of salvation. They must see their sin, and that the only remedy for that sin is My cross. Through My cross, multitudes will come home to the heart of the Father. They can't earn it; they can't do any works to gain entrance and access into My kingdom. Throughout the ages many have tried to enter this door with indulgences, good works, and by putting on a plastic face of holiness and righteousness, but I have seen through all the masquerades, and I will pull back the veil, the lies, and the deception that the enemy has used to blind the minds of unbelievers, and even My own children in this hour.

"It is the cross that saves a soul, and it works in a soul a deep, agonizing repentance that will bring the inner changes that I desire to see. Nothing else will save and liberate a soul. The cross—My cross alone, as it is embraced by a soul, will bring that one into liberty and freedom. No other works, no other pattern have I put into effect—but My blood, the blood of My cross. I alone paid the debt, and by My grace and the power of My Spirit, a soul can now be set free. My cross frees a soul from the bondage of trying to keep the Law, for now in My power, in My Spirit, I will cleanse internally, and give that soul the power to walk in holiness, for without holiness no one will see Me. They must be in

Me—My righteousness—My holiness—and My works through them—My will alone being accomplished. In Me alone can you be pleasing to the Father. He will accept nothing else.

"Repent—put on sackcloth My children, for out of sorrow will come joy! Tear your hearts and not your outer garments. Your righteousness is as filthy rags before Me. Come to Me, and I will remove the rags and give you My robe of righteousness. Those who sow in tears will reap in joy! Now is the time to repent children—not tomorrow. Do not put this off until tomorrow! Turn from your wicked ways. Come to Me and confess your individual sins, and then My blood will wash them away. Cover your sin no more: your lying, greed, idolatry, hate, and bitterness. Confess it all and you will be brought into the fullness of liberty and freedom—even the abundant life that I have promised you! Self-will must be abolished from your heart. Repent and do My will alone. Ask Me for My will in your life, and truly I will reveal it to you. Repent children—the hour is late! The hour is dark with wickedness and sin. Come—for I love you! I will forgive you, indeed, I already have! Oh prodigal children, come home to the heart of the Father and delay no longer. I love you!" Jesus
(Given to me on September 21, 2011)

But know this, that in the last days perilous times will come: For men will be lovers of themselves, lovers of money, boasters, proud, blasphemers, disobedient to parents, unthankful, unholy, unloving, unforgiving, slanderers, without self-control, brutal, despisers of good, traitors, headstrong, haughty, lovers of pleasure rather than lovers of God, having a form of godliness but denying its power. And from such people turn away!

2 Timothy 3:1-5

Does this sound like the generation that we live in? I believe that this description fits our era in more than any other past generation. Many in our nation, and in the nations of this world, love the pleasures of this world more than God. Not only in the world do we see this, but also in a multitude of churches throughout the world. Where are the passionate, wholly committed believers who will give up everything for Christ?

God has shown me that the wave of glory that is coming will awaken millions upon millions of people in the Church to a passionate, radical commitment to Christ in this hour. Yes, there are committed believers now, but they are few and far between; there is a *Remnant*, but the Lord is about to come and visit His Church with a fire and glory that we have never seen or experienced. This fire will bring forth in our hearts an agonizing, godly sorrow that will set us free from our deep-seated sin and fears and lift us up to a height that we have never known.

God is about to resurrect a dead, dry Church, that will no longer deny His power to radically free them on the inside. They will not doubt that the Spirit can transform them into the image of Jesus! They will no longer be just hearers of the Word, but doers of the Word. For too long the Church has lived in idolatry and unbelief, but now, in the power of the Christ's cross, millions will be awakened to a new, fresh zeal for Jesus, and they will walk in the resurrection power of the living Savior!

How will this be accomplished? Is it possible, in this late hour, for a company of true believers to come forth and bring the radical changes that need to be made in the Church and in this world? Yes, for nothing is impossible with God! The Lord is coming to His Remnant in this hour, and will accomplish this radical work through the power of His cross, and many of God's children will submit to this work because of the revelation of Christ's love, mercy, and grace. It will be an accelerated work that will consume sin and idolatry—with a fire so intense that the passion of Jesus will explode in the hearts of His true children! Are you ready for this work to be done in your heart? The catastrophic judgments that are coming to our nation, and to the nations of this world, will bring a fire that will be *"seven times hotter"* than any fire we have ever known.

As we open God's Word, we will see that what Christ accomplished on the cross is a *finished* work—a solid foundation on which we can stand on in the coming storms, and it will show us what *our* part is—in order for us to walk in the wholeness and freedom that Jesus purchased for us.

THE CROSS OF CHRIST AND ITS TRANSFORMING POWER

> *For Christ also suffered once for sins, the just for the unjust, that He might bring us to God, being put to death in the flesh but made alive by the Spirit.*
>
> 1 Peter 3:18

For He made Him who knew no sin to be sin for us, that we might become *the righteousness of God in Him.*

2 Corinthians 5:21

THERE CAN BE NO transforming work in our lives apart from the cross of Christ. This is the solid ground on which our lives must be built, for apart from repentance through His cross, there can be no strong foundation under us. If our lives are built on anything else other than the shed blood of Christ and His sacrifice for our sin, our foundation will be weak, faulty, and cracked, and it will eventually crumble. His cross alone will reveal the deep depravity that lies hidden in our souls; it is the only pathway to freedom.

When we bow at the foot of the cross, it is only then that this transforming work will begin as God reveals to us our sin and rebellion. The Holy Spirit is the One who convicts us of sin, and we will know deep brokenness as we see how we have broken His Ten Commandments. The Ten Commandments are the Lord's plow that will break up the fallow ground in our hearts. There are many who do not see their deep sinfulness. Proverbs 30:12-13 says, "There is a generation that is pure in its own eyes, yet it is not washed from its filthiness. There is a generation—O how lofty are their eyes! And their eyelids are lifted up." I believe that we are living in this generation, for multitudes have set their own standards for righteousness, and not God's holy standard that is laid out for us in His commandments.

Sin must be exposed by the Law in order for us to see our utter depravity and our helplessness to free ourselves. When this work is done in a soul, they will begin to see and feel their desperate need for a Savior. Only then can someone even begin to walk in true repentance. You see, sin is not so much the *fruit* of sin—outward acts such as disobedience, hate, or rebellion—but the *root* that is in a person's heart, which is living a life of independence apart from the will of God. The root must be dealt with, the sinful nature, for this is what the Lord dealt with on the cross. Without a new nature, the nature of Christ implanted into our spirit, we will never enter the kingdom of God. We may try to patch up our lives with good works and religious activity, but this will never save us or bring that "new birth" into our spirit-man. We must come to the place where we depend on the Lord alone for salvation, the Holy One of Israel in truth. (See Isaiah 10:20.)

Jesus destroyed the heredity of sin in our lives through His cross, and unless we are *"born again"* by His life—by this "new heredity"—we can never be free from the clutches of sin and death! Sin is not so much what we *do*, but it is *who we are*, and without the life of Christ pulsating through our lives, we can never be holy. *Holiness is Christ living His life through us.* There is nothing—absolutely nothing—that we can do—to ever be good enough in ourselves. This is a death blow to the pride of man and is the reason why so many prefer "religion" instead of the truth of who we are apart from Christ.

There was only *one* sacrifice that is acceptable to the Father—the shed blood of His Son, the sacrifice that Jesus made on the cross of Calvary. He paid our debt of sin in full. The blood of goats and bulls in the Old Testament was only a foreshadowing of Christ's sacrifice for our sin. "For it is not possible that the blood of bulls and goats could take away sins" (Heb. 10:4). These Old Testament sacrifices covered their sin, but they could never free them from sin on the inside. Only the blood of Jesus, through the eternal Spirit, who offered Himself without spot to God, can cleanse our conscience from dead works to serve the living God. (See Hebrews 9:14.)

Jesus became sin for us that we might *become* the righteousness of God in Him. God's Word shows us that in Christ, because of His sacrifice, we can now be made holy on the inside. We no longer have to wallow in sin, or be bound with a myriad of strongholds, but as we believe His Word and apply it to our lives, we can be liberated into the abundant life that Christ has promised us.

We have a *better* covenant in Christ:

> Not according to the covenant that I made with their fathers in the day when I took them by the hand to lead them out of the land of Egypt; because they did not continue in My covenant, and I disregarded them, says the Lord. For this is the covenant that I will make with the house of Israel after those days, says the Lord: I will put My laws in their mind and write them on their hearts; and I will be their God, and they shall be My people. None of them shall teach his neighbor, and none his brother, saying, "Know the Lord," for all shall know Me, from the least of them to the greatest of them.
>
> -Hebrews 8:9-11

When God called Moses to come up to Him on Mount Sinai, he lingered with the Lord for 40 days and 40 nights, "And when He had made an end of speaking with him on Mount Sinai, He gave Moses two tablets of the Testimony, tablets of stone, written with the finger of God" (Exod. 31:18).

In the book of Exodus, we see that because of the Moses' delay on the mountain, the children of Israel willfully broke the covenant by having Aaron make gods to go before them. Aaron made them a golden calf head; they offered burnt offerings to it and "sat down to eat and drink, and rose up to play." (See Exodus 32:1-6.) God informed Moses of what was happening and said, "I have seen this people, and indeed it is a stiff-necked people! Now therefore, let Me alone, that My wrath may burn hot against them and I may consume them. And I will make of you a great nation." But Moses pleaded with the Lord and "the Lord relented from the harm which He said He would do to His people." (See Exodus 32:9-14.)

Here we see the seriousness of idolatry, and how God feels about it, not only at that time so long ago, but even now—with this generation, and with His own people. God has not changed; He is the same yesterday, today, and forever! Now when Moses came down from the mountain and heard and saw what the children of Israel were doing, his "…anger became hot, and he cast the tablets out of his hands and broke them at the foot of the mountain" (Exod. 32:19).

I believe that these "tablets of stone" represented their hardened hearts. Many of God's children still have hard hearts and are living in the Old Covenant, trying to be good enough in themselves, and not living in obedience to God's will. Many still live in the flesh, and have not truly repented with godly sorrow for their willful ways. As Moses cast the tablets out of his hands, and they were broken at the foot of the mountain, so, too, must our hearts be broken deeply for breaking the commands of the Lord. We must admit to the Lord and to each other that of our own strength or ability we cannot keep His "laws" and then yield our lives fully to the Lord to accomplish His work in us. Only in the transforming power of the Spirit can we be changed internally, and be given the power to walk in holiness. We have been kept "under guard" by the law, kept for the faith which would afterward be revealed. The law was our "tutor" to bring us to Christ. It was meant to teach us that we can't keep the law in our own strength. The Old Covenant is a ministration of death. We read the 10 commandments, but trying to keep the law and the commandments in our own strength we realize we do not have the ability to keep them. When we realize no matter how hard we try on our own we keep failing. It is meant to bring us to the end of ourselves—to bring death to any hope of freeing ourselves from the bondage of sin. But those who have truly come to Christ in faith no longer need a tutor, for they have found in Christ the fulfillment of the law, and the power to walk in holiness. You see, we were kept in a prison of law so that we would see and feel our desperate need for the grace of God, and yet so many, because of the lack of repentance in their souls, do not yet feel their desperate need for Jesus; they are still walking in the Old Covenant. (See Galatians 3:19-26.)

Grace was never meant to be a license to sin, but it shows us the way to Christ and the path of true repentance and holiness. Out of the brokenness in our hearts we find that only Christ is holy, and that what needs to die in us is our self-righteousness and sin. Many are still in their sin, for there is no transforming power in them to change. Only in Christ's atoning sacrifice will our entrance to heaven be secured. We must allow the transforming power of His cross to puritfy us deeply; this is the only path to holiness. We can now be cleansed on the inside and have His law written in our minds and hearts; we can now come to know the Lord in a most intimate way. We can be changed and liberated on the inside; we can have "boldness to enter the Holiest by the blood of Jesus, by a new and living way which He consecrated for us, through the veil, that is, His flesh" (Heb. 10:19-20).

In the Old Testament the high priest could only go behind the second veil in the temple once a year—and not without a blood offering. But now, because of Christ's sacrifice, the veil has been torn, and we can come boldly to the throne of grace. Do we truly realize what Christ has done for us? "…let us draw near with a true heart in full assurance of faith, having our hearts sprinkled from an evil conscience and our bodies washed with pure water." We must not doubt the sufficiency of Christ's sacrifice, but "…hold fast the confession of our hope without wavering, for He who promised is faithful." (See Hebrews 10:22-23.)

Those who are in the flesh can never please God; they are denying that the power of the cross alone frees them. They are still making daily "blood sacrifices" that will never free them from their sin! The law can make nothing perfect. (See Hebrews 7:19.) A New Covenant, ratified with the blood of Jesus, can now cleanse our consciences, and we can be freed from the dead works of the flesh. We are now free in the power of His cross to follow the Spirit and obey His will in all things—to do God's will, not our own. We can know the deep, intimate love of our heavenly Father; we can *really* know Him! His desire is to take us past the "outer court," through the "holy place," and into the very "Holy of Holies."

Christ has made the way for us to enter in, but we must appropriate this finished work into our lives and embrace our cross daily. Only then will we be able to experience the transforming power of His cross. Will it cost us? Yes, it will cost us all of our sin and rebellion. There must be repentance, a yielded heart, and a full surrender to the internal work that the Spirit of God desires to do in us. We will find that His grace is sufficient, for it is God who works in us, to will and to do His good pleasure. (See Philippians 2:13.)

If we desire to follow the Lord, we must deny ourselves, take up our cross, and follow Him. If we save our life, we will lose it, but if we lose our lives for His sake, we'll find it. (See Matthew 16:24-25). Our cross will involve suffering, but Jesus will be with us every step of the way.

When Jesus laid down His will in the garden at Gethsemane, He cried out that if it was possible, He wanted to have the cup removed, but He prayed, "Not My will, but Yours, be done" (Luke 22:42). In the laying down of our wills to do the Father's will there will be great suffering at times, but we will be strengthened in the inner man—the new life of Christ within us, our spirit-man—to endure it. We must be willing to pay the price to be changed internally. As we submit to the work of the cross in our lives, it is here that we will begin to be transformed into the image of Christ. (See Romans 8:29.) God's desire is not only to give us a new nature, but to make us whole—spirit, soul, and body; we must be willing to die to our sin and selfishness and go through the suffering that is necessary in order to be made new. God wants our hearts to be broken and pliable so that His will can be accomplished in and through us.

In Joel 2:12-13, it says, "'Now, therefore,' says the Lord, 'turn to Me with all your heart, with fasting, with weeping, and with mourning.' So rend your heart, and not your garments; return to the Lord your God, for He is gracious and merciful, slow to anger and of great kindness; and He relents from doing harm." The Word tells us to "… circumcise the foreskin of your heart, and be stiff-necked no longer" (Deut. 10:16).

Jesus longs to remove the veil from our faces so that we can gaze upon His glory. We will be transformed more and more into His image and go from glory to glory, through the power of His Spirit. (See 2 Corinthians 3:18.) This will only be accomplished as we go through the trials of life—for *pain is a purifier*. The impurity must be removed from our hearts through the fires of deep repentance. As the veil was rent in two at Christ's death, so does the Lord desire to cut away the foreskin, the hardness from our hearts, and reveal to us our idolatry and the deep sin that we try so desperately to hide from Him. This work must be done in our hearts if we are to ever live in His overcoming power and victory. We will now see how the Spirit works out this godly sorrow and repentance in our lives.

TRANSFORMED THROUGH REPENTANCE AND HUMILITY

He who covers his sins will not prosper, but whoever confesses and forsakes them will have mercy.

Proverbs 28:13

As GOD BEGINS TO uncover our sin through His cross, His desire is to begin to rend our hearts and make deep internal changes in them. Freedom from sin will begin to fill our lives as we confess our sins and are open and honest before the Lord and others. True repentance can never be worked out in our souls as long as we wear a mask and cover up our sin.

What is *true* repentance? Is it saying a sinner's prayer at the altar, but then going back into the world to do our "own thing" and live a lifestyle of sin? There are multitudes sitting in pews with a false sense of security, but they have never truly *turned from their sin* and given their lives to Christ.

They believe because they have said "I'm sorry," and have prayed a little prayer that they are now safe and are covered by God's grace no matter how they live. This is *not* the path of true repentance, but is a *"false gospel"* that is being preached throughout the world. Paul said, "What then? Shall we sin because we are not under law but under grace? Certainly not!" (Rom. 6:15).

The horror and deadliness of sin is not preached in most churches in our nation. They do not see that sin, like cancer, will bring death, unless the blood of Jesus cleanses their souls through true repentance. Where are the preachers like John Wesley and Charles Spurgeon who will tell God's people the truth about their sin and their need to walk in holiness and repentance daily? True repentance is walking in the fear of the Lord, knowing that all of the sins of the heart must be confessed to the Lord in deep repentance. True salvation and repentance can only come through the Spirit of God as the truth of God's Word is preached: the truth of sin, judgment, heaven, and hell. God desires truth in the inward parts, and in that hidden part He will make us to know wisdom. (See Psalm 51:6.)

Sin is lawlessness, and its penalty had to be paid with the spotless blood of Jesus, through His cross, in an excruciating death.

So few know the fear of God in our generation; many, even in the Church, take sin lightly. Through deep, agonizing repentance we will begin to see the horror of sin in our lives and in the hearts of those around us.

True repentance begins with a turning away from all known sin in our lives as the Holy Spirit reveals to us how deeply we have sinned against a holy God and how we have willfully broken the commandments of God. God wants to see change and repentance in our hearts, so that our sins may be blotted out and that times of refreshing may come from the presence of the Lord. (See Acts 3:19.) God not only wants the unsaved to repent, but His desire is to rend the hearts of His children, so that He can send times of refreshing—the rain from heaven that will bring in His mighty end-time revival. This revival must start in the hearts of His children, and then the Lord will bring in the final harvest of souls.

True repentance will always bring exposure and a stripping of those things that are unholy and dark in the hearts of God's children. Many are covering deep, hidden sin, but the Lord sees it all. The Holy Spirit desires to bring conviction of sin to God's people, *not* condemnation.

The Word tells us that for everything there is a season, and I believe that now is the time to tear open our hearts through repentance so that the Lord can bring His holiness into us, and prepare us for our heavenly home. It is time to weep so that we can reap the Lord's joy, and to mourn so that we can dance. (See Ecclesiastes 3: 4, 7.)

Exodus 33:6 says, "So the children of Israel stripped themselves of their ornaments by Mount Horeb." God desires to strip us of all pretenses. His desire is to uncover us and show us our sin in order to restore us to His heart. We use "ornaments" to cover up deep, hidden sin, and some of these may be religious works, busyness and even involvement in church activities. It is time to break up our "fallow ground," and seek the Lord diligently, until He comes and rains righteousness on us. (See Hosea 10:12.)

When Jesus, Peter, John the Baptist, and many others began their ministries, it was always in the foundational truth of repentance. (See Matthew 3:2, 4:17, Acts 2:38.) Without repentance, which produces holiness, nothing else will stand in our lives. We will walk in deception and in our own works. Everything else in our lives will be tainted. Our foundation will be faulty, and it will only be a matter of time before we will fall, along with any ministry that we have built on "sinking sand."

The first transforming work of the cross must be the exposure of sin in our lives; this exposure is a work of the Spirit that will bring brokenness and sorrow. Our prayer must be, "Search me, O God, and know my heart; try me and know my anxieties; and see if there is any wicked way in me, and lead me in the way everlasting" (Ps. 139:23-24). We do not even know our own hearts for the Word tells us that "The heart is deceitful above all things, and desperately wicked; who can know it? I the Lord, search the heart..." (Jer. 17:9-10).

Sin is a *heart* issue. It will destroy our relationship with the Lord and with others. God's passionate desire is to restore us to His heart, but it will not happen apart from true and deep repentance. In the book of Mark we read, "For from within, out of the heart of men, proceed evil thoughts, adulteries, fornications, murders, thefts, covetousness, wickedness, deceit, lewdness, an evil eye, blasphemy, pride, foolishness. All these evil things come from within and defile a man" (Mark 7:21-23). Truly the New Testament standards have been raised to a higher level in Christ. More than anything else we need a deep heart cleansing by the blood of the Lamb.

When David sinned so deeply against the Lord, we see how God used the prophet Nathan to expose his sin. When confronted, David did not cover his sin, and in Psalm 51, we see that he cried out: "Against You, You only, have I sinned, and done this evil in Your sight..." (v. 4).

The Word tells us that "*If* we confess our sin, He is faithful and just to forgive us our sins and to cleanse us from all unrighteousness" (1 John 1:9, emphasis added). There must be a confession of sin before we can be forgiven and cleansed from our sin. This promise is *conditional*.

We must come back to preaching the Ten Commandments of God in order to bring an understanding of what sin is. It will produce the deep brokenness in our hearts that God so longs to see. Many, even in the Church, are living in fornication, adultery, lying, gossip, and idolatry, and because God's truth and the holy commands of the Lord are not preached, they no longer feel the convicting power of the Holy Spirit in their lives. The catalyst that will bring true repentance in God's people is the preaching of the truth of God's holiness and His standards for our lives.

True repentance produces godly sorrow for our sins as the Spirit reveals the deep, hidden sin and iniquities in our souls. "For godly sorrow produces repentance leading to salvation, not to be regretted; but the sorrow of the world produces death" (2 Cor. 7:10). Godly sorrow produces a repentance that will bring a tearing in our souls—the sorrow that is in God's heart over our sin. It is a sorrow that brings internal changes into our hearts. It is not feeling bad because we've been caught, or even saying "I'm sorry"—but it is a drastic change of direction as we allow the Spirit to cut the sin out of our hearts—at the root. We must allow the ax of God to be laid at the root of our sin as His fire burns up all the chaff in our hearts. (See Matthew 3:10-12.)

The sorrow of the world brings tears that make a person *feel sorry for themselves* because of the exposure of sin in their hearts. God has placed His finger on their sin, but they do not truly want to change, or face their deep sin. Immediately they put the blame on someone else, because they refuse to take responsibility for their sin. They say: "Everyone is against me; I'm always the bad guy!" True repentance says: "I see my sin and my part in this situation, and I am truly sorry. God help me to repent so that You can bring the changes into my heart that are necessary." Do you see the difference? Godly sorrow will bring change because the law has done its work in bringing true sorrow for sin. Other repentance is often from mere selfishness coming from wounded pride.

True repentance will always involve an active return to God, and it always begins with honesty; honesty is a form of repentance. We must turn from the denial of our sin and confess our rebellion against the will of God. True repentance will open our hearts to the truth of God in His Word, and we will realize how we have lived our lives in unbelief and independence—doing our own will and not God's. Repentance is facing the truth of our sinfulness—that we are deserving of an eternal hell because of our sin. True repentance will strip away our self-hatred and the hatred that we hold in our hearts toward others. What will come forth is true humility, tenderness, and love. In true repentance our souls come alive, and we begin to walk on a path of freedom, wholeness, and victory. We will see our lives released from the *power* of sin.

When I think of repentance, the prodigal son in Luke 15:11-32, comes to mind. His was a true repentance coming from a heart that was deeply broken over his sin. The restoration with his father was revealed in their embrace, and it was celebrated in great joy. True repentance will always manifest in a heart-to-heart restoration with our heavenly Father. When there is true sorrow for our sin, one of the fruits that we will begin to see is *joy*. Those who sow in tears will reap in joy. As we bow low before the Lord in humble recognition of our sin, God will comfort our waste places, and make our wilderness like Eden; our desert will be like the garden of the Lord, and joy and gladness will be found in us, as will "thanksgiving and the voice of melody." (See Psalm 126:5, Isaiah 51:3.)

The apostle Paul lived a *lifestyle* of repentance that was *progressive*, even as ours should be. In 1 Corinthians 15:9, he said that he was the "least of the apostles." In Ephesians 3:8, he states that he was "less than the least of the saints," and near the end of his life, he states in 1Timothy 1:15 "… Christ Jesus came into the world to save sinners, of whom I am chief." As we grow in the Lord, and as He draws us closer to His light, we will see, more and more, the darkness and depravity that is hidden in our hearts. We must walk in the light as He is in the light, for then the blood of Jesus will cleanse us from all sin. (See 1 John 1:7.)

We must "bear fruits worthy of repentance" (Matt. 3:8). We must "turn to God, and do works befitting repentance" (Acts 26:20). Remember that you will know a tree by its fruit. The fruit of repentance starts with hearing the Word of God and then obeying it.

Penance is not the same as *repentance*. Penance does not see or acknowledge how deadly sin is; it believes that if you try hard enough you can make the changes that are necessary. It tries to pay the Lord back with "works of the flesh" that can never pay for sin or eradicate it. Penance brings hardness of heart, and it refuses to bend its knee to the lordship of Christ.

True repentance frees us from shame, for our sin will be uncovered, and we will no longer have anything to hide. It will free us to love and laugh again, and we will be thankful for every affliction that the Lord has allowed in our lives to bring us to this place of freedom. (See Psalm 119:71, 75.)

The brokenness, painful emotions and Godly sorrow of true repentance and complete openness before the Lord cannot be numbed, though many try through food, entertainment, sex, drugs, greed, materialism, or the works of the flesh. It will honestly face the truth about the condition of one's soul, and will do whatever is necessary to bring forth this reconciliation with God and with others. Its fruit will show forth in a passion to love and forgive all who have hurt us, and through a willingness to do God's will. There will be a pursuit to find the reason for which God has created us, and then a passion to prepare for the vision that God gives us. It is seen in a thirst and longing for God Himself, not only for what He will give us.

Repentance will bring forth the process of sanctification that will yield the fruit of holiness and humility in our lives. To be sanctified is to be set apart; to be a purified vessel of honor, a vessel that can be used for the purposes of God.

Repentance looks like the tax collector, who "…standing afar off, would not so much as raise his eyes to heaven, but beat his breast, saying, 'God be merciful to me a sinner!'" (Luke 18:13).

Penance looks like the Pharisee, who "…stood and prayed thus with himself, 'God I thank You that I am not like other men —extortioners, unjust, adulterers, or even as this tax collector. I fast twice a week; I give tithes of all that I possess'" (vv. 11-12).

The Word of God tells us that "…everyone who exalts himself will be humbled, and he who humbles himself will be exalted" (Luke 18:14). "And what does the Lord require of you but to do justly, to love mercy, and to walk humbly with your God?" (Micah 6:8).

True repentance will birth *humility* in our hearts. The deep root of pride must be confessed, or we will never know freedom from the doubts and fears that plague our lives. We must humble ourselves in the sight of the Lord, and then He'll give us grace, and will raise us up. (See James 4:5-6, 10.) We must seek earnestly to have a deeper knowledge of the Lord, but also of ourselves and our true hearts, or we will never have the depth of humility that God desires us to have.

Romans 12:16 tells us not to set our minds on high things, but to associate with the humble. We must not be wise in our own opinion. We must not do anything through selfish ambition or conceit, but in lowliness of mind we should esteem others better than ourselves. We must look out not only for our own interests, but also for the interests of others. (See Philippians 2:3-4.) Even in our deep trials we can look past our own difficulties and pray and help those around us who are also struggling; this brings healing to our own souls.

1 Peter 5:5-6 tells us to be clothed with humility, "for 'God resists the proud, but gives grace to the humble.' Therefore humble yourselves under the mighty hand of God, that He may exalt you in due time."

There is nothing that will humble us more than deep brokenness through godly tears of sorrow. The Lord desires to place upon us a mantle of humility so that He can raise us up and do His works through us in this hour. Humility will come as we humble ourselves in the fiery trials of life that are meant to cleanse us from our sin. Will we submit to this deep work in our souls?

TRANSFORMED IN THE DARK NIGHT OF THE SOUL

Who among you fears the Lord? Who obeys the voice of His Servant? Who walks in darkness and has no light? Let him trust in the name of the Lord and rely upon his God.

Isaiah 50:10

As WE WALK THE path of true repentance, many times the Spirit of God will draw us into the wilderness, just like He did Jesus after His baptism. (See Matthew 3:16-4:11.) Jesus was tempted of the devil, and He knew a time of suffering, hunger, and thirst in order to prepare Him for ministry. This was a sign of favor from His heavenly Father—not disapproval. Jesus came out of His "wilderness journey" filled with the Spirit, and empowered to do the works of His Father.

Many times we do not understand the ways of the Lord, for when He takes us into a dark place of trials in our lives, we often doubt and question His love for us. Little do we realize that He is preparing us in our spiritual desert, and His intention is to rid us of the things of this world. He empties us, so that He can fill us with His Spirit and power. We want to skip the cross and the desert place of death, and run directly to the miracles, signs, and wonders. But God cannot entrust us with His power until we are broken and cleansed, and this work will be accomplished in us as we yield to the Lord in this "dark night of the soul."

The dark night of the soul is a "journey in darkness," a time when we cannot see, nor can we understand, where the Lord is leading us. Abraham, our "father of faith," walked through this "dark night" when he followed God, not knowing where he was going. It is a faith journey and a time of suffering great temptations. During this season in our lives, our understanding is darkened and our senses are mortified, for we cannot understand what God is doing with our own *natural* reasoning. Our faculties, passions, affections, and desires sleep. At times we feel great fear in our souls, for walking in the unknown will bring up what is deep within our hearts. We cling tightly to His hand in trust as we stand on His Word. This is where we will begin to "walk by faith, and not by sight."

God is drawing us into His light, and all that is natural in us becomes dark. As the brightness of His glory overshadows us, it will blind and weaken us, much like looking directly into the sun in the natural world. We can also liken this process to the way fire acts upon a piece of wood; first it dries out all the water that is in it, then it turns deepest black in color as the fire draws all that is contrary to the nature of the fire. Finally, in this process, it will begin to heat the outside of the log and give heat. The dark night will remove the things of the world from our souls and reveal our black, hidden sins. God will remove all that is not like Him during this process in order to bring us into union with Himself, even as the fire will not stop burning the wood until it completely consumes and becomes one with it. God's fire will do the same in our own souls as we yield to His love and submit to this deep work in our souls.

True death in the spiritual realm is very much like a physical death in the natural. God begins to bring us into a new life in His Spirit as the old is cut away and put to death. This is not an overnight process. It will require much patience as the fruit of long-suffering is developed in us. In God's kingdom, death must come before Life—this is why Jesus tells us to pick up our cross daily and follow Him.

During this process our wills become dry as He takes us into the desert and empties us. He empties us in order to unite us with His will and purpose for our lives. We suffer deepest affliction as He removes even our former spiritual blessings in order to draw our souls completely into Him. It is here that God is purging our souls and beginning to possess us fully. Many begin to turn from the Lord at this point, because they are not willing to surrender all. In the desert, Christ becomes our "manna"—our "Bread;" it is in the wilderness that we find that He *alone* truly satisfies.

Another suffering we will go through in this dark night is the feeling of being emotionally dead. God is in the process of detaching us (in a healthy way) from everyone and everything in order to fulfill His purposes in and through our lives. We will love others more than we ever have, but we will no longer have relationships that are controlling or dysfunctional, for God will be our all in all, our "first love."

God's purpose is to detach us from this world and bring us to a glorious end—*union with Him*. At times we will feel a sense of abandonment, but God's purpose in taking us into this dark valley is to empty us of all that is not of Him. He "hollows us out" in order to fill us with Himself. The Lord will be Light to us as we sit in darkness, and when we fall He will pick us up. (See Micah 7:8.)

Our souls will long for Jesus in this night season as they never have before, and we will earnestly seek Him. (See Isaiah 26:9.) This is where "deep calls unto deep," and we will begin to hear and understand the language of heaven. In this darkness, true spiritual revelation will come to us. All of God's true children will experience this dark night, but for some it will be to a lesser or greater degree, according to the will of God.

Jesus longs to fashion us into a new vessel for His glory and honor. As a young Christian, there was a time when the Lord led me to Jeremiah 18:4-6, which says, "And the vessel that he made of clay was marred in the hand of the potter; so he made it again into another vessel, as it seemed good to the potter to make." As I continued to read, Jesus spoke these words directly to my heart, "O house of Israel, can I not do with you as this potter? Look, as the clay is in the potter's hand, so are you in My hand, O house of Israel." Instead of the word "Israel" in this verse, He had me put my name in it. This truth comforted my heart as I realized that I was on the His wheel being conformed into His image. My circumstances seemed to be spinning out of control, but I believed my life was fully in His hands. It is at this very place in our lives that God is removing the doubts and fears and filling our hearts with His faith, the faith of the Son of God.

We have all been marred because of sin, but the Lord takes us like a piece of clay and begins to mold us and make us into "vessels of honor." There will be times when we will have to go into the furnace of affliction, but this must not surprise us. (See 1 Peter 4:12.) We will experience a fire that is "seven times hotter" than anything we have ever known. There will be times when we will be set aside, in order to dry out, and we will feel as if we are of no use to God, but this is all a part of what we must go through, just like the clay pot must go through many different processes in order to be made into the vessel that its maker wants it to be. It must yield to the pressure that comes from the potter's hands. As clay in our Potter's hands, we must submit to this process in order to be changed and purified.

God desires to reveal Himself to us in new and fresh ways in this dark night. It will not be easy, for the crucifixion of the flesh is painful and difficult, but in His grace, He will never give us more than we can bear. We must be like the grain of wheat that falls into the ground and dies. (See John 12:24.) As we die to our sin and self-will, we will bring forth a harvest of righteousness. If we allow ourselves to be put to death in the flesh and in our "soulish" nature, we will find that the life of Christ will begin to be formed in us, and as the process continues, we will explode with His resurrection life and power. We will be able to say with Paul, "I have been crucified with Christ; it is no longer I who live, but Christ lives in me; and the life which I now live in the flesh I live by the faith in the Son of God who loved me and gave Himself for me" (Gal. 2:20).

In this dark night our heavenly Father will prune the useless branches off of us, even branches that may look *good*, but are not His *best* for our lives. This pruning is necessary if we are to become fruitful branches in His kingdom. When God began to prune me and take me through this dark night, I fought Him for years, not realizing that the death that I felt working in my soul was actually bringing forth His light, life, and presence. Many lack a true understanding of the ways of God, but I believe in this hour that true apostles, pastors, teachers, and prophets are rising up and will teach the *whole* truth of God's Word to the Body of Christ.

How will God perform this work is us? In Exodus 23:30, it says, "Little by little I will drive them out from before you, until you have increased, and you inherit the land." We see here that this is not an overnight process, and it is during this season of suffering that the Lord will develop patience and trust in our hearts. As we yield to this work, we will find ourselves being lifted up into a new light and glory.

As the Lord brings us into deeper waters of suffering, we will find ourselves in the midst of a furious storm. The Lord desires to take us to the "other side of the lake," but we must first learn to trust Him in the midst of the storm. There will be times when we will feel as if He is sleeping in the boat, and we'll say, "Teacher, do You not care that we are perishing?" (Mark 4:38). We'll learn that it is at this very time that our Lord desires to develop faith and trust in us, and to uproot fear and unbelief from our souls. In the very midst of this darkness the Lord will begin to strip us of our idols and the worldly dependence that we have on others. God will begin to reveal our foundation and show us the sin that lies covered deep in our souls. All of our carved images shall be beaten to pieces, and all our idols God will lay desolate. "Therefore I will wail and howl, I will go stripped and naked; I will make a wailing like the jackals and a mourning like the ostriches." (See Micah 1:6-8.)

As God draws us deeper into His heart, we will find that His Word will penetrate our souls as a sharp sword, and He will begin to cut away our sin. Paul experienced this process through a multitude of trials—he was in severely beaten, frequently in prison, and often faced death. From the Jews, five times he received 40 stripes minus one. Three times he was beaten with rods; once he was stoned, and three times he was shipwrecked. On his frequent journeys he faced perils of water, robbers, his own countrymen, the Gentiles, the wilderness, and among false brethren. He experienced weariness, toil, sleeplessness, hunger and thirst, fasting, and cold and nakedness. It was through these trials that Paul "suffered the loss of all things" in order to gain Christ. His deepest desire was to know Christ, and "the power of His resurrection, and the fellowship of His sufferings, being conformed to His death" (Philippians 3:8-10). In addition to all this, Paul carried daily his deep concern for all the churches. (See 2 Corinthians 11:23-28.)

So many of God's children want the power of the Spirit in their lives, but they are unwilling to go through this dark night of the soul, the place where we must be stripped of our sin, and where at times we will feel the darkness of sin obliterate the light of His presence in our souls. It is not that He has left us, but that He is drawing so near to us. Like it says in Psalm 18:19-21, He will bow the heavens and come down with darkness under His feet. He will fly to us on the wings of the wind, and make *darkness* His secret place. His canopy around Him is dark waters and thick clouds of the skies. "From the brightness before Him, His thick clouds passed with hailstones and coals of fire." Verse 15 says, "Then the channels of the sea were seen, the foundations of the world were uncovered at Your rebuke, O Lord, at the blast of the breath of Your nostrils."

Can you see that the darkness we experience in the midst of our trials is because of the nearness of His presence? He is on His way to deliver us from all of our enemies, but because of His brightness and glory there is a "dark canopy" around Him. This is for our protection, so that we will not be destroyed in His fiery presence! This darkness is the "secret place" that He will draw us into, in order to speak to us as He reveals His hidden truths to us. The Lord told Moses that He would come to him in a thick cloud. (See Exodus 19:9.) It is in this cloud that His glory is revealed to us.

In Luke 9:28-36, we read about the encounter of Peter, James, and John with Jesus when He was transfigured before them on the top of the mountain. Jesus appeared in His glory, "...and when they were fully awake they saw His glory and the two men who stood with Him." Peter wanted to make three tabernacles, one for Jesus, Moses, and Elijah. "While he was saying this, a cloud came and overshadowed them; and they were fearful as they entered the cloud."

Jonah experienced his dark night in the fish's belly, and he cried out to the Lord in his affliction and said:

> For You cast me into the deep, into the heart of the seas, and the floods surrounded me; all Your billows and Your waves passed over me... The waters surrounded me, even to my soul;

the deep closed around me; weeds were wrapped around my head....the earth with its bars closed behind me forever; yet You have brought up my life from the pit, O Lord, my God.

-Jonah 2: 3, 5-6

Jonah suffered in darkness because of disobedience; he felt that he would be in this prison forever. We may feel that our fiery trials will never end, but they will; they ended for Jonah, and they will end for us.

Jeremiah felt this dark night many, many times as he walked in obedience to the Lord's will. In his pain he cried:

I am a man who has seen affliction by the rod of His wrath. He has led me and made me walk in darkness and not in light. Surely He has turned His hand against me time and time again throughout the day. He has aged my flesh and my skin, and broken my bones. He has besieged me and surrounded me with bitterness and woe. He has set me in dark places like the dead of long ago. He has hedged me in so that I cannot get out; He has made my chain heavy. Even when I cry and shout, He shuts out my prayer. He has blocked my way with hewn stone; He has made my paths crooked.

-Lamentations 3:1-9

Jeremiah cried out in his pain, but in the second half of Lamentations 3, he makes many confessions of faith. The chapter ends with great confidence in God: "I called on Your name, O Lord, from the lowest pit. You have heard my voice: 'Do not hide Your ear from my sighing, from my cry for help.' You drew near on the day I called on You, and said, 'Do not fear!' O Lord, You have pleaded the case for My soul; You have redeemed my life" (Lam. 3:55-58).

God desires that we cry out to Him in the midst of our suffering, that we release our emotional pain to Him and not cover our grief and questionings. If we bring our pain to the Lord He will come and speak words of comfort, and we'll find relief through trust and faith in the midst of our greatest trials. Read the Psalms of David, and you will see that he was always honest about what he felt; we must be, too.

There is one thing that I would like to make clear in the midst of this teaching: the "dark night of the soul" does not only come to the disobedient in order to bring them back to God's path, but also to the

Lord's true servants, so that they might be drawn closer to Him and to bring an even greater purity to their souls. Job was an obedient servant, and so was Paul, but they suffered deeply in order to bring God's comfort and salvation to a multitude of souls. Little did Job realize that many people would be comforted because of his dark night of suffering. Do you think Paul realized the extent to which God would use him in the midst of his excruciating pain? Paul's light and understanding grew as he walked with God; it was progressive in his suffering, but I do not believe that he knew the *full extent* of what his suffering would accomplish while he was yet on earth, and neither will we. God's purpose is much higher than we realize, and we must trust Him even when we do not understand His ways. His ways are perfect—whether we understand them or not!

Are we afraid to enter this dark cloud, this place where we will be transformed and see the glory of God? Our God dwells in the dark cloud, and when we walk through the "valley of the shadow of death" we must fear no evil, for the Lord is with us, protecting us and keeping us safe in the midst of our dark night. It is here that all of our doubts and fears will be exposed, and if we allow Him, He will remove them in His blazing fire of love.

In this place we'll find that He has hedged us in, behind and before, and laid His hand upon us. If we try to run from Him at this time, we will find that we cannot flee from His presence. If we feel that our bed is made in hell, we will find that He is there, right beside us. We'll say: "'Surely the darkness shall fall on me,' even the night shall be light about me; indeed, the darkness shall not hide from You, but the night shines as the day; the darkness and the light are both alike to You." (See Psalm 139:5-12.)

In the darkness of our suffering we feel alone, but the Lord is never so near to us as when we feel forsaken and unloved. He will never leave us or forsake us; He knows everything that we are suffering. Jesus felt forsaken, and so did Job, and so have many of God's saints throughout the ages. When we suffer emotional pain we must realize that our "feelings" are not the *truth*. We must stand upon His Word in the darkest night that we go through, for He is faithful. It is in these very times, if we stand upon His Word and praise Him in the midst of the storm, that we will see glimpses of His lovely face. The veil within our hearts will begin to tear, and we will begin to know Him in a way that we never dreamed possible. There is a *valley* that we must walk through if we are to come to that place of full trust and surrender to His will.

Jacob wrestled with the Lord during his dark night, and so will we. He had a great fear in his soul because his brother Esau wanted to kill him; he had to overcome the "fear of man." He cried out to the Lord from the depths of his heart, and this is what we must do in all of our struggles. (See Genesis 32:9-11.) Don't be ashamed of your weakness and fears, but release them to the Lord; openly and honestly confess them. He is merciful and understands us completely. He knows that we are made of dust. Our weeping will endure for the night, but joy will come in the morning! In Genesis 32:24 it says that Jacob was left alone, and a Man wrestled with him until the breaking of day. At times we will find ourselves left alone as we go through our dark night, for no one, no friend or family member can go through this with us; it is God alone that we must face in our sin and struggles. We must wait on the Lord and wrestle with Him until the light of Christ breaks through our souls and we are delivered.

As Jacob wrestled with God, he was touched, and the socket of his hip came out of joint. Jacob would not let Him go until He had blessed him; this is when Jacob's name was changed, for he had struggled with God and with men, and he prevailed. From then on Israel (Jacob) limped on his hip . (See Genesis 32:25-31.)

In this place of weakness, we will find, as Paul did, that when we are weak, we are then strong in Christ. Paul gloried in his weakness, so that the power of Christ would rest upon him. As Jacob was weakened when God touched him, so will the Lord touch some area of our soul in our struggles, and we will be greatly weakened *in the natural*. We will learn how to rely and lean completely on the Lord. God changed Jacob from the inside out, and because of this change, peace filled his soul. Because of the heart change in Jacob, the Lord made even his brother Esau to be at peace with him. God changed Esau's heart toward his brother, and if we allow the Lord to change *us,* we will find that He will make our enemies to be at peace with us.

The Lord showed me years ago that when He was on the cross, during His horrible, dark night, He could endure His suffering as long as He could see the face of His Father, but when that dark cloud of sin came and He could no longer see His Father's face, it was then that He died of a broken heart. In our trials we have His promise that He will never leave us or forsake us; we may *feel* abandoned, but He is always with us.

He was, "poured out like water, and all His bones were out of joint. His heart like wax, melted within Him. His strength was dried up, and his tongue clung to His jaws. His hands and feet were pierced, and He could count all His bones." (See Psalm 22:14-17.) He died an excruciating death in a depth of suffering none of us will ever fully understand or ever experience. We will never understand fully what it cost our Savior when He took upon His sinless body the filth and sin of the world. What we suffer in comparison is what the apostle Paul calls a "light affliction" and it is, no matter how painful or devastating we may feel that it is.

When Betsie and Corrie ten Boom were imprisoned in one of Nazi Germany's most dreaded concentration camps, in the midst of hellish suffering and cruelty, Betsie said: "There is no pit so deep that God's love is not deeper still." Even as Betsie and Corrie experienced the presence and love of Jesus in their dark night, so will we know the comfort of the Holy Spirit in our suffering. He will be with us and will even bring us joy in the midst of sorrow. We *will* suffer in this world, for "It has been granted to us on behalf of Christ, not only to believe in Him, but also to suffer for His sake" (Phil. 1:29).

What will our dark night look like? It will be different for everyone. For me it was a deep depression as the abuse from my past surfaced. It came to me in a cloud of fear and terror as I witnessed loved ones turn to drugs and sex for relief from their sorrows. I suffered excruciating pain as my marriage began to crumble before my eyes. My *night* enveloped me as I was slandered and misunderstood by those around me. I felt separated and abandoned by my loved ones, and even from those that I loved in the church. As dark as this night was, never did I feel completely abandoned by the Lord. Even though I could not feel His presence, or see Him in my circumstances, still I *knew* in my deep heart, even in my spirit-man, that He was with me. It was there, when all His waves and billows were crashing over me, that the Lord commanded His loving kindness in the daytime, and in the night His song was with me. Deep was calling unto deep inside of me. (See Psalm 42:7-8.) It was in this very place that the Lord revealed to me His deep heart of love, and began to remove the roots of fear and unbelief.

For you, it may come as a debilitating illness, where you will have to cling tightly to His promises for healing. It may come as one of your children is caught in a trap of drugs or alcohol, or as your spouse betrays you by having an illicit affair. For many it will come as a financial crisis and you will have to cry out to Jesus as "Jehovah-jireh" —God the provider. It may even come through the death of a loved one. It may come from the pain of incest, or in the grief you experience as your spouse emotionally abuses you. It will be during the crisis times in our lives that we will learn to walk by faith and not by sight. Your heart may not feel even a glimmer of hope at this time. There may be times of paralyzing fear, when you will feel you cannot even pray, but I promise you, that if you cling to Jesus and stand on His Word, He will see you to the other side of the lake. The clouds will break, and you *will* see the sun again. During this time you will have to stand on the solid rock of God's Word and not listen to the words of unbelief and fear that many will speak to you. During this season of death, you will have to cling to the Lord like Jacob did, until the morning breaks in your soul. When you are in the midst of these dark clouds, always remember that the sun is still shining above them. Keep praising, trusting, and crying out to Jesus. He will not fail you!

In our wilderness, God will feed and nourish us, and give to us "water out of the rock." God never failed His children in the wilderness—they failed Him! Jesus will feed us when we're hungry, for He is the "bread of life." He is the "bread" that comes down from heaven; one may eat of it and not die. (See John 6:48-51.) He will quench our thirst in the parched desert, for whoever drinks of the water that He gives them will never thirst, and it will become in him a fountain of water springing up into everlasting life. (See John 4:14.) He wants "rivers of living water" to flow out of our hearts, and we will experience this if we allow the Lord to remove the weeds and rocks from our souls—the sin that is hindering the flow of this water. (See John 7:37-39.)

God will provide a "table in the wilderness," but the children of Israel did not believe He would do so for them. Will we be guilty of this same sin? They said, "'Can He give bread also? Can He provide meat for His people?' Therefore the Lord heard this and was furious…and anger also came up against Israel, because they did not believe in God, and did not trust in His salvation" (Ps. 78:20-22).

My prayer is that we will trust Him fully in our dark night, knowing that He will feed us and care for us no matter what comes our way. We must have faith in the goodness of our God, especially in the dark trials and judgments that are about to come to our nation, and the nations of this world. Feed on the Word day and night, and do not allow the lies of the enemy to penetrate your mind. Our faith will be perfected in the "dark night of the soul" that He takes us through.

We want *instant* deliverance, but that is not the way of the Lord. We must persevere until we come to the place of freedom in Christ—no matter how long it takes. This is where the *fire of delayed answers* will purify us deeply as we wait on the Lord.

As we wait patiently for the Lord in the midst of our fiery trials, we will be able to say with the Psalmist, "He also brought me up out of a horrible pit, out of the miry clay, and set my feet upon a rock, and established my steps. He has put a new song in my mouth – praise to our God; many will see it and fear, and will trust in the Lord" (Ps. 40:2-3).

TRANSFORMED THROUGH IMPLICIT TRUST AND TOTAL SURRENDER

I beseech you therefore, brethren, by the mercies of God, that you present your bodies a living sacrifice, holy, acceptable to God, which is your reasonable service.

Romans 12:1

"Surrender is the key—surrender is the key that will unlock the riches in My storehouse. Rest is a ceasing from your own striving, ceasing to do your own will, whether it's sunny or stormy, joyful or painful, whether or not things are going your way, or another's will is being done—a will that overrides yours.

"I never saw a human factor in anything that touched My life. I lived in perfect obedience and trust and did the Father's will only. I never sought to do My own will. This, My children, is how you must learn to live—deny yourself in the little things as well as the big, according to My Father, and your Father's will.

"There will be times when you must confront others and the devil—but you must be led by My Spirit always. See no human hand in your life—see no demonic attack —only the hand of the Father. When your life is fully surrendered to Me, you can know, without a doubt, that nothing can touch your life apart from My will, and this alone will bring great and deep peace in your soul. Don't see the enemy or others as having the 'upper hand,' but see My heavenly hand, the hand that rules and holds the universe in the palm of His hand—the Sovereign Ruler, whose Kingdom rules over all—as having everything under His control. I will allow nothing apart from My will.

"When you are under attack, whether from the enemy or his attacks through others, run to Me—come to Me—and you will find that no weapon formed against you will prosper. You are in the palm of My hand when you are fully surrendered. I will

allow no one— nothing—to destroy you; I am only out to crucify those things that are keeping you from My intimate love—those things alone I will burn up. I will never hurt who you truly are in Me.

"Rest and embrace these truths, My children. I'm on My way to show you the way of the Master—not many ways or thoughts—but the way of your God.

"I will make you fruitful in the barren land. As you are emptied and surrendered to Me <u>fully</u>, you will know the fullness of My Spirit, and I will lead you into that promised land— where you will find My fullness and love in a measure that is incomprehensible to you.

"Trust Me now, children. Surrender—cease from your own works and striving. I alone have 'measured up' and am perfect. My life—My perfection—will be known by you only through a full surrender of all: everything you have, everything you are—all your loved ones, desires, and longings. <u>All</u> must be laid on the altar of sacrifice, even as Abraham sacrificed Isaac to Me in his heart. When he surrendered fully in his heart his most cherished treasure— it was then that I could take full possession of My servant—it was then that he entered fully into My rest.

"So come—come close. Do not be afraid. Open your hearts and open your hands, and as I take every idol from your heart, I will then fill you with My glory and My presence!

"I am asking for all this day. Nothing less will do. I will not accept 99 percent. Only 100 percent full and complete surrender to Me is acceptable. If you hear Me this day and respond in obedience, I will bless you beyond measure! I love you, and I, your God, am calling you this day." -Jesus
(Given to me on August 23, 2011)

As we continue our journey in the dark night, God will lead us to a place of total surrender and submission to His will. If we refuse His loving discipline in our lives and continue to live in self-will and rebellion, we will never enter fully into the inheritance that He has for us or be delivered fully from our doubts and unbelief.

When we think of sin, most of the time we think of individual sins, such as lying or stealing, but sin is a *disposition* that says, "I have a right to do what I want—when I want. I have a right to live my own life and make my own choices." This root of rebellion is bound strongly to the root of unbelief, which will not trust or submit to the lordship of Christ. Eve believed the lie that God was holding back His best from her, and in unbelief decided to make her own choice apart from God's perfect will for her life. When we have this mind-set, we walk in deception and unbelief and only by the grace of God can we be freed.

God's desire is that we surrender every part of our lives to Him —our past, present, and future. We must be willing to lay down our own wills and desires *daily*, for only then will we be able to say as Paul did, "...I die daily." (See 1 Corinthians 15:31.) As we embrace our cross fully and learn to trust and surrender to His will, we will come forth out of our wilderness experiencing His freedom and life, but if we run from Him in fear and unbelief, the loss will be great. God's desire is to give us a glorious inheritance, but the choice is ours.

I love what Oswald Chambers says in his book, <u>My Utmost for His Highest</u>:

The preaching of today is apt to emphasize strength of will, beauty of character—the things that are easily noticed. The phrase we hear so often, "Decide for Christ" is an emphasis on something Our Lord never trusted. He never asks us to decide for Him, but to yield to Him—a very different thing.

It is not "head knowledge" that will save us, but a surrender of our sin, hearts, and even our very lives. You see, Jesus doesn't want our works, but He wants our hearts fully abandoned to Him. The surrender must be complete in this hour, and that means loving Jesus above those we most cherish in this world. Jesus said, "He who loves father or mother more than Me is not worthy of Me. And he who loves son or daughter more than Me is not worthy of Me" (Matt. 10:37). This is a surrender that only a few teach and preach about today, but it is one that many in China, India, Iran, and other nations know much about. Many have been abandoned and cast out, even tortured and killed because of their commitment to Christ; they have chosen Jesus in spite of their devastating losses. I believe in the days ahead, as the persecution heightens in our own nation, we, too, will have to make some extremely painful choices that will reveal where our loyalty lies! Our losses will be great, but our reward is eternal.

He is calling us to a *radical* surrender to Him and to His will in this hour. Without this full surrender, we will be in grave danger as greater fires come into our lives, for we will find ourselves spiritually weak. Trials are meant to make us strong in the Lord so that we can stand firm in faith, no matter how fierce the storm. These fires will remove every fear and obstacle from our hearts, and all that would hinder us from riding His wave of glory. Many of God's children feel that they are ready for what is coming, but the Lord has shown me that there are multitudes in the Church that are still bound in fear and unbelief; they trust Him when the weather's mild, but in the coming storms they will shake like leaves if they do not draw closer to Him and give up everything.

How can we surrender fully to Him if we do not trust Him? Our trust in Christ must be complete; it must be *implicit*, which means having *no* doubts or reservations. Trust brings us to a place where we will never doubt the Lord or His ways, but must fully believe and stand on His Word, no matter what the situation looks like. God will take us through many fiery trials in order to strengthen our faith and deepen our trust in Him.

The Word says that for a while we will be grieved by various trials, so "...that the genuineness of your faith, being much more precious than gold that perishes, though it is tested by fire, may be found to praise, honor, and glory at the revelation of Jesus Christ" (1 Pet. 1:7). Our faith must be tried in the fire if it is to be a *genuine* faith, for anyone can trust the Lord when the sun is shining. It is in the storms of life that we will find that our anchor is secure in Christ. God can, and will, bring us to that place of full trust as we surrender to Him in these trials, and we will say as Job did: "Though He slay me, yet will I trust Him" (Job 13:15). It will be worth all the suffering we go through to come to this place!

How can we fully surrender to Him, or give our bodies to Him as a living sacrifice, unless we have total trust in His goodness and mercy? As we study the Word, we will come to understand God's character and ways more fully, and we'll learn to trust Him more deeply as we experience His manifest presence and love personally.

Moses and Joshua spent time with the Lord in intimate communion with Him, and that is why they lived a life of faith, not doubting His love, provision, or promises to them. There is nothing more important in our lives than spending time with Jesus, worshipping Him, and listening to the still small voice of the Spirit. This alone will eliminate much of the doubt and fear that plague our lives at times. We spend hours with our husbands, wives, loved ones, and friends in order to get to know them more deeply and intimately, and the same holds true in our relationship with Jesus. He is calling us to draw close to Him in this hour and desires that we sit at His feet as Mary did. God wants us to choose the "good part, which will not be taken away." (See Luke 10:39-42.)

We put so much confidence in man at times, but the Word says that "It is better to trust in the Lord than to put confidence in man" (Ps. 118:8). Man at times will fail us, but we must not compare the Lord to man, for "God is not a man, that He should lie, nor a son of man, that He should repent. Has He said, and will He not do? Or has He spoken, and will He not make it good?" (Num. 23:19).

Titus 1:2 says, "...in hope of eternal life which God, who cannot lie, promised before time began." If we truly believe that the Bible is the written Word of God, why do we not believe the more than 7,000 promises that He has made to us in it? We can trust the One who died for us! As we examine our hearts, we must repent deeply for not trusting Him in our personal lives. Our God is not a man, and He will *never* fail to keep His Word to us. There may be delays and setbacks, but in the end He will not—He cannot—fail a child of His who is fully surrendered to Him. When there is failure, we must examine our own hearts and ask ourselves where we have been disobedient to His will and commandments. We must always remember that many of His promises are conditional; we must do *our* part.

God promises us that he who puts his *trust* in Him shall possess the land, and shall inherit His holy mountain; the condition is *trust*. (See Isaiah 57:13.) Fear will always bring "a snare, but whoever trusts in the Lord shall be safe." (See Proverbs 29:25.) If we trust the Lord fully in the days ahead, there is nothing that we need to fear.

God's Word—not our own thoughts—must be our anchor. The Word says that those who trust their own hearts are fools. We must trust in the Lord with all of our hearts, and not lean on our own understanding. (See Proverbs 3:5.) Leaning on our own understanding, or on someone else's opinion, will often get us into trouble. We must seek the mind and the wisdom of the Lord in every situation we find ourselves in.

Jesus is our stronghold in the day of trouble, and He *knows* those who trust in Him (See Nahum 1:7.) Does Jesus know you? Do you fully trust Him? To those who trust Him fully He would say:

"'For I will surely deliver you, and you shall not fall by the sword; but your life shall be as a prize to you, because you have put your trust in Me,' says the Lord " (Jer. 39:18).

As we trust the Lord, and embrace our cross in full surrender to the Father's will, we will find that little by little the Holy Spirit will begin to take possession of our souls and our bodies. We will feel a new vibrancy and life begin to fill our inner being. There will be times when we will even feel our bodies energized with this new life as we wait upon Him in praise and worship.

In the desert of our souls, God is creating in us a hunger and thirst for righteousness. In the wilderness we will long more deeply to see His face and will desire to know Him more intimately. This dark night will bring us to the end of ourselves, for we will see that no good thing dwells in our flesh. (See Romans 7:18.) Through our poverty of spirit, all of our "dead works" will begin to dry up, and we will begin to see His hand and His works in *all* things. We will realize that apart from Jesus we can do nothing.

The Word tells us in Matthew 7:13-14, that we must "Enter by the narrow gate; for wide is the gate and broad is the way that leads to destruction, and there are many that go in by it. Because narrow is the gate and difficult is the way which leads to life, and there are few who find it." Jesus is telling us that the way to life is difficult—not easy. We are to expect tribulation, persecution, and trouble. Praying, going to church, and doing good deeds are part of the Christian life, but these works alone will not secure a place for us in heaven. It is not by works of righteousness which *we* have done, but according to *His mercy* that He saved us. (See Titus 3:5.)

What is this narrow way, this narrow gate that we must go through in order to find life? It is only through His cross, as we repent and surrender our lives fully to Jesus that we will enter through this narrow gate and find Life. Jesus is the Way, the Truth, and the Life. *He* is the narrow gate that we must go through. Our sins must be confessed and fully surrendered to Jesus, and then He will begin the process of cleansing our souls and bodies from all sin. You see, our spirit-man came alive at the new birth—when we came to Jesus and asked Him to forgive us. Many of us rejoiced with great joy because we knew Jesus came in to set up His throne in our hearts. Our spirit-man was made new, for old things passed away, and we knew we had a new nature. But the "soulish" realm—our mind, will, and emotions—were still a major mess, at least for most of us. As a young Christian, there were times when I doubted that I was even saved. After learning the truth about the need for our souls and bodies to be delivered and healed *after* the new birth, it was then that I began to be strengthened in faith concerning my salvation. You see, I thought that because I still had evil thoughts, bitterness, and anger after accepting Christ, I couldn't possibly be saved. I didn't understand the difference between the spirit, soul, and body. Many still are bound with unbelief and fear because of this lack of understanding in the way that we are made.

Many fail to realize what Christ has done because they cannot get past their *feelings* of guilt and shame. It's a done deal; we only need to believe it, and act on the truth of God's Word. Our sin nature no longer has to be dealt with, because the sin that was in our spirit was—past tense—crucified with Christ. Our spirit-man is now alive because of Christ's sacrifice on Calvary. When we truly repent and receive Christ into our hearts, our spirit-man is resurrected by the power of His cross, but that does not mean that our souls and bodies are automatically freed. There are "graveclothes" from our past that need to be loosed from us, even as they had to be removed from Lazarus. When we truly repented of our sin, we, like Lazarus, came out of our tombs of death. Our sin is forgiven, but we are still "wrapped" with strongholds in our souls, and with sins of the flesh in our bodies. We must still deal with these areas in our souls and bodies through repentance and transformation. As we have seen, we must never take sin lightly. The "washing of the water by the word," and the fire of the Spirit through our surrender and obedience, will finish this work inside of us. There is still a great need for the renewing of the mind, a surrendering of our will to His, and for a deep healing in our emotions if we are to see ourselves freed fully from doubt and unbelief.

In the transforming work of surrender, God is asking us to give Him every part of our lives. God is asking us to sacrifice to Him what is natural in this life, in order for the spiritual to come forth in us. Everything that is natural in us must be transformed into the spiritual through obedience and through the process of the cross. We are called to be spiritual beings who glorify God on this earth, and if we walk in the flesh we cannot be pleasing to Him. Only through obedience and sacrifice can this work be accomplished in us. Even our spirit must be laid on the altar of sacrifice, we must hold nothing back. Jesus died for us so that we would no longer live for ourselves, but for Him. (See 2 Corinthians 5:15.) Our bodies are the temple of the Holy Spirit, who is in us, and we are *not* our own. We were bought with a great price—the blood of God's dear Son. We are called to glorify God in our bodies and spirits, which belong to Him. (See 1 Corinthians 6:19-20.) We no longer belong to ourselves, but to Jesus, the One who redeemed us and now desires to sanctify us fully!

God is calling us to present our bodies to Him as a living sacrifice, holy and acceptable to Him. This includes our entire being—our whole personality—the deepest place in our hearts. This is a total surrender—not just a mental assent to this truth. This process must be *worked out and appropriated* into our very lives, or we will lose the fullness of His life that He so desires to give us. He wants us to experience what Paul talked about when he said "it is no longer I who live, but Christ lives in me." (See Galatians 2:20.)

As the Lord sits on the throne in our spirits, our souls and bodies must now learn to submit to Him, and be in subjection to Him. Jesus must now become the only King inside of us. The Lord must sit on the throne of our hearts, for there can no longer be two kings. We must abdicate the throne in our hearts to Jesus, and then as we yield full control to Him, little by little the Spirit will begin to take control of our minds, wills, emotions, and bodies.

In this transforming process of surrendering our soul and body to Jesus, the "inward man" must break through the "outward" man. We must build up this inward man by our "most holy faith" until we become strong in the Spirit's power. God's Spirit within us will break through our mind, will, and emotions, and our five physical senses. It will then be "Christ that lives in me." The best illustration that I can think of is Gideon's army. When he divided his men, he "put a trumpet into every man's hand, with empty pitchers, and torches inside the pitchers." When they went to face the enemy, Gideon told them to blow the trumpets and break the pitchers. It was then that the enemy was defeated. (See Judges 7:16-25.)

In the wilderness, God is emptying us like those pitchers were emptied, and filling us with His Holy Spirit—His "Torch," that alone will defeat the enemy. The pitchers had to be *broken* in order for the light to shine through, which illustrates how our souls must be broken and shattered in order for the life of Christ to shine through us. It is then that we will walk in the power of the Spirit and experience great victory over our enemies.

Our souls and bodies greatly affect our spiritual life and progress in the Lord. The spirit, soul, and body are *interconnected*. When we grow weary and depressed from trials and hardship, we must be on guard, for it is then that we are more vulnerable to the insidious lies of the enemy. We must make sure that the helmet of salvation is intact and hold on to God's Word even more tightly. There will be times that our bodies will feel weak, whether from lack of sleep or even sickness, but we must run to the Lord and cry out to Him for strength to stand firm in the battle. We must get the rest we need, or it can affect our *spirit-man,* and he may weaken. When we disobey, or are weary through weeping because of our deep wounds, we must all the more feed our souls on God's Word and spend time in His presence building up our faith and trust in Him. God's desire is to make us completely whole—spirit, soul, and body—so that we might be strong and do exploits in His name. (See 1 Thessalonians 5:23.) This is the glorious end that the Lord has in mind for us in the tests of life: to be true overcomers, victorious over our enemies, and be able to take hold of our full inheritance.

TRANSFORMATION OF THE MIND

For those who live according to the flesh set their minds on the things of the flesh, but those who live according to the Spirit, the things of the Spirit. For to be carnally minded is death, but to be spiritually minded is life and peace.

Romans 8:5-6

WITHOUT A FULL SURRENDER of our minds to the Lord, and daily meditation in the Word, we will never enter our promised land, or be freed from doubt and unbelief. Our minds affect every part of our lives including our relationships (how we view ourselves and others), and if not renewed in the Spirit can actually cause us to lose our inheritance. Our minds can even affect our bodies by bringing in sickness and disease because of negative thinking. Depression, and even psychosomatic illnesses, which have real physical symptoms, can be experienced by those who have a "diseased mind." You've heard of hypochondriacs: people who have persistent conviction that they are sick, or will be sick. They experience pain that is very real to them, even when there is no true illness in them—so powerful is the human mind.

Our thoughts will transform our lives, either for good or for evil, for the Word says, "...as he thinks in his heart, so is he" (Prov. 23:7). How do we truly see ourselves? Many would say the right words, "Oh, I'm a child of God. I am victorious. I am greatly loved!" But God sees our deep hearts. Many say these words, but they are hollow; they do not really believe this in the core of their being. The Spirit desires to work in our deep heart, that place where we hardly go, and don't really know. (See Jeremiah 17:9.) Do we truly believe that the trial we are in is because of God's deep love for us? Can we truly thank the Lord for the trial, or are we struggling with deep feelings of rejection?

In Numbers 13:33 we read, "...and we were like grasshoppers in our own sight, and we were in their sight." As God's people faced their giants in the wilderness, they saw themselves as grasshoppers and not the victorious warriors that God had called them to be. They had the wrong focus, for they looked at their own frailty and weakness and not on the greatness and power of their God! We, too, fail many times, because we look at the mountains and giants before us and *believe the lie* of the enemy that we can't overcome them. We must look past these giants and see our mighty God standing over them—our victorious God! The focus of our mind must be changed, and this can only be done as our minds are renewed daily through meditating on the Word day and night, as Joshua did, and *applying* it to our lives. Only then will we have good success, and our way will prosper in the Lord. (See Romans 12:2, Joshua 1:8.) Our minds must be fully surrendered to the Lord until we have His mind, "the mind of Christ," fully developed in us. (See 1 Corinthians 2:16.)

As we set our minds on things above and not on the things of this world, we'll find the "peace of God that passes all understanding." (See Colossians 3:2, Isaiah 26:3.) Our minds must be controlled by the Holy Spirit, and we must take every negative thought captive to the obedience of Jesus. (See 2 Corinthians 10:5.) A practical way to do this when a negative thought surfaces is to replace it with a Scripture from God's Word. For example, when a fearful thought tries to enter your mind, say: "God has not given me a spirit of fear, but of power and love and a sound mind" (2 Tim. 1:7). The *feeling* of fear may not immediately leave, but as you continue to stand on this promise you will be able to face this giant in the strength of your God.

As we learn the ways of the Lord, we see that human reasoning is the opposite of trust, for the Word says that we are not to lean on our own understanding. (See Proverbs 3:5.) There will be many times in your life, as there are in mine, when we will not understand what the Lord is doing in situations that are right now so painful. There were times, many times, when I could not see the hand of God in my situation. It *looked* so devastating. It was at those times that I had to learn to trust the promises of God and not lean on my own understanding, for if I did, it would have emotionally destroyed me. If we refuse to give up our carnal reasoning, it will lead only to death; it will destroy our relationship with God, and some may even take their very lives.

This is a very serious issue for many of God's children. If we choose to stand on the solid rock of God's Word, no matter what it looks like, it will eventually lead us to life and peace. To be "spiritually minded" is to have Christ's mind in every situation. (See Romans 8:6.) We can, in the power of the Spirit, gird up the "loins" of our minds, but it will be hard work, and we will feel death come to our own reasoning. This is the work of the cross, crucifying our carnal reasoning. I believe that this is one of the reasons why Jesus suffered the crown of thorns on His head. When Jesus wore the crown of thorns and His brow was pierced He was in so much pain that His thoughts were numbed—they came to a place of death. It is painful to crucify your own reasoning, but it must be done if we are ever to be free from the chain of unbelief in our lives. Our thoughts must be surrendered and submitted fully to the authority of Christ. We must manage and discipline our minds to think only thoughts of truth and goodness. This is something God will *not* do for us. He will help and strengthen us in the power of His Spirit, but we must do *our* part.

Philippians 2:5-8 tells us that we are to have the "mind of Christ," and that Jesus made Himself of no reputation, taking the form of a bondservant, and coming in the likeness of men. Jesus humbled Himself and became obedient to the point of death. This is the kind of mind God wants to develop in us. A bondservant has no rights of his or her own, but does only what the master tells him or her to do. They are totally submitted to doing their master's will. Do we have a humble mind like this? Are we surprised when God takes us into a fiery trial, or do we get offended when someone slanders our name? As we meditate on the life of Christ we will see just how much pride and stubbornness yet remains in our hearts. Jesus never felt a need to defend Himself, for He knew who He was.

We will be changed more and more into the likeness of Christ as we meditate on "...whatever things are true, whatever things are noble, whatever things are just, whatever things are pure, whatever things are lovely, whatever things are of good report, if there is any virtue and if there is anything praiseworthy—meditate on these things" (Phil. 4:8).

As we embrace our true identity in Christ by what the Word tells us, not by what others say or by what the world's standard are, we will then be transformed into His likeness.

In Christ you are:
- Included (Eph. 1:13).
- A saint (Eph. 1:18).
- The salt and light of the earth (Matt. 5:13-14).
- Chosen (John 15:16).
- God's co-worker (2 Cor. 6:1).
- Alive with Christ (Eph. 2:5).
- Raised up with Christ (Col. 2:12).
- Seated with Christ in heavenly places (Eph. 2:6).

- God's workmanship (Eph. 2:10).
- A holy temple (1 Cor. 6:19).
- God's child (John 1:12).
- Justified (Rom. 5:1).
- Christ's friend (John 15:15).
- A member of Christ's body (1 Cor. 12:27).
- A citizen of heaven (Phil. 3:20).
- Anointed and sealed by God (2 Cor. 1:21-22).
- Born of God and the evil one cannot touch you (1 John 5:18).
- Are blessed in the heavenly realms with every spiritual blessing (Eph. 1:3).
- Holy and blameless (Eph. 1:4).
- Adopted as His child (Eph. 1:5).
- Forgiven (Col. 1:14).
- Not in want (Phil. 4:19).
- Victorious (1 John 5:4).
- Blameless (1 Cor. 1:8).
- Crucified with Christ (Gal. 2:20).
- More than a conqueror (Rom. 8:37).
- The righteousness of God (2 Cor. 5:21).
- Safe (1 John 5:18).
- A new creation in Christ (2 Cor. 5:17).
- Redeemed from the curse of the Law (Gal. 3:13).

As we meditate on the truth of God's Word, we will find ourselves changing, little by little, until our minds are fully renewed in the Spirit.

In our dark night, as our natural senses enter into the peace and rest of God, we will find a new wisdom—a light that transcends the darkness of our natural reasoning. As Christ's mind becomes more and more formed in us, there will be a *spiritual knowledge* and *discernment* in difficult situations that will amaze us, and a wisdom given to us that we'll know is from on High. This will be the Lord's mind in us, giving us a spiritual understanding that we have never known before. Death must come to our own reasoning *first*, and then we will gain a new understanding in many situations that once puzzled us. It is worth going through this dark valley in order to have Christ's mind developed in us more fully.

Even as Christ suffered for us in the flesh, we must arm ourselves with the same mind, and realize that "he who has suffered in the flesh has ceased from sin" (1 Pet. 4:1). Our minds must embrace the truth that we, too, must suffer in the flesh, in order to be freed from sin and walk in holiness.

TRANSFORMED THROUGH SURRENDERING OUR WILL

DYING TO OUR OWN *will*, by surrendering it fully to the Lord, is a deep and painful process, but as the Word tells us, "For to you it has been granted on behalf of Christ, not only to believe in Him, but also to suffer for His sake" (Phil. 1:29).

In going through this deep process, we will find that our *will* is the mental faculty by which we make our daily choices. I would even say that in the laying down of our will before the Lord, we are giving Him our very life. What more can we give to the Lord than our daily decisions, desires, dreams, and the longings that we hold onto so tightly? In giving our will, we are giving our *all*—our very reason for living. The will is the very center of our lives—it is who we are. In the giving up of our will to the Father, we embrace our cross fully, even as Jesus did, and we are then set free from every selfish ambition and the unbelief that has plagued our souls for so long.

Our will is the captain of our souls; it will determine our destiny on earth and, ultimately, our eternal destiny. Every day we make hundreds of choices, and this is where we crucify our own will in order to do the Father's will.

As a young Christian, one of the very first things that the Lord said to me was: "There is *one* thing that I will never take by force from a human soul, and that is man's will!" God will *never* force a soul to love and serve Him. Joshua had a strong word for God's children when he said, "Choose for yourselves this day whom you will serve." (See Joshua 24:14-15.) This is a choice that every human soul must make, and no one can make it for them. Because of a lack of repentance, many have chosen a willful, rebellious lifestyle, and the Lord will hold every soul accountable for his or her choices. God has set before each one of us life and good, death and evil—the choice is ours. God has given us a great and valuable gift in giving us a free will, but we must see that if handled wrongly by the choices we make, it can ultimately lead us to death and destruction. We must treasure this gift deeply and ask the Holy Spirit to help us make godly choices.

Jesus, in great agony, began to sweat drops of blood as He surrendered His will to the Father in the garden of Gethsemane. He knows the struggle that we sometimes have in our wills, when we must choose to do His will instead of our own; this is where deep brokenness is worked out in our lives. This is where our cross comes into the picture, and as it is embraced we will find our hearts and desires changed drastically. Unbelief will be burned up, and true faith will begin to rise up in our hearts. You see, our own will and works must be laid at the foot of the Christ's cross; our sustenance must be to do the will of the Father, and our deepest desire must be to "finish His works." (See John 4:34.) God's Word says, "If you are willing and obedient, you shall eat the good of the land; but if you refuse and rebel, you shall be devoured by the sword" (Isaiah 1:19).

We must *choose* to do the Lord's will by an act of our will, and not by what we are *feeling*. Our feelings will many times get us into trouble if we allow them to rule our lives. We must obey and do what is right, no matter what others say or believe about us. As we obey the Lord, our feelings will eventually line up with the truth of God's Word, and we will say: "I delight to do Your will, O my God" (Ps. 40:8). We need great endurance at times, so that after we have done God's will, we may receive the promise. (See Hebrews 10:36.)

Unbelief must be crushed in our lives, and the only way to do this is by yielding our will fully to Christ and putting our flesh to death by the power of the Spirit. The world is passing away, as is the lust of the world, but "he who does the will of God abides forever." (See 1 John 2:17.)

When I think of how this process is worked out in a will that is unbroken, the first thing that comes to my mind is what a horse owner has to put his *unbroken* horse through. I don't know if you can relate to this, but I sure can! As a horse bucks and fights the one who is trying to break him, so did I scream and yell at God in the process that He was taking me through. I thought that He was destroying me, but all He wanted to do was break my stubborn will and unyielding soul! A horse is of no use until he is "broken," and God knew that I would be of no use in His kingdom until my stubborn will lined up with His. As the horse's independence has to be broken, so did I need to come to a place of total reliance and dependence on the Lord—as we *all* do. To die to our own will is truly a deep work of death in us. It takes much grace from the Lord and undying love and patience on the part of our Maker in order for us to submit to this work.

At times, the laying down of our will brings great anguish, but the longer we hold onto our own will and fight God's, the longer we'll wander around that mountain and stay in a desert place as the children of Israel did. If we continue to resist His will, our hearts will not know His rest or His deep abiding peace. God's desire is to refresh and renew us, and this will only come as we surrender all!

The Lord uses many different tools to break us, and they are never the tools of our own choosing. Even as Jesus couldn't crucify Himself—*others* nailed Him to the cross—so will God use those around us to bring the needed death to those areas that are in rebellion to His will. (See Proverbs 27:17.) We submit to the work of the cross as we willingly yield to the Father during our process of death. God will arrange the circumstances that will lead us to our breaking. Sometimes the thorns will come through the painful remarks from loved ones, and sometimes through false accusations. Some of the sharpest nails will come through the Body of Christ as we are rejected and maligned by those we love deeply. Jesus was wounded in the house of His friends, and so will we be. (See Zechariah 13:6, Psalm 41:9.) The Lord may use a family crisis, a wayward child, or a crushing illness. God has many ways and means by which this work will be accomplished. He will never destroy us or crush our spirits. His design is to make us one with Him and His will—but know this, the cross is *always* painful.

Paul, the apostle, struggled in his will greatly, and asked the Lord three times if He would remove the thorn that was in his flesh. (See 2 Corinthians 12:7-10.) God's response to Paul was that His grace was sufficient for him—and it will be for us also. Paul could boast in his infirmities, he even took pleasure in them so that the power of Christ could rest on him. Do we want this power to rest on us in order to be lifted up from all of our doubts and fears? In our weakness we will find the same power that Paul did, but our wills must be crucified, and then Christ will be lifted up *in* us.

We pray for God's will to be done on this earth as it is in heaven, but are we willing to die to our *own* will in order for *His* will to come to pass? (See Matthew 6:10.) Jesus lived to fulfill the will of the Father—what is *our* purpose in life?

If we do not surrender our will to the Lord, and instead continue to live a selfish life, we will not bear fruit for eternity—souls will be lost—and Christ's ministry in us will never come to fruition. There will also be an eternal loss that will never be regained, and our reward in heaven will be greatly diminished. It is not worth living your own life and doing your own thing; this will only bring forth a barren and empty life.

In a dream, some time ago, the Lord showed me a large cross lying on the ground in a stadium. There was lots of activity all around, and many people were running to and fro. When they came to this cross, all of the people in this stadium (which I believe represented many people in the Church) just ignored it and walked over it—as if it wasn't even there. The Lord told me that many wear a cross around their necks, in their ears, and even on their fingers and wrists, but so few are willing to pick up their cross and embrace it in order to be free from their sin. Many even have it tattooed on their skin and wear clothes with crosses printed on them, but where are those who are marked with the cross in their souls—those who have died to their own will and follow only the Lamb? We must learn to walk in our wills, not in our own fleshy desires and longings.

As I went through the Psalms in my concordance, I found that there are about 200 times where the writers said, "I will."

They say, I *will*...

- Teach transgressors God's way.
- Praise Him.
- Obey Him.
- Worship Him.
- Delight in Him.
- Bless Him.
- Extol Him.
- Lift up my hands to Him.
- Bow before Him.
- Sing to Him.
- Trust Him.
- Walk in His truth.
- Call upon Him.
- Be glad in Him.
- Pay my vows.
- Not fear.
- Speak of His testimonies.
- Rejoice in Him.
- Keep His statutes.
- Give thanks.
- Not forget His Word.

- Hope continually.
- Magnify Him.
- Seek the Lord early.
- Pray.
- Confess my transgressions.
- Declare my Iniquities.

Not once did I see that anyone said, "I will bless You, Lord, when I feel like it," or say, "Father, I am too depressed to praise you," or "I'll bless You when I feel better!" But it does say, "I will bless the Lord at all times, His praise shall continually be in my mouth" (Ps. 34:1). As we learn to bless Him when our hearts are heavy with grief, we will find that it is a sacrifice well pleasing to the Lord. (See Psalm 116:17.)

Obedience to the will of the Father is not an option, for the Word says that we cannot enter the kingdom of heaven unless we obey Him, and that can only come through the breaking of our wills. (See Matthew 7:21.) Jesus learned obedience by the things that He suffered, even though He was God's Son. (See Hebrews 5:8.) As we submit to the Father, we'll learn obedience through the trials and sufferings that crush our wills.

It must become our passion to obey the Father, even as it was the Lord's. God doesn't want our *sacrifices,* but our *obedience.* (See 1 Samuel 15:22.) As we obey, intimidation and the fear of man will be released from our hearts, and we will find a new freedom to serve the Lord with our whole heart. No more will this hideous sin of unbelief mar our relationship with the Lord. As our wills become one with His, there will be a new strength and power in our souls, but we must fall on the Rock, Christ Jesus, and be broken, so that we can know His healing love—there is no other way. (See Matthew 21:44.) *Wholeness* will come into our lives as we allow the Spirit to heal our broken hearts. (See Psalm 147:3.) We must be still on the Potter's wheel and allow the Lord to remake us into His glorious image. As this love enters us, we will no longer walk in unbelief, but we will know that we are deeply loved by the Father and we will finally be able to take hold of all His glorious promises. This is the path to wholeness—the path of total victory in Jesus.

Paul was "poured out as a drink offering," as he lived a life of unconditional surrender to his Lord. If our lives are to be "living sacrifices," we, as Paul, must be crushed like grapes and broken like bread. Only as we make a full surrender to Christ will we be true servants, and out of our brokenness others will be fed through our lives. (See 2 Timothy 4:6, Matthew 14:19-20.)

God is calling us to suffer according to His will, and not because of our foolishness. (See 1 Peter 4:19.) Let's submit our souls to our faithful Creator and allow His knife to cut away the deep anger, bitterness, rebellion, and unbelief that is deep in our hearts. His fiery sword will release us from the iniquitous roots that are binding us.

As we are willing to go the way of the cross, and lay down our wills in full surrender, only then will this work be accomplished. May none of us resist and rebel against God's will like the children of Israel did, but submit to Him fully.

Let's pray:

> *"Oh Father, forgive me for going my own way and for resisting Your will for my life. I desire this day to make an unconditional surrender to Your will—no matter what the cost. Take my will and make it wholly Yours this day. I desire to walk on the path that You have foreordained for my life. I lay down my own desires and plans, and ask that You accomplish Your plan and purpose for my life. May I be as broken bread and poured out wine—for the glory of Your name. In the name of Jesus I pray. Amen."*

SURRENDER OUR EMOTIONS—FOR HEALING

> *They have also healed the hurt of My people slightly, saying, 'Peace, peace!' when there is no peace.*
>
> Jeremiah 6:14

> *He heals the broken hearted and binds up their wounds.*
>
> Psalm 147:3

IN MANY CHURCHES SIN has not been revealed, and our deep, gaping, infected wounds have been covered with a band aid. Many have been taught by their leaders that Jesus took all their pain and afflictions, and that all their sin has been washed away, but this is not the *whole* truth. They have not expounded to God's people the importance of repentance through the confession of their sins, and millions are ultimately living in idolatry and rebellion, and are feeling little or no guilt. (See 1 John 1:6-10.) Little has been taught about the cross and our daily need to die to sin and self, but now is the time and season when God will come with His purifying fires and refine us deeply!

The Word of God tells us that there is a time to weep, and a time to mourn. (See Ecclesiastes 3:4.) This is the time and season for deep cleansing, and for the healing of our emotions as we prepare our hearts fully for the coming of the Lord.

We all know how strong our emotions can be at times—those feelings of joy, sorrow, hate, rejection, anger, grief, loneliness, intimidation, guilt, jealousy, loss of control, and love. These emotions spring up at times with no conscious effort on our part. These feelings, whether intense or mild, are a God-given gift from the heart of our loving Creator. Feelings, in themselves, are not sinful, but they must be harnessed and expressed through the Spirit of God. The Word says, "'Be angry, and do not sin': do not let the sun go down on your wrath" (Eph. 4:26).

Many of us have been taught that *all* anger is sin, and so we have shoved it down, repressed it, and developed roots of bitterness in our lives. There is a *righteous anger* from the Lord that our hearts can experience when we see how destructive and hellish sinful acts are. The Lord will show us what to *do* with this righteous anger, for it will always be constructive. We have a right to be angry about the injustices of life, but we never have a right to hold onto hate and unforgiveness against those who have wounded us. It's what we *do* with the anger that will determine if it is a righteous anger or if it is demonic in nature.

In my life, I pushed the anger down and ignored it. I was terrified to admit that I was angry; I thought that all anger was sinful. Because I refused to deal with this anger in a godly way, eventually it became a root of bitterness in me, and even turned into a murderous rage inside of me. If I would have known the Lord and His ways, I would have come to Him and confessed my rage and pain and would not have suffered such agony and pain for those years. I *should* have been angry that my father abused me, but the way I handled it was not godly. I suffered for many years with a deep, excruciating depression because of this denial. My soul was in torment, and my fears were overwhelming. For years I suffered with panic-attacks that would all but wipe me out—physically and emotionally—but thanks to the mercy and grace of God, He has taught me the principles that you are now reading, and I have been set free from these tormenting fears and depression. Once I acknowledged how deeply my father had hurt me and the hate and anger that I felt toward him, I began to experience a new joy and vitality that gave me the strength to go on to victory. Righteous anger will spiritually energize us to help others in their afflictions and will move us into the plan that God has for our lives.

There will be times when we will feel like Jeremiah did when he cried out: "Why is my pain perpetual and my wound incurable, which refuses to be healed?" (Jer. 15:18). Or we'll groan as the children of Israel did because of their hard bondage. (See Exodus 2:23.)

There were times when I felt my wounds would never be healed, for my heart was filled with unbelief, but there came a time, in the midst of my suffering, that it no longer mattered what I felt or saw. I *knew* God had healed and delivered me, and that it was only a matter of time before this healing would manifest.

Our Father is filled with emotion, and we must always remember that *we* are made in *His* image; we were made to express deep emotion. He is a God who experiences love, joy, anger, pain, rejection, grief, and compassion. His heart feels the full intensity of these emotions, where we at times just feel these emotions mildly. God desires to share with us His very own heartfelt emotions, the depth of His love, and the grief of His heart over our sin. The Lord sings over us, and even rejoices over us with gladness—just because of His delight in us. (See Zephaniah 3:17.)

If our emotions are not fully surrendered to Jesus, the enemy can come in and express *his* personality through us—his hatred, rage, and anger through our *unhealed* emotions. If we do not allow the Lord to come into our deepest wounds and heal us with His love, the enemy will continue to control areas of our lives with his strongholds and will keep us in a place of fear and unbelief. Our emotions must be surrendered to God, or they will affect every other area of our lives, and our faith in Christ will be diminished.

Jesus, in the days of His flesh, when He had offered up prayers, did so with "vehement cries and tears" to His Father in heaven, and He was heard because of His godly fear. (See Hebrews 5:7.) There will be times in our lives when we will identify strongly with the Psalmist when he wrote, "My tears have been my food day and night, while they continually say to me, 'Where is your God?' (Ps. 42:3). There were many days of copious tears in my life as the enemy came and tormented me with the lie that God had left me, but God was faithful, and through the years I came to a place of deep security in the Lord's love. God's desire, through the brokenness, was to bring me to a place where I would no longer doubt His love or waver in my faith and trust in Him.

Many in our society, especially men, are afraid to express their deep emotional pain, but we must follow Jesus' example and express our deep pain and anguish. For years, many of us have stuffed down our grief and pain, and then we wonder why we are depressed or have a body filled with sickness and disease. God wants us to come to Him, whether in the agony of tears for our sin or in the pain of our feelings of rejection. We must no longer wear a mask and act as if everything is okay, but we should learn to be honest about our emotional pain as we open our hearts wide to the Lord. Many of us have hidden our anger, grief, and pain for so long that only with the Spirit's help are we now able to express our hearts to Jesus. He understands our pain, and it says in Isaiah 53:3-4, that He was "… despised and rejected by men, a Man of sorrows and acquainted with grief." Jesus bore our grief and carried our sorrows. Jesus felt all of the pain that we have ever experienced, but to a deeper degree. He is patient with us when we struggle with hate and anger, because He knows the depth of our wounds. His desire is to heal and perfect us in His love. The joy of the Lord will be our strength in the midst of our deepest pain. It took the Lord a long time to reach down into the depths of my sorrow, and in the midst of my screaming pain He soothed me with His tender love in a way that is beyond description.

Elijah suffered greatly with depression after his victory on Mount Carmel, and when he was threatened by Queen Jezebel, he ran for his life. When he had traveled a day's journey into the wilderness, he sat down under a broom tree and prayed that he might die. Elijah then slept, and suddenly an angel touched him and said, "Arise and eat." Elijah ate and drank, and then slept again. The angel came back to him a second time and said, "Arise and eat, because the journey is too great for you." He then survived on the strength from that food for 40 days. (See 1 Kings 19:4-8.) God's servant had a powerful victory on Mount Carmel, but that did not keep him from suffering in his emotions when he was attacked by the enemy.

We will find on our journey, like Elijah and the children of Israel did, that we must guard our hearts and emotions. We must also make sure that we get adequate rest for our bodies, for as we have learned, our spirit, souls, and bodies are interconnected. We need the strength of the Word of God in our souls daily, for it will strengthen and nourish us. We must never allow ourselves to become depleted—never! When the enemy fights hard against us, we must daily run to the secret place of prayer and communion with our Lord and feast on His manna from heaven, for we have a High Priest who is touched by the feelings of our infirmities. (See Hebrews 4:15.)

Many times I failed the Lord because of the deep emotional pain in my soul, even denying in my heart His great love for me. I was much like the apostle Peter who said that he would never be made to stumble, and that even if he had to die with Jesus he would not deny Him. Peter *did* deny Him, three times, just as the Lord predicted; he then wept bitterly. (See Matthew 26:31-35, 69-75.) Peter's heart was shattered into a million pieces, but he needed this brokenness in order to see his own weakness and sinfulness—and so do we. After this happened, Peter needed deep inner healing in his emotions because of wounded self-love and shame. Jesus loved His servant, for Peter was not only His disciple, but an intimate friend of His. I love the Lord's heart of compassion, for the Word shows us that Jesus appeared to Peter *personally* to restore him. He knew how deeply his heart was hurting, and Jesus took him aside—*alone*—just like He'll do with us when He comes to heal us. The Lord brought deep healing to Peter's soul as He freed him from his guilt and shame.

Jesus wants to take us back to those times when we denied Him and sinned so horribly against Him, even back into our childhood wounds that are not yet healed. Many of these unhealed wounds are from parents who may have rejected us and told us we were nothing or worthless—or they could have come from sexual or physical abuse that has not been exposed to Christ's healing light. He takes us back to those times in our past that we have covered up in grief and shame in order to release our pain and heal us fully. We are a product of our past, but the Lord can use our past as a steppingstone into our glorious future with Him. His desire is to break the strongholds in our past—those things that are still binding us in the present—in order to bring us into our glorious inheritance in Christ. He will not allow the past to enslave us if we are *honest* with Him and allow Him to fully uncover the abuse, fears, and pain that are yet keeping us bound. The faster we can open to His love, the sooner we'll enter into our promised land!

As we open fully to His love, we will find that the heart of the Lord is tender and kind. At times we may feel *humiliated* and *exposed* in our grief and pain, but He will gently draw us to His heart and touch those deep wounded places inside of us. This is where all the doubt, unbelief, and fear will begin to be eradicated from our hearts. In openness and honesty we must allow Him to cut those deep wounds; we will find that His perfect love will remove all the doubts and fears from our lives. The poison and infection in our wounds must be lanced deeply in order for them to be healed. It *is* okay to grieve our losses; this is a normal process. When someone dies that you love dearly, it is normal to weep and grieve their loss. In the same way, we must give ourselves time to grieve over the *death* of our childhood—this is part of the healing process. As we allow the love of the Father to enter into our deep wounds, we will find our emotions liberated. We'll begin to feel a freedom in every area of our lives.

Some of God's children are "frozen" emotionally because they have not let go of the bitterness of their past. This is what happened to the children of Israel in the desert. God wanted to melt their icy emotions, as He does ours, but they would not allow their fiery trials to burn away the hardness in their hearts.

If there is still bitterness and unforgiveness in our hearts, this hardness will keep us from experiencing the deep love of the Father. This is where repentance and godly sorrow are such a help to us; this sorrow will free our souls to love. The rejection, bruises, and lies of the past must all be exposed to the fire of God's love. Our loved ones have hurt us and our friends have betrayed us, but as we receive the love of the Father and absorb the truth of who we are in Christ, we will begin to come to life in our emotions. We'll feel a love and joy we have never known. As His healing presence fills us, we'll know that Jesus will never leave us or reject us, and all doubt concerning His love will begin to leave. It will be worth the pain that we go through to reach this place of wholeness and freedom.

There is coming a day when "…God will wipe away every tear from their eyes; there shall be no more death, nor sorrow, nor crying. There shall be no more pain, for the former things have passed away" (Rev. 21:4). Amen!

SURRENDER OUR BODIES—FOR CLEANSING AND HEALING

… present your bodies a living sacrifice, holy, acceptable to God, which is your reasonable service.

Romans 12:1

Or do you not know that your body is the temple of the Holy Spirit who is in you, whom you have from God, and you are not your own?

1 Corinthians 6:19

THE LORD DESIRES TO take full control of all three parts of our being. He starts in the inner man (our spirits) then the "soulish" realm and finally our bodies. We are healed from the inside out. He wants *every part* of us, and He is asking us to surrender our bodies, the "outer court" of our "temples" to Him for His use and for His glory. As we surrender our bodies fully to Jesus, He is then able to accomplish His will and purpose through us on this earth. As we give our bodies to Him as a living sacrifice, He will take full possession of us and deliver us from the works of the flesh.

God has given us a *natural* body, for we live in a *natural* world. This is our "suit of skin," and it has served us well in this world. He has endowed our body with five natural senses: *sight, hearing, taste, smell,* and *touch.* These senses are good, but if they are not fully yielded to the Lord, they can be the gates that the enemy will use to enter into our lives. We are the ones that can open or close them—to good or to evil. They are a gift from God, and to live in this world they must be used, but our natural senses must also experience the "dark night," even as our souls must. This is where, if we embrace our cross, we will develop our *spiritual senses* and *discernment* in the Spirit of God.

Most of the children of Israel lived *only* in their natural senses; they allowed their senses to control them. They longed to go back to Egypt and eat the foods they once enjoyed there. They wanted to enjoy their "fleshy" pleasures, and did not want to go through the discipline and death to their flesh in order to be changed into the children of faith that God intended. This is where they would have been transformed into the spiritual, faith-filled children that God wanted them to be. They felt the cost was too great for them; they would not give up their natural reasoning and desires in exchange for the faith walk, which required death to their old way. Many in the Church feel the same way: As long as things are easy, they continue to walk with Jesus, but when the fire comes, they pull back into the world, just as the children of Israel did.

In Joshua 10:5, it says that the "five kings" of the Amorites camped before Gibeon and made war against it. In verse eight, the Lord said that He would deliver them into Joshua's hand. In verse 16, it states that the five kings fled and hid themselves in a cave. In verses 24 and 25, the men of Israel brought out the kings that were hidden, and put their feet on the necks of these five kings, they then proceeded to kill them and hang them on five trees.

I believe that these five kings represent our five natural senses, and that we must not be controlled or governed by them. We are to take dominion over them, and at times we will have to put to death our natural senses in order for our "spiritual senses" to come forth in us! We must be ruled and governed by what God's Word tells us, and not by our flesh. The Word tells us that the "flesh lusts against the Spirit, and the Spirit against the flesh;" they are contrary to one another—herein lies the battle. (See Galatians 5:16- 17.) If we "live according to the flesh" we will die, "but if by the Spirit we put to death the deeds of the body, we will live." (See Romans 8:13.)

When pain and sickness come, we must not let our senses or our natural reasoning rule, but we must stand on the Word of God which states: "By His stripes we are healed" (Is. 53:5). When we are going through a valley of suffering, we must not allow fear to enter in by what we see or hear, but we must believe that when we "walk through the valley of the shadow of death," God will be with us, according to His Word in Psalm 23. We must walk by faith and not by what we see with our natural eyes. When we drink the bitter cup of suffering, we must believe that His cross will make the bitter taste of these waters sweet. (See Exodus 15:25.)

Paul, the apostle, had to discipline his body and bring it into subjection—and so must we. (See 1 Corinthians 9:27.) His natural senses did not rule his life or control him; he developed his spiritual senses and walked in the power of the Spirit. As we grow in our faith walk and no longer allow our natural senses to dominate our lives, we will then walk in Christ's victory and have the power to overcome the lusts of the flesh. The enemy will at times try to bring darkness into us through the gates of our senses; we must always guard them by allowing in only those things that are pure and holy. Our eyes and ears must no longer feast on ungodly entertainment or unholy books, but we must fill our hearts and minds with those things that are pleasing to the Lord. As we "present our members" to Him as "instruments of righteousness," it is then that our "whole body will be filled with light," and there will be "no part dark." (See Romans 6:13, Luke 11:36.)

Paul bore in his body the *marks of Christ*; the dying of the Lord Jesus, so that the life of Jesus would be manifested in his body. (See Galatians 6:17, 2 Corinthians 4:10-12.) Paul was so filled with the Spirit that his very flesh pulsated with the life of Christ, "so that even handkerchiefs or aprons were brought from his body to the sick, and the diseases left them and the evil spirits went out of them" (Acts 19:12). You see, it wasn't Paul's life, but the life of Christ *in* Paul that flowed in healing power, even saturating his flesh and clothing. God so desires to use us in this way, but are we willing to pay the cost? Christ wants to be "magnified in our bodies," but the sins of the flesh must be dealt with ruthlessly! (These sins are listed in Galatians chapter five.) We must discipline our bodies and bring them under subjection. (See 1 Corinthians 9:27.) Through the power of the Spirit in us, our sensual appetites can be crucified.

There may be times when we will cry out, "O wretched man that I am! Who will deliver me from this body of death?" (Romans 7:24). It will be hard, but it will be worth the loss and pain in our lives in order to be brought into the glorious liberty of the sons of God. (See Romans 8:19-23.)

As we grow in the Lord we will discover as Paul did, that in Christ we are already free; we only need to believe it and allow the Spirit to work it out in us as we yield our natural senses, these "kings," fully to Him. (See Romans 7:25.)

Here are a few ways that these natural senses can hinder us:
- With **sight**, the flesh lusts and at times desires things that are unholy. What are our eyes gazing upon: the things of this world or the beauty of the Lord? In chapter three of Genesis, we read that "when the woman *saw* that the tree was good for food, that it was pleasant to the eyes…she took of its fruit and ate" (Gen. 3:6, emphasis added). Eve took her eyes off of the Lord and did what He explicitly commanded her *not* to do; she allowed her fleshy desire to take control of her.
- The second "king" is our **hearing**. We hear many voices crying out to us in this hour, but we must ask Jesus to open our spiritual ears to hear *His voice* above every other. We must cast down the lies of the enemy, and even our own reasoning when it contradicts the Word of the Lord.
- The third "king" is our sense of **smell**. Satan has entrapped many with this sense. Smell brings desire and can allure our senses. Proverbs 17:7 tells of an immoral woman who seduced the young man and perfumed her bed with myrrh, aloes, and cinnamon. (See Proverbs 7:17.)
- The fourth "king" is our sense of **touch**. The Lord tells us to "…Come out from among them and be separate … do not touch what is unclean" (2 Cor. 6:17). There are so many idols, so much ungodly entertainment, so many drugs and vices in this world that the enemy tries to entrap us with, but we must flee every dark temptation and run to the "secret place." Let's

"...cleanse ourselves from all filthiness of the flesh and spirit, perfecting holiness in the fear of God" (2 Cor. 7:1).

- The last "king" is **taste**, which represents our appetite, what we eat and drink, not only in the natural, but in the spiritual. Jesus wanted the children of Israel to learn to feast on Him— the "Bread" from heaven, even His very life, but they longed for the "fleshpots" of Egypt. In Numbers 11:4-6, we read that the children of Israel wept and said, "Who will give us meat to eat? We remember the fish which we ate freely in Egypt, the cucumbers, the melons, the leeks, the onions, and the garlic; but now our whole being is dried up; there is nothing at all except this manna before our eyes." God's desire was to empty them, to dry up the things of the world in their souls and in their flesh, but they resisted the work of the Lord greatly. They did not want the manna—the life that God was offering them. All they wanted was to satisfy their sensual desires. May we take this as a lesson from the Lord and not allow our fleshy desires to rule our lives. Let's "taste and see that the Lord is good," and be fully satisfied in Him alone. (See Psalm 34:8.)

My prayer is that we would see with His eyes, hear when He calls, smell His sweet fragrance, touch His deep heart, and taste of His goodness!

Do we truly believe that God desires to heal us physically, as well as spiritually, emotionally, and mentally? God's Word says, "Who forgives all your iniquities, Who *heals all your diseases*, Who redeems your life from destruction, Who crowns you with loving kindness and tender mercies..." (Ps. 103:3-4, emphasis added). God's holy will is to heal our bodies, but there are times, as in the case of Job, when our faith will be tested in this area. Job had some deep-seated fears and unbelief in his heart that the Lord desired to expose so that He could deliver him and heal his deep heart. In our times of illness, when the fire is heated up in our bodies, many times God will expose deep roots of unbelief and sin. Multitudes have lived in doubt and unbelief for so long, and have been so conditioned by this world and those around them, that most of the time they run to doctors, medications, tranquillizers, and prescription drugs. Many, even in the Church, look at this as a normal course of action. Shouldn't our first course of action be to run to the throne of grace, and cry out to the Lord in our sicknesses? His desire is that we would learn to stand on His Word in the midst of our trials, and wait for Him to heal us and set us free. This may be one of the main reasons why we see so little physical healing and deliverance in our nation. In many other nations, because of poverty and a lack of medical care, they cry out desperately to the Lord for healing, and many times they are instantly healed. They may be poor in the natural, but they are rich in faith and are seeing many signs and wonders in their midst. God wants us to believe for healing and deliverance in every part of our lives, including the healing of our physical bodies.

One of the curses for disobedience is found in Deuteronomy 28:59-60. It says that if the Israelites didn't observe all the words of His law, He would bring "...serious and prolonged sicknesses." He would also bring back on them, "... all the diseases of Egypt," of which they were afraid, and that these diseases would cling to them. Disobedience will always bring the discipline of the Lord, and it may come through physical affliction.

Not all who suffer physically, or who have died prematurely, were disobedient to the Lord, but God will try us and test us, and we must stand in faith—no matter what we see or feel. I believe that He will give back to us "double for our trouble," like Job was rewarded and restored after his ordeal! Job was a righteous man, and part of the reason for his fiery trials was to bring him to a place of greater revelation in the sovereignty and goodness of his God. The Lord desired that Job would come to know Him more deeply and intimately as his soul was purified in these fires of suffering.

Illness in our bodies may be showing us that there is some "soul sickness" in an area of our lives that needs to be touched and healed by the Lord. We must get on our faces before the Lord and seek Him earnestly. We must allow the Spirit to penetrate our hearts and expose anything that might be causing the sickness. There may be some sin, some unforgiveness, or a bitter root that needs to be pulled out of our hearts. If our minds are not renewed and we are dwelling on negative thoughts, this, too, could affect us physically. I believe one of the main reasons for sickness is our lack of faith and trust in His healing power. We need to grow up the spirit-man in us, until our faith becomes as strong as a mountain. Jesus came to set us free in *every area* of our lives, if we will first believe His promises. As our souls prosper, we will find greater health and strength coming into our bodies. (See 3 John 2.)

Once we personally hear a word from the Lord concerning our illness, we must then step out on the *waters of faith* until we see our healing manifested. Sometimes our symptoms may even seem to get worse for a time, but if we stand on the Word, the promises that God has given us, we will see our bodies healed—to the glory of His name. We must put all of our fears down; they must once and for all be burned up in our hearts or we will continue to wander in *our* wilderness and may even die there.

"… the chastisement for our peace was upon Him, and by His stripes we are healed" (Is. 53:5). There may be a fiery delay in our healing, but I believe with all my heart, that if we earnestly seek Him, repent, and obey His commands, in His perfect timing "The Sun of Righteousness shall arise with healing in His wings" (Mal. 4:2).

May our prayer be as Paul's when he said, "…according to my earnest expectation and hope that in nothing I shall be ashamed, but with all boldness, as always, so now also Christ will be magnified in my body, whether by life or by death" (Phil. 1:20). Amen!

SURRENDER OUR TONGUE—FOR BLESSING

> *Do all things without complaining and disputing, that you may become blameless and harmless, children of God without fault in the midst of a crooked and perverse generation, among whom you shine as lights in the world.*
>
> Philippians 2:14-15

> *If anyone among you thinks he is religious, and does not bridle his tongue but deceives his own heart, this one's religion is useless.*
>
> James 1:26

WORDS ARE MORE POWERFUL than we could ever imagine. The world was created as God *spoke* the creation into existence. "Then God *said*, 'Let there be light;' and there was light. Then God *said*, 'Let there be a firmament in the midst of the waters'… Then God *said*, 'Let the waters under the heavens be gathered together into one place'" (Gen. 1:3, 6, 9, emphasis added). God *spoke*, and the creative force of His words brought forth what He had spoken. Words have a *substance*, and a *force* behind them that will bring forth either good or evil. The Word says in Proverbs 18:21 that "Death and life are in the power of the tongue, and those who love it will eat its fruit." Jesus said, "For out of the abundance of the heart his mouth speaks" (Luke 6:45). This is a deep heart issue in our lives. What is in our hearts will eventually come out; this is where we need purification.

As we have learned, we will reap what we sow, and the words we speak are like seeds that we plant in our hearts and in the hearts of others. The harvest that will come forth will either produce good fruit—or death. If we are sowing words of doubt and fear, hatred and animosity, disunity and gossip, we must realize that the harvest that will come forth will be deadly to our spiritual life and to our future. This is what happened to the children of Israel; they spoke words of death—and this is what they reaped in their lives. God's judgment will come to whisperers and gossips, backbiters, haters of God, and boasters; those who practice such things are worthy of death. (See Romans 1:29-32.)

What we sow with our lips we will surely reap; we will bring forth either life to ourselves and others or a harvest of death and destruction by the words we speak. When we talk positively at church but then go home and cry about how the devil is destroying us, are we not negating the Word of God in our lives? We say: "With God all things are possible," and "By His stripes we are healed," but then we talk in fear and unbelief about our parent's cancer or heart condition, and we hope that these illness will not take *our* lives. Unless we repent, we will reap what it says in James 1:6-7, which states, "… for he who doubts is like a wave of the sea driven and tossed by the wind. For let not that man suppose that he will receive anything from the Lord."

When we gossip, in the sight of God it is as if we are murdering those we speak against, for our desire is to ruin their reputation. Once we speak out words of death, they may never be able to be taken back. Families have been torn apart and friendships forever destroyed because of poisonous words that have been spoken. A life is easily torn down through hateful words, and it is so hard to build that life back up again!

If these seeds of destruction are not taken out of our hearts early in life, they will take root like weeds and will be difficult to uproot later in life. They may even become bitterness in our hearts that will defile many. If we allow the soil in our hearts to be broken up through deep, godly sorrow, the Lord will then be able to remove these roots from our lives.

Many times as I was growing up, I heard the words, "You are nothing— you will never amount to anything." These words that were spoken to me brought a curse into my life that crippled me for many years. Even after I came to Jesus, these words played over and over in my mind—until my mind was renewed in the Word of God. I wept many tears before the Lord as He spoke *words of life* to me and released me from the lies of the enemy. Those words shattered my soul, and for many years I struggled with God's call on my life because of them.

Never underestimate the power of the words that you speak. We must be *aware* of the words that we speak daily over our lives. Words are creative, and there is either life or death in them. Are our words filled with thanksgiving that God is bringing health and providing for us? Do we claim the victory and the delivering power of God, even when we struggle with besetting sins and the addictions that try to bind us? So many times we confess what we feel or see in the natural, but God desires that we stand upon His Word—no matter what we feel or see. This is where we learn to trust Him; it is where we will begin to develop the fruit of the Spirit in our lives.

When the children of Israel were thirsty in the desert they said, "Why have you brought up the assembly of the Lord into this wilderness, that we and our animals should die here?" They *spoke death* over their own lives and cursed themselves by their words of destruction; the Lord fulfilled what they had spoken, and everyone in that generation died in the wilderness—except Joshua and Caleb. Only their children went into the promised land. (See Numbers 20:4, 14:3, 26-28.) Their words killed their destiny and brought death to them; they never entered into the blessings of His great promises for their lives.

Matthew 15:11 says, "Not what goes into the mouth defiles a man, but what comes out of the mouth, this defiles a man." The enemy inhabits the negative words that we speak; we must give no place to the devil. Let's confess the promises of God—not the problems! We must, with the help of the Lord, break our negative speaking patterns through repentance and by meditating on the Word of God. Negative words will only deepen the root of unbelief in our souls, but words of faith will fill our hearts with light and joy. Feed your faith, and starve your doubts, by confessing the truth of God's Word over every circumstance in your life. The *blood of Jesus* and the *word of our testimony* are the arsenal that will blast the enemy out of our lives. We must use this creative force that God has given us to bring forth life into this dark and negative world that we live in. Daily we must pray: "Set a guard, O Lord, over my mouth; keep watch over the door of my lips" (Ps. 141:3).

Words spoken over us or about us, especially by a parent or authority figure in our lives, will bring strongholds and bondage into our lives. These word curses must be broken in our lives if we are to be fully freed. In Isaiah 54:17, it says, "No weapon formed against you will prosper, and every tongue which rises against you in judgment you shall condemn." It is never the *person* that we condemn, but we condemn the *words* that have been spoken against us. We break the power of these words off of our lives in the name of Jesus. We cancel the curse by speaking God's positive words over our lives and the lives of our loved ones—and also by forgiving those who are persecuting us. We come against these negative words with the powerful blood of Jesus; through the power of the cross these curses will be broken in our lives. As we do this, the boulders and hindrances that have been blocking the flow of God's Spirit in our lives will be removed.

It is important that we, as God's people, know how to confront the giants that come against us. We know how the children of Israel blew it when they spoke in unbelief concerning their enemies, but now I want to show you how King David faced his giant in the power and victory of God's Word.

David had spent much time in the desert with his God as he cared for the sheep. He communed with the Lord, he spent hours worshipping his Creator, and he came to know the Lord's faithfulness and protection when the wild animals came after his sheep. This is a major key to our victory: spending much time with the Lord and getting to know His love and character. David did not meditate on dark thoughts but continually sang his love songs to the Lord. Faith controlled the voice of David, and faith will control our tongues as we grow in our knowledge of the Lord. Faith was released through the tongue of David as he sang and worshipped, even as it was released when Paul and Silas sang and worshipped in their prison experience. As we release our faith through words of trust and songs of worship, the Lord is then able to move mountains out of our way and fulfill His plan and purpose for our lives. Other captives will hear us, and they, too, will be freed from their chains.

When Israel went out to battle, they sent the worshippers out in front to lead them, and the sound of their praises scattered and defeated their enemies. It will do the same for us. On the same note, the walls of Jericho fell down flat when God's people shouted in victory. The walls in our hearts and lives will come down also, but we must lift up a shout of praise. This is where we learn to give thanks in everything, "for this is the will of God" concerning you. (See 1Thessalonians 5:18.)

In Isaiah 30:32, we read, "And in every place where the staff of punishment passes, which the Lord lays on him, it will be with tambourines and harps; and in battles of brandishing He will fight with it." We have only just begun to realize the power and victory that can be unleashed against our enemies through our praise and worship. God's ways are not our ways, and what seems foolish to many are the very tools that the Lord will use to bring the enemy down. His high praises in our mouths can bring down the strongest giant in our lives.

As David was strengthened in his faith walk with the Lord, he was then able to go up against the Philistine giant. He *faced* his giant, and so must we confront those giants that try to bring us down. We must face our fears and painful circumstances, knowing that in Christ we will overcome them. David spoke these words of faith even *before* his victory and said, "Your servant has killed both lion and bear; and this uncircumcised Philistine will be like one of them, seeing he has defied the armies of the living God...The Lord who delivered me from the paw of the lion and from the paw of the bear, He will deliver from the hand of this Philistine" (1 Sam. 17:36-37). David took five smooth stones with his sling and approached the Philistine. The giant tried to instill fear into David's heart by saying, "Come to me, and I will give your flesh to the birds of the air and the beasts of the field" (1 Sam. 17:44).

Our enemies will try to bring fear into our hearts also, but we must face them. In my many battles with darkness, there have been a many times when I heard the voice of the enemy threatening to "kill" me, or saying, "you are cursed," but I always responded to him with the Word and said, "It is written" just like David did when he said, "You come to me with a sword, with a spear, and with a javelin. But I come to you in the name of the Lord of hosts, the God of the armies of Israel, whom you have defied. This day the Lord will deliver you into my hand, and I will strike you and take your head from you...for the battle is the Lord's, and He will give you into our hands" (1 Sam. 17:45-47).

David then took out one stone and slung it; the stone struck the giant in his forehead, and the giant fell on his face to the earth. The stone, representing the Word of God, will cause our giants to fall. God not only wants us to use His Word against the enemy to make him fall, but He also desires to give us His flaming sword, so that we can cut off his head as David did. (See 1 Samuel 17:49-51.) God showed me that as we cut off our enemy's head with His sword—His anointed Word spoken through us—our victory will be *complete*, and even the *root* of our iniquity will be cut away. We will experience a power and strength in and through our lives that we have never seen before! Glory to God! I find it very interesting that David had four stones left in his bag, and as I researched this, I found out that this giant had *four* descendants! David had *total* victory over his enemies! (See 2 Samuel 21:22.)

What comes out of our mouths will determine our present and future, and it will even release us from our past. Spoken words are so powerful, and in the sight of God so serious, that Jesus said, "But I say to you that for every idle word men may speak, they will give account of it in the day of judgment" (Matt. 12:36).

In the book of James, it says that if anyone does not stumble in word, he is a perfect man, able also to bridle the whole body. It speaks of the tongue being a fire, a world of iniquity, unruly, evil, and full of deadly poison. Our tongues can defile the whole body—no *man* can tame the tongue. Many, with the tongue, bless our God and Father, and with it they also curse men who are made in the image of God. Out of the same mouth proceed blessing and cursing, "...these things ought not to be so" (Jas. 3:2-10). The Spirit of God alone can control our tongues as we yield to Him fully. Yes, it is a process, but by faith, and in His power, He will take control of the words that come forth out of our mouths. In order for this to happen our hearts must be cleansed, for out of the abundance of the heart the mouth speaks. We must daily renew our minds in His Word, and yield our members to the Lord—only then will we be His instruments of righteousness. It is God who is at work within us, but we must yield and surrender fully to Him in order for this work to be accomplished.

We must speak to the challenges that rise like mountains in our lives, just as Jesus did when He was tempted in the wilderness by Satan. Every time He was tempted, He came against Satan with the Word saying, "It is written," as seen in Matthew 4:1-11. When we're weak we must say: "Lord, Your strength is made perfect in my weakness" or "I can do all things through Christ who strengthens me." (See 2 Corinthians 12:9, Philippians 4:13.) In fear you can say: "God has not given us a spirit of fear, but of power and of love and of a sound mind" (2 Tim. 1:7). As that mountain looms large before you, say: "In the name of Jesus come down, for '...With men this is impossible, but with God all things are possible!'" (Matt. 19:26, 17:20). Speak the Word—speak the Word—speak the Word, and you will see those mountains come down!

Holy words must come forth out of our mouths, not negative words filled with doubt and fear. When we truly get a glimpse of the Lord as Isaiah did, we will cry out as he did. "So I said: 'woe is me, for I am undone! Because I am a man of unclean lips, and I dwell in the midst of a people of unclean lips; for my eyes have seen the King, the Lord of hosts.' Then one of the seraphim flew to me, having in his hand a live coal which he had taken with the tongs from the altar. And he touched my mouth with it and said: 'Behold, this has touched your lips; your iniquity is taken away, and your sin is purged'" (Is. 6:5-7). Will the Lord do any less for us if we truly repent of the vile words that we speak? He will come to us with His fiery love and burn out of our hearts and lives all that is unholy and impure. Do we believe His Word, or will we forever doubt the power of His cross in our lives? By His grace and through the power of His blood this work will be done—*if* we would only believe!

May Psalm 19:14, be our earnest prayer: "Let the *words of my mouth* and the meditation of my heart be acceptable in Your sight, O Lord, my strength and my Redeemer" (emphasis added).

SURRENDER OUR BITTERNESS AND UNFORGIVENESS—FOR FREEDOM

> *And be kind to one another, tenderhearted, forgiving one another, even as God in Christ forgave you.*
>
> Ephesians 4:32

> *If someone says, "I love God," and hates his brother, he is a liar; for he who does not love his brother whom he has seen, how can he love God whom he has not seen?*
>
> 1 John 4:20

THERE IS NOTHING AS destructive or defiling to our souls as bitterness and unforgiveness. This strong root is tied tightly to unbelief, and it stems from the anger that many feel because they are not living the *abundant life* that God has promised them. They blame their circumstances, spouses, the Church, and others for their misfortune. Jesus desires to give them a life of freedom and joy, but bitterness and unbelief have blocked the flow of His life in many of His children. Many have a root of anger against God because of their hard circumstances, but instead of bowing their knee to the Lord and repenting for their sin and rebellion against Him, they blame God for their hard life and refuse to take responsibility for their lives. Their *response* in their difficulties is what's binding them, not God.

Moses greatly feared that the children of Israel would stone him because of their anger and hate. (See Exodus 17:4.) This sin was tightly woven to their unbelief, for they did not believe that God would care for them and bring them into their promised land. They refused to believe God, and consequently bitterness was their lot in life. The poison of bitterness filled their hearts, and it was only a matter of time before they would perish in their sin. Today, many are bound with this same root of bitterness, and only in true brokenness and repentance will they be freed.

In our own lives we must learn to release to the Lord those who have wounded us, and secondly, we must release them from all obligations to pay us back. God's children would not release those who had so deeply wounded them in Egypt. Their wounds festered, and with their bitterness and unforgiveness they defiled many. (See Hebrews 12:15.) This is a warning to us, for if we refuse to let go of our past hurts, neither will we enter into our inheritance in Christ, and we'll be in danger of dying in our own wilderness of sin. Only as we release our hurts from the past will we be free to live in the present. Forgiveness will release us from the people that have hurt us. If we are *willing* to forgive, our Father will give us all the grace that is necessary to release others.

After her release from the Nazi concentration camp, Corrie ten Boom still struggled with hate and unforgiveness against those who hurt her and her sister. Her desire was to be freed from the bitterness and hate that still, at times, tried to take hold of her, and the Lord heard her earnest prayer. Years later, when Corrie was preaching at a meeting, a man came up to her and rejoiced because of his new found forgiveness in Christ. For a moment Corrie recoiled as she realized that he was one of her former prison guards. She knew that in herself she could not forgive him, but when she reached out her hand to him in faith, the love of God poured through her into this man that she once hated. What a miracle this was for Corrie, and the Lord will do the same for each one of us, *if* we are willing to forgive. By an act of our will we *choose* to forgive, and as we move out in faith God will give us His own love and all the grace that we need to forgive. Forgiveness is a *choice*—not a *feeling*.

Forgiveness is a *process* that will take time through honesty, repentance, godly sorrow, and allowing the Spirit to open our wounds and bring the deep healing that we so desire. I know that in my life it was a choice, but it took a long time before I actually experienced the release of God's love in my heart toward my father. What helped me tremendously was the revelation of my own wickedness and failures. It was then that I began to see my father as a deeply wounded man—a victim of Satan—and not a heartless abuser.

Forgiveness must become a *lifestyle*. When Peter asked Jesus if he was supposed to forgive his brother up to seven times, Jesus replied that it is not up to seven times, but up to "seventy times seven," that's four hundred and ninety times, which implies "continually." As we forgive, it releases God to forgive us. (See Mathew 18:21-22.) Whenever we pray, if we have anything against anyone, we must forgive them, so that our Father in heaven may also forgive us our trespasses. (See Mark 11:25-26.) If our enemy is hungry we must give him something to eat, and if he is thirsty, give him water to drink. Jesus wants us to be true sons of the Father, "…for He makes His sun rise on the evil and on the good, and sends rain on the just and on the unjust (Matt. 5:45). His desire is to remove the hard rock of unforgiveness from our souls, so that He can pour His love through us to others.

His Word tells us not to resist an evil person; if they slap us on the right cheek we are to turn the other to him also. If anyone wants to sue us and take something from us, we must give them even more. We are to give to him who asks us, and we must not turn away those who want to borrow from us. We are to love our enemies and bless those who curse us; we are to do good to those who hate us, and pray for those who despitefully use and persecute us. (See Matthew 5:39-44.) Wow! Do you see how this goes against the grain in us? This is why we must go through the deep fires of suffering, so that the hard outer shell of our souls will be burned away. It is the heart and the life of Christ that must be formed in us in order for us to live this life of love and forgiveness. God's work of grace will not come forth in us if we refuse to forgive. God always works on the principles of grace and mercy.

The Word says that whatever we loose on earth will be loosed in heaven. We must release others from the debts that we feel are owed to us—and even go the "second mile!" (See John 20:23, Matthew 5:41.) It's the principle of sowing and reaping: As we sow forgiveness in our lives by forgiving others, we will reap God's forgiveness and healing.

As we release the ones who hurt us, we will be released from *our* hurt, but this might take some time to work through if the wounds are deep. It took time for the Lord to open my deep wounds and bring the healing that I needed, because the emotional pain was so deep. We must *own* our pain and *embrace* it before we can be released from it. We must not take our pain lightly and say: "It was no big deal." It *is* a big deal that we were sexually, emotionally, and physically abused. Our betrayals and rejections have wounded us deeply, but our Lord can heal our deepest wounds. If we deny our pain we leave ourselves open to a root of bitterness. We must be honest about the pain: embrace it, feel it, and then give it to Jesus. Never, never, deny your pain; confess it and tell Jesus that you are willing to forgive them.

When we acknowledge and feel our pain in the abuse that we have suffered, it is then that our deepest hate and anger, even our unbelief in God's love and care, will come up to the surface. This must come up, for if we deny our pain, the enemy will come in with lies and deception, and we'll never see the truth of our sin and our deep need for godly repentance. God will give you much grace in this, but if you push it down and never deal with your pain, you will become numb in areas of your life. You will experience *misplaced* anger, and may even take it out on someone you deeply love. Always deal with your anger; admit it—for God already knows it's there. He loves you and will set you free from these roots of bitterness as they are revealed and released from your life.

Honesty and repentance are major keys in our healing, and as we deeply repent, we will be delivered from all unbelief. Do you see why the enemy doesn't want us to be honest about our pain, and why so few churches teach this truth? It is only in the knowledge of the truth, the truth of who we are and what is in our hearts, that we will be freed. Without truth, we will live a life of deception and will never enter into our glorious inheritance. We will live in a prison of torment if we aren't honest about the hate in our hearts. We may not see the bitterness in ourselves, but believe me, other do! Bitterness will always work its way to the surface, whether it's through a fiery trial, a relational difficulty, or even road rage. (See Matthew 12:34.) We must forgive "from our hearts," as the Bible says, and this is a work that only the Holy Spirit can do in us. (See Matthew 18:35.)

As we deal with our wounds, and receive God's grace and mercy, it is then that Jesus can give us His heart to see the wounds that are in others, and that they, too, have been victims and pawns in the hands of Satan. This truth brought deep healing in my heart concerning my own father. He was a pawn in the hands of the enemy. I chose to forgive my father, but it took time before I truly forgave him from my *heart*. Some years after my father's death, I remember driving my car and pulling over to a quiet street; I wept profusely for not having a loving father on this earth. The Lord spoke to my heart and told me that my father was deeply sorry for the pain that he had caused me. As I opened my heart there seemed to be a *spiritual transaction* of love and forgiveness between my father and me. I can't explain what took place, but that day a deep healing came into my soul. God can, and will, heal us deeply—if we cry out to Him from the depths of our hearts.

Jesus meant it when He cried from the cross and said in Luke 23:34, "Father, forgive them, for they do not know what they do." God desires to reveal the heart of His Son *to* us, and ultimately *in* us. He longs to forgive *all* our iniquities, and to heal *all* of our diseases, but how can He when we hold onto resentment and refuse to release those who have hurt us? (See Psalm 103:3.)

Unbelief will be a as a chain around our soul until this stronghold of hate is uprooted from our hearts. We pray, "God, forgive us our debts, as we forgive our debtors," not even thinking about what we are saying. If the Father would forgive us, as we forgive others, would we even be forgiven at all? We must examine our hearts and let no root of bitterness remain, no matter what was done against us in the past. We must bear with one another and forgive, and if anyone has a complaint against us, even as Christ forgave us, so must we forgive those who hurt us (Col. 3:13). Always remember: Forgiveness is never cheap; we need only to gaze upon the cross of Christ.

Are we willing for the Lord to show us the "plank" in our eye, in order for us to see more clearly? (See Matthew 7:1-5.) Only as we humble ourselves before the Lord and realize that except for His grace, we, too, are capable of the vilest sin. Forgiveness is the key that will release love, joy, faith, health, and the glory of God in and through our lives. This is a *major* key to our freedom in Christ.

Pride, more than any other sin, will block us from receiving God's forgiveness. One of the greatest examples I can find in the Word is from Luke 7:36-50. In these Scriptures we read that Jesus went to the house of a Pharisee named Simon, and as He sat down to eat, a woman in the city, who was a sinner, came and brought an alabaster flask of fragrant oil. She "stood at His feet behind Him weeping; and she began to wash His feet with her tears, and wiped them with the hair of her head; and she kissed His feet and anointed them with the fragrant oil." Simon, the Pharisee, spoke to himself saying, "This Man, if He were a prophet, would know who and what manner of woman this is who is touching Him, for she is a sinner." Jesus answered him and told a parable about a creditor who had two debtors, one owed five hundred denarii, and the other only fifty. These debtors had nothing with which to repay, so he freely forgave them both. Jesus asked Simon, "...which of them will love him more?" Simon answered, "I suppose the one whom he forgave more." Jesus answered, "You have rightly judged."

Simon's heart was so hard, so full of pride, that he gave no water for the feet of Jesus when he entered his home. He gave Jesus no kiss, nor did he anoint his feet with fragrant oil. On the other hand, this woman, who had so many sins, was forgiven because of her deep repentance, brokenness, humility, and gratefulness to Jesus for cleansing her (v. 44). In receiving Christ's forgiveness, she was freed from her past and went home in peace. Simon was unable to receive the Lord's forgiveness at that time because of his pride and his judgmental heart against this woman. How can one be freed from sin and receive the forgiveness of the Lord if they do not see themselves as sinners? Simon was just as sinful in his pride and arrogance as this woman, but he could not see it.

We must ask the Lord to show us our sin and pride, and only then can we be freed from our sin and receive His abundant mercy in our lives. We must ask God to break us and show us the roots of unforgiveness that are tied so tightly to unbelief in our lives or we will remain as hard as Simon and never enter into the abundant life of victory that He won for us so long ago. This woman's brokenness released faith in her heart to receive the Lord's love; we must allow God's fire to do this same work in us.

Unless we receive the Lord's forgiveness deep in our hearts, neither will we be able to truly forgive *from our hearts* those who have deeply wounded us. We will see them as great sinners and will sit in hardness of heart and pride as Simon did, judging them from an impure heart.

God help us to see our desperate need to receive Your forgiveness daily. "If You, Lord, should mark iniquities, O Lord, who could stand? But there is forgiveness with You, that You may be feared" (Ps. 130:3-4).

SURRENDER OUR FEARS—FOR LOVE

> *The Lord is my light and my salvation; whom shall I fear? The Lord is the strength of my life; of whom shall I be afraid?*
>
> Psalm 27:1

> *To grant us that we, being delivered from the hand of our enemies, might serve Him without fear, in holiness and righteousness before Him all the days of our life.*
>
> Luke 1:74-75

FEAR IS A DEVASTATING, controlling stronghold in the lives of millions upon millions of souls in this hour. It is a feeling of alarm and a sense of impending doom. Many who are bound with fear feel that a foreboding evil will harm or destroy their lives—and the lives of their loved ones. There's a sense of danger, terror, dread, and sometimes a constant state of apprehension, even when there is no sign of danger in their lives or in their circumstances. Even the apostle Paul said in 2 Corinthians 7:5, "For indeed, when we came to Macedonia, our bodies had no rest, but we were troubled on every side. Outside were conflicts, inside were fears."

You see, all of us have fears on the inside to some degree. When we are in conflicts, struggles, and sufferings, it is then that these fears begin to surface. But even as Paul overcame his struggles by trusting and obeying the Lord—so can we. We must never allow the fears in our hearts to control us, but as we face them the Lord will deliver us, for He is faithful. I have told others in their times of struggle with fear, that it is only a feeling and that these feelings cannot destroy them. Satan comes with a loud roar to try to frighten us off of the path that the Lord has us on, but as we continue to walk forward, we will gain the victory in Christ every time. I know at times we actually feel a physical terror in our flesh, but we must remind ourselves that what we feel in our souls and flesh can never destroy us! We must run to the secret place, our prayer closet, and cry out to the Lord with our whole heart, and He will comfort us.

Recently, I ran to the Lord in a time of great struggle with fear, and as I meditated upon Psalm 91, I found great comfort. The next morning He confirmed this Word through my devotional and even in the church service that I went to that morning. God is faithful to comfort us in our deep distress!

I believe that Job suffered from a deep sense of fear, as seen in Job 3:25, when he said, "For the thing I greatly feared has come upon me, and what I dreaded has happened to me." I believe God desired to free Job from those deep-seated fears so that He could reveal His love to him in a depth Job did not know.

Job suffered greatly through many devastating trials, but at last he came to see the Lord in His sovereignty and power. When he truly *saw* the Lord, he repented deeply, and the Lord restored double to him for all his anguish. Job needed to see that his fears, though they were greatly realized in his trials, were not able to destroy him or his relationship with his heavenly Father. Though he suffered the "loss of all things," as Paul did, he realized that his inner life, his spirit and soul, was completely protected in his Maker, and that nothing could ever separate him from the love of God. He had a revelation of God in his suffering that surpassed all of the head knowledge he had, for God opened his eyes to see Him, and Job was freed from all his fears (Job 42:5). God did not want to destroy Job, but to free him and make him whole.

God has not given us a "spirit of fear," as stated in 2 Timothy 1:7. In this Scripture we see that fear is an evil spirit. Many times this spirit enters into our hearts through a traumatic experience in our lives or from some abuse that we have suffered. Sometimes these spirits manifest themselves in panic attacks or in a terror of the unknown. This spirit will dominate and control our lives unless we face these giants and bring them down by speaking the truth of the Word of God against them. We must not be passive against these spirits, but aggressive, as we run toward Satan's roar! I have suffered panic attacks for most of my life, and I empathize with those who suffer them, but we must never give in to self-pity. We must build up our faith in the Lord through His Word, and face these giants in the strength of the Lord. Many times I ran away in fear from these giants, but I found out the hard way that if we turn and run from them, there is no armor or protection for our backs. We must put up the shield of faith and aggressively move forward toward our giants as David did; we must not back down until we experience the total victory of the Lord over them. We must, "Strengthen the weak hands, and make firm the feeble knees. Say to those who are fearful-hearted, 'Be strong, do not fear! Behold your God will come with vengeance, with the recompense of God; He will come and save you'" (Is. 35:3-4).

The children of Israel focused on their giants and not on the greatness of their God; this was their downfall. Only Joshua and Caleb saw the bigness of their God, and said, "If the Lord delights in us, then He will bring us into this land and give it to us, 'a land which flows with milk and honey.' Only do not rebel against the Lord, nor fear the people of the land, for they are our bread; their protection has departed from them, and the Lord is with us. Do not fear them" (Num. 13:30-33, 14:1-9). We, too, must focus on God's greatness—and *not* on our giants.

In order for Job to come out of his pit of fear, he needed to see God in a new and glorious light. This new vision of God is what delivered him from all his fears. The children of Israel saw time and time again the miracle-working power of God, and yet they still *focused* on their smallness and the bigness of their enemies. Proper perspective on the omnipotent power of our God will free us from all of our fears—the choice is ours. When Peter focused on Jesus in the midst of the storm, he could walk on the water, but as soon as he took his eyes off of Jesus he began to sink. The same will happen to us if we do not keep our eyes on Jesus in the midst of our storm. We must pray for a greater revelation of the enormity and power of our God.

The "perfect love of Jesus" will cast out of our hearts every deep-seated fear. Those who are afraid have not been made perfect in His love. (See 1 John 4:18.) No matter what dark valley we walk through, we need never fear any evil, for the Lord is with us. (See Psalm 23:4.)

We must never fear man, for this will always bring a snare into our lives. (See Proverbs 29:25.) Fear, hate, and unbelief are a demonic "three braided cord" that must be broken fully in our lives if we are ever to receive our inheritance in Christ.

There is only one healthy fear—and that is the "fear of the Lord." God's Word says, "And do not fear those who kill the body but cannot kill the soul. But rather fear Him who is able to destroy both soul and body in hell" (Matt. 10:28). The Lord must be hallowed; He must be our fear and our dread, for it is a fearful thing to fall into the hands of the living God. (See Isaiah 8:13, Hebrews 10:31.) There is a godly fear and respect that we must have for the Lord, and not an attitude that says, "I think I'll talk to the 'big man upstairs.'" This is blatant disrespect and irreverence against a holy, awesome, and all-powerful God. I have a beautiful, intimate relationship with Jesus, but I honor and respect Him as the King of the Universe. We must bow low before the Lord in humble adoration and brokenness, for He has shown us great mercy and love in all of our failures and sin. As we truly fear our Mighty God, the angel of the Lord will encamp around us and deliver us, and we will suffer no want. (See Psalm 34:7, 9.) "The Lord takes pleasure in those who fear Him, in those who hope in His mercy" (Ps. 147:11).

Recently I went to a basketball game to watch my 11-year-old grandson play. His team had lost every game in the season and this was their final game. As I looked at the opposing team I saw that they were twice their size in height and weight. They had green t-shirts, and I immediately nicknamed them the "green giants." I heard that this team had not lost one game in three years. Immediately, I thought about the movie, "Facing the Giants." I cried out to the Lord from my heart and asked if He would grant my grandson's team a victory that day, though the odds of them winning in the natural looked slim. When the game was about to begin, Nate looked at his opponents and I could see him shake his head back and forth. I knew he felt fear and that he doubted they could beat them. I remembered that God's children in the wilderness felt fear when they faced their giants, and I prayed that my grandson and his teammates would not look at the size of their opponents.

At the very start of the game the *green giants* immediately gained eight points, and you could see that Nate's team needed a miracle. Little by little, as the game progressed, Nate's team pulled together remarkably. Throughout the whole game they managed to keep the score ahead of the green giants as they focused on their plays and techniques. Their teamwork, stamina, and focus were outstanding, to the amazement of all who watched them. The last seconds of the game were the most intense, and I even felt the Lord's anointing upon me as I cried out for my grandson's team. The excitement and joy I experienced that day was overwhelming as I watched his team win by two points!

God immediately began to show me the parallel between these two teams and His children of faith who face their giants daily. We have a big God who is on our side, and because of Calvary the victory is already won. Love, unity, and teamwork will be seen in the lives of His true children in the final hour, and as we trust the Lord fully in the midst of our battles and refuse to look at the size of our opponents, we, too, will come forth victorious.

I believe this word from Lord sums up why the "fear of the Lord" is so important in our lives:

> *"I am a loving Father, but I am also stern. Doesn't My Word say that every child I receive is scourged?" (See Hebrews 12:6.) "How many preach this message? My children need to have a healthy fear and respect for their Heavenly Father, for He is a Holy God: perfect, powerful, almighty, all-knowing, invincible, and the One who holds the planets in His hands. Is He not to be feared, My child? A healthy fear is good, for if more of My children had it, they would cease sinning and taking their sin lightly. I love My children, daughter, and it is in deepest love that I use the rod and whip, not to hurt them or break their spirits, but to break their hearts and stubborn wills so that I can pour My love into them and show them how much I love them. Tell them I love them and will never stop loving them. They are Mine, and I will comfort them in all their distresses. Tell them, child. Make sure they know how deeply I love them. They are standing on a firm foundation of love, and all that I do, all that I allow into their lives, comes from a heart of perfect love. My love is perfect, and this love is perfecting them completely. Run to Me, children; cast off the*

works of darkness and put on the armor of light! I am coming. I'm on My way! Prepare your hearts! I love you!" -Jesus
(Given to me October 2011)

"Whenever I am afraid, I will trust in You. In God (I will praise His Word), in God I have put my trust; I will not fear. What can flesh do to me?"

(Ps. 56:3-4).

"I sought the Lord and He heard me, and delivered me from all my fears"

(Ps. 34:4).

"The wicked flee when no one pursues, but the righteous are bold as a lion"

(Prov. 28:1).

SURRENDER OUR FINANCES—FOR HIS ABUNDANCE

For the love of money is a root of all kinds of evil, for which some have strayed away from the faith in their greediness, and pierced themselves through with many sorrows.

1Timothy 6:10

THERE IS ONE FINAL area I would like to speak about that is so important in our lives. If we do not surrender this area, we will be forever bound with unbelief, and will be unable to receive the bounty that the Lord has for us. How can we say we're believers if we hold on tightly to our money and don't believe that God is able to provide for our every need? It says in Malachi 3:8-11, that we rob God when we do not give tithes and offerings to Him. A tithe is 10 percent of our income, but it also speaks of robbing Him by withholding the *offerings* that He tells us to give. The tithe belongs in the storehouse, where you are spiritually fed, and the offerings go wherever He tells you to give them. God tells us that when we disobey in this area of our lives, we are "cursed with a curse" (v. 9). Do we believe this? If we truly did believe His Word, it would cause us to tremble and repent before Him. In verse 10 God promises us that if we bring all the tithes into the storehouse He will open up to us the windows of heaven and pour out for us such blessings that there would not be room enough for us to receive it. When we obey the Lord in this area, God will rebuke the devourer for us, so that we can prosper financially. Not only will it be monetarily, but also in every area of our lives. When God brought the children of Israel out of Egypt, He had the Egyptians (the enemy who robbed them) pay them back for all their years of suffering in their hard labor. (See Exodus 12:35-36.) God will restore to us also the years that the locust has eaten. (See Joel 2:25.)

The Word of God says, "Give and it will be given to you: good measure, pressed down, shaken together, and running over will be put into your bosom. For the same measure that you use, it will be measured back to you" (Luke 6:38). This is a major principle in the kingdom of God: If we withhold our money from the Lord, or anything material, God cannot prosper us. We will also find ourselves spiritually stunted in our growth, for greed will fill our hearts and it will affect our walk with Jesus. The Lord talked much about money; I encourage you to study God's Word on what it has to say about finances.

There are many principles that God teaches us through Paul in 2 Corinthians 9:6-14. The first one is that "God loves a cheerful giver." God wants us to give with trust and joy, not grudgingly, for when we give in fear it shows us that we do not believe that the Lord will care for our needs, or that there will be a blessing that will come from our obedience to His Word. God's Word tells us that He is able to make all grace abound toward us, "having all sufficiency in all things" and "an abundance for every good work." By releasing our money, we release our faith and God's righteousness in us. As it is written: "He has dispersed abroad, he has given to the poor; his righteousness endures forever."

Will we hold onto our money in disobedience and unbelief, or will we plant it as seeds before the Lord into good ground and watch the abundant harvest that comes forth from it? We may not see the fullness of the harvest that we have planted on this earth, but in eternity we will. On that day we'll see the souls that were saved, the needs of the poor that were met, and the work of love and trust that was developed in our hearts through our faithful obedience to the Lord. When we ask in faith, God will even supply the *seed* for us to plant. The Lord will multiply the seed we have sown and increase the fruits of our righteousness. You may ask, "How can the fruits of our righteousness be increased through our giving?" All we have to do is look at the life of Jesus and His cross to see what giving can produce in our lives.

I believe that how we handle our money, almost more than anything else, will reveal to us the condition of our hearts. When we give our finances completely to the Lord—we give our very hearts to Him. We work hard and sweat to earn our living, and how we spend our money shows us where our desires lie. The Word says, "For where your treasure is, there your heart will be also" (Luke 12:34). Righteousness is also released through our obedience to His Word. We must obey God even when it hurts, even when we don't see a financial breakthrough before us. This is a walk of faith and trust; doubt in this area must be forever buried in the deepest grave.

When others see our generosity and obedience to the Lord, it will bring glory, honor, and praise to our King. Always remember: God sees the gift when it is given in love, obedience, and joy. The widow's mite brought more joy to Jesus than any of the other gifts that were given into the treasury because she gave her *all*. (See Mark 12:41-44.) God is also looking at our motives as we give, and more than anything else He wants our whole hearts. Selfishness will bind us in unbelief; we must forever be released from this gross sin. Only as we surrender our pocketbook to the Lord fully, and hold nothing back from Him, will we be released into His glorious freedom and joy! Let's be liberal givers in every area of our lives and hold *nothing* back from our Lord and King.

Chapter 5: God's Heroes of Faith

But let us who are of the day be sober, putting on the breastplate of faith and love, and as a helmet the hope of salvation.

1 Thessalonians 5:8

Now the just shall live by faith; but if anyone draws back, My soul has no pleasure in him.

Hebrews 10:38

As we have already discovered, our faith must be *walked out* every day of our lives, not by what we see or feel, but by the Word of God. It will be very hard at times, but as we face our giants of fear, insecurity, and unbelief, and allow them to come to the surface, the fire of God's love will then burn them out of our hearts.

Just today I had to face a situation that caused great fear to rise in my heart. I spent time with the Lord in prayer, the Word, and in His presence before facing this situation. The Lord assured me that everything would turn out according to His will as I trusted Him fully.

I realized many years ago that when we confront painful and difficult situations, we must see it as a spiritual battle, not a battle against flesh and blood. There are giants that work through those who are not committed to the lordship of Christ, even people who may be in church every Sunday. We must face our fears, spend time with Jesus, and then go forth in the victory that He has already won for us. It may not always turn out the way we want it, but the Lord's will shall be accomplished in us, for our hearts will be changed, and in the end all will come together according to His will and purpose for our lives.

The trouble lies in the "process," for this where we struggle at times. God is more concerned about our *character* than our *comfort*. We must walk out what we have learned, and sometimes we will literally shake in our boots, but if we are faithful to obey His Word and do it God's way, in the end we will always come forth as the victor. We must embrace our uncomfortable feelings and bring them to the Lord. It is in our times of deep turmoil and suffering that He does His deepest work in us; this is where our hearts are circumcised.

If we defend ourselves and try to "save face" in the times of slander and lies, we will not be broken sufficiently, and the life of Christ will not be able to manifest through us. God will vindicate us in His own time and in His own way, but for now we must embrace our cross, walk in truth, and cling to Him tightly. Does it matter if others see us in a negative light? Even Jesus was slandered and was of no reputation, and would we vindicate ourselves? God's purpose through all of this is to transform us and create in us a faith that is unshakable and unquenchable in the face of every fiery affliction. It is when you are in your fiery trials "that the genuineness of your faith, being much more precious than gold that perishes, though it is tested by fire, may be found to praise, honor, and glory at the revelation of Jesus Christ…" (1 Pet. 1:7).

Faith is a creative force, a substance that can only be released through the life of the Son of God in us. It is in this fire, when the outer shell is burned away, that His faith will be released through us. Faith works only through God's love, and He desires that we would be His *vehicles* of love. Through our words and actions God would release His faith. We must do only those things that we see the Father doing—this alone is "walking in the Spirit."

Faith is the substance of things hoped for, the evidence of things not seen. (See Hebrews 11:1.) This faith of Jesus in us is something that we can hold onto, and we can actually feel it in our spiritual bones—our spiritual "knower." When this faith is imparted to us, it is more real to us than anything we see or feel in the natural. Many walk in their own feelings and fleshy desires and are claiming things that are not God's will, but their own; this is why we do not see the full manifestation of the Lord's glory in the Church. It's been our will and works, and not the works of the Lord that have been manifested. This is where repentance and the fire of God are so desperately needed in the Church in this hour. I believe this is the season when the Spirit of God is about to visit us and bring a fire so hot that all of our fleshy, "soulish" works will be burned up. Through repentance and brokenness, the faith of the Son of God will be fully released in the hearts and lives of God's children. We will walk in "heavenly places" in Jesus, and accomplish His works in this final hour, but this will only come as we surrender fully to His work in us.

Faith will flow through us like a river when we learn to praise and worship God in humility and brokenness. Doubt will be removed and faith released as we allow God's fire to purify our hearts deeply. We are called to be children of faith—children of destiny—but all rebellion and self-will must be burned up in us.

In Christ, we've been:

> ...circumcised with the circumcision made without hands, by putting off the body of the sins of the flesh, by the circumcision of Christ, buried with Him in baptism, in which you were raised with Him through faith in the working of God, who raised Him from the dead. And you, being dead in your trespasses and the uncircumcision of your flesh, He has made alive together with Him, having forgiven you all trespasses, having wiped out the handwriting of requirements that was against us, which was contrary to us. And He has taken it out of the way, having nailed it to the cross. Having disarmed principalities and powers, He made a public spectacle of them, triumphing over them in it.
>
> -Colossians 2:11-15

We are raised with Christ through faith and are forgiven by faith. (See Ephesians 2:8.) Believing that we have been circumcised in the cross of Christ, we must now appropriate this *finished* work into our lives. In the midst of seeming failures and setbacks, in our dry and desolate times, we claim and proclaim the finished work of the cross, and by faith we will be raised into that high and holy place in the heavenlies. It is by faith that we work out our salvation. It is by faith that our hearts are cut and circumcised, but it is a real work that is accomplished in our souls. Many just want to "reckon" themselves dead in Christ without allowing the Spirit to convict, cut, and purify their souls. Jesus wants not only people of faith, but a *holy people*—who will walk with Him in purity. Our faith must be worked out in practical ways, and what the Father is looking for is the likeness of His Son in our souls. In Christ we are holy, righteous, and clean, but this must be worked out daily in our lives. There is a righteousness that comes forth through faith when we truly believe the promises of God, but "faith without works is dead." (See Romans 9:30, James 2:20.)

Everything that God gives us is received by faith, for the Word says that "without faith it is impossible to please Him…" (Heb. 11:6). Day and night we must saturate our souls with God's Word, for "faith comes by hearing, and hearing by the word of God" (Rom. 10:17). There is a fight of faith that we must all fight, and if we are not speaking the Word of God daily, we will be weak spiritually. (See 1Timothy 6:12.) Each of us has been given a "measure of faith," but this faith must be built up daily in God's Word (Rom. 12:3).

The spiritual battles that we will go through will strengthen us as we submit to God, resist the devil, and are steadfast in faith, knowing that the same sufferings are experienced by our brotherhood in the world. (See James 4:7, 1 Peter 5:9.) As we take the "shield of faith" we will quench all the fiery darts of the evil one. (See Ephesians 6:16.) As we stand firm in faith against the lies of the enemy, and as we take steps of obedience, we will then activate the life of Jesus in us, and *His faith* will be released through us. In the dark days ahead, we are going to find many, many opportunities to stand in faith as our economy shakes, and as we find trouble on every side. Some Christians would say, "None of these things will happen to me, for I walk in faith." As we have seen, walking in faith does not mean that you will not go through suffering, but rather we will walk in peace and joy and as "more than a conquerors," in the midst of grossest darkness and suffering. If you study the lives of God's saints through the ages you will find that every one of them went through deep and dark trials and they came out victorious. Their faith and trust in God was strengthened and purified as they walked as true children of faith.

Without the presence and the power of the Spirit of God, we will not have the strength or stamina to walk on His path. We must come to know the Spirit personally, by spending time with Him in prayer, and by listening to His voice daily. Before Jesus left His disciples to go home to His Father, "He commanded them not to depart from Jerusalem, but to wait for the promise of the Father…" He also told them that they would receive *power* when the Holy Spirit came upon them, and that they would be His witnesses in Jerusalem, and in all Judea and Samaria, and to the end of the earth. (See Acts 1:4, 8.) What makes us think that we can do anything without the leading and the power of the Holy Spirit in our lives?

Apart from Him we can do nothing! We must wait in His presence until we are filled and empowered, and then go forth in obedience doing only those things that we see the Father doing. This is the *normal* Christian life. So many look at a life lived in obedience to the Word and in the power of God as a radical walk, but I say this is the way every child of God should be walking. We must no longer judge our walk by what others say or do, but we must live by the truth of the Word of God and walk according to what we read in His holy Word. We have been deceived, inoculated against the truth through false teachings and false prophets. It is high time that we shake off the chains of unbelief—the lies that we have believed for so long. This is an hour of freedom and liberty for the children of God—*if* they would only *believe* and *receive* it!

"There is therefore no condemnation to those who are in Christ Jesus, who do not walk according to the flesh, but according to the Spirit... For as many as are led by the Spirit of God, these are the sons of God" (Rom. 8:1, 14). We see here that if we walk according to the Spirit there is no condemnation, but what about those who walk in their flesh? God is bringing a holy fire that will expose all the works of the flesh. We have seen it many times in the past as God revealed fornication, adultery, lust, and greed in some leaders in the Church, but what we will see now is an exposure of evil on a wider scale than we have seen before. Many in leadership positions who call themselves Christians and those in the five-fold offices in the Church, will now experience this strong fire of God. God is calling us to repent and to follow the Spirit alone in this hour; all fleshy works will now be burned up. A submission to the Spirit will not be an option, and truly, it never was! Only those who are *led by the Spirit* are sons of God. We are freed from the law and legalism in order to do the Father's will, not our own. God has freed us from the control of the *evil one*, but many still submit to the unhealthy control of dysfunctional people around them; they find it hard to say, "No," because they are yet people-pleasers. Many of God's children are doing church ministries that God has not asked them to do, and because of this, they are missing out on the plan that God has for their lives. God sees this as disobedience.

I remember a time early in my walk with the Lord when I was involved in many church ministries. I was doing them out of love for the Lord, but one night, as I knelt in prayer, the Lord spoke to my heart and showed me that much of what I was doing was not His will for my life. I was trying to *earn* God's approval by doing many church activities, which the Bible calls *"the works of the law."* My motives were not pure, and the Lord told me to lay down those ministries at His feet. He comforted me and told me that He knew that I did those works out of love for Him, but that He did not want *them*—He wanted *me*, and a heart of obedience in doing His will alone. How many in the Church consult Jesus before they get involved in ministries that He has not even asked them to do? We must examine our hearts and see if we are doing the Father's will or our own. We will waste valuable time if we are doing our own will, and will find that these works will burn up before us on the Day of Judgment. God wants us free to be who He created us to be—to be forever free from being men-pleasers. We must say, "Yes" to God's will and "No" to every lesser work in this hour. God has broken the bands of our yokes and made us to walk uprightly. He has brought us out of the land of Egypt so that we would no longer be the slaves of men. (See Leviticus 26:13.)

As we walk in the Spirit, we will not fulfill the lusts of the flesh; we will not be under the law. (See Galatians 5:16, 18.) Only in the Spirit is there freedom from sin, and the grace to walk on His path of obedience. In the Spirit, we will find the strength to endure the persecutions that are coming—when all of hell will rage against us. Following the Spirit will free us to accomplish His will on this earth. It is then, and only then, that we will be judged by the "law of liberty."

Releasing hate and bitterness will allow the Spirit to purify us as we become *doers* of the Word and not *hearers* only. Only in the Spirit can we be free from our sin and the works of the law; in the cross of Christ this will be accomplished! Our repentance, good works, sacrifices, and obedience can never justify us before the Father—they are the *fruit* of our faith in Him.

Let's walk in the footsteps of our father Abraham:

> ...who, contrary to hope, in hope believed, so that he became the father of many nations, according to what was spoken, "So shall your descendants be." And not being weak in faith, he did not consider his own body, already dead (since he was about a hundred years old), and the deadness of Sarah's womb. He did not waver at the promise of God through unbelief, but was strengthened in faith, giving glory to God, and being fully convinced that what He had promised He was also able to perform. And "therefore it was accounted to him as righteousness."
>
> -Romans 4:18-22

Abraham is called the father of all who walk in faith. As we follow his example and do not consider the deadness of our circumstances and the barrenness that we see in our lives, we, too, will come to a place where we will no longer waver in our faith or in the promises that God has made to us. Only those who are of faith are the sons of Abraham. (See Galatians 3:7, 9.)

We will become strong warriors in His kingdom, and bring great glory to our Father as we walk in faith—and *truly* believe His promises. We will be fully convinced that God will bring to pass what has promised us. It will be worth all the suffering, shakings, and trials to come to this place of stability where we will be perfected, established, strengthened, and settled. (See 1 Peter 5:10.)

Our times of crushing and brokenness are meant to heal us and remove the doubts and fears that are deep within our hearts. God wants us stable, "not like a wave of the sea driven and tossed by the wind." (See James 1:6.) For too long we have lived an "up and down" spiritual life. By the grace of God we must no longer live by what we see or feel. Yes, at times, there will be tears, but we will walk on a level plane, for His fire will complete in us His perfect work.

Jesus is the "...author and the finisher of our faith." Our confidence lies in His *finished* work on the cross and on the truth that He who has begun a good work in us will complete it. (See Hebrews 12:2, Philippians 1:6.)

God's Overcomers

> *I have fought the good fight, I have finished the race, I have kept the faith.*
>
> 2 Timothy 4:7

God's overcomers are His warriors, His champions of faith, who are "more than conquerors." (See Romans 8:37.) As God's ambassadors they "die daily"—they put down their own will to do the will of the Father. Their lives are marked with great suffering, but in the midst of the darkness they say: "For Your sake we are killed all day long; we are accounted as sheep for the slaughter" (Rom. 8:36). They are persuaded that nothing can separate them from the love of God. (See Romans 8:38-39.) They have overcome the fear of death, and all doubt has been eradicated from their souls through the fiery furnace that they have gone through. The smell of smoke does not rest on them, for the fragrance of heaven alone fills their hearts and lives. (See Daniel 3:27.)

Hebrew warriors, Shadrach, Meshach, and Abed-Nego, walked in faith and trust, so are we called to walk as lights in this dark world so that others can find their way home to the Father's heart. So many of God's children walk in darkness; they speak His Word and claim His promises, but their words are empty and hollow because they live a powerless life, devoid of God's holiness. As we have seen, the outer shell of our lives must be crushed in order for the Lord's life to flow through us. We can stand on His Word and speak it, but it is only as we die to our own wills and ways that the full manifestation of His life and power can flow through us. We must go through the cross before His resurrection power can be released in us. This is where we learn to overcome and win the victor's crown.

Now is a time of great acceleration in the Spirit. God is moving in unprecedented ways in this hour to free His children from the yokes of sin and the bondages that have held them captive for years. Those who have "ears to hear" what the Spirit is saying in this hour will be freed from all the darkness that has held them captive for years. They will burn with His fire of holiness, and the seeds of truth that have been planted in their souls will now explode within them, bringing forth His Life as they surrender all and embrace their cross with a radical abandonment to His will. They will not stroke the flesh of man, preaching and teaching only the portions in the Bible that are uplifting, but they will preach the *whole* counsel of God. These radical warriors have chosen to fear God and not man, no matter what the cost!

David Wilkerson, who has recently gone on to be with His Lord, was such a hero of faith. He was a true prophet of God. In the midst of rejection and ridicule, not only from the world, but even from the Church, he spoke the truth of God's Word fearlessly. As God's children, are *we* willing to speak the truth, the whole truth, and nothing but the truth to His people? I have vowed to be a God-pleaser and not a man-pleaser; I pray you will make this same commitment to the Lord in this hour.

I heard the Lord speak this word to me:

> *"Hear, oh barren ones; hear, oh deaf ones! Know that My coming is soon! Know that this time of dispensation is coming to an end —and My Kingdom is about to come forth in My children, through My true children!*

"Captives will be released, blinded eyes opened, and deafened ears will now hear the sound of My voice through My true prophets, through those who fear no man, through those who are fearless in Me!

"I will raise up a Remnant, a company of true believers who will speak truth; they will not fear man, nor the devil, but will speak the words that I put in their mouths. They will not fear the face of man, but will proclaim my whole truth, not just parts of it—the parts that tickle the flesh of My children. 'Those days are over with,' says the Lord your God. 'Those days are forever gone!' For My judgment is here, and I will begin this fire in My House, in those places where they proclaim and teach My Word. I will in mercy deal with leadership: teachers, pastors, prophets, and all who say that they are Mine! We will see in this hour those who are truly Mine, for only in truth, the whole truth, will My ministers stand. If they reject My truth in this hour and refuse to repent, I say in deepest love, they will no longer stand before My people and preach or teach. I am serious, serious in this hour! For My eyes are a flame of fire that will pierce through the hypocrisy and compromise that I see in the hearts of My children!

"Daughter, a new stream, a fresh stream of truth is about to flow through My body, and as this stream of truth flows through My body, it will wash away all the filth and debris out of the hearts of My children.

"I need ministers of righteousness who will look for favor from no man, but only from Me. I have found a people, few in number, but strong in My Spirit, who will accomplish this work.

"Be steadfast—be strong—and look only to Me! This work shall be done quickly now, for I, by the power of My Spirit, will do a quick and powerful work in this hour. Trust Me. It shall be accomplished; I promise you! Thus says your Lord!"
(Given to me on October 13, 2011)

How do we as God's children overcome the world? We must, without mercy, slay the giant of unbelief in our souls—through faith. For "...this is the victory that has overcome the world—our faith." Those who have been born of God and who truly believe that Jesus is the Son of God, will wear the victor's crown. (See 1 John 5:4-5.) Those who embrace God's truth will rise up as true children of faith. The faith of the Son of God will arise in our souls like the "morning star," and we will go forth conquering, no more to be conquered. (See Galatians 2:20.)

These overcomers have committed their souls completely to Christ; they boast in the cross of Jesus, and are dead to the world. (See Galatians 6:14.) The faith of Christ permeates their whole being, and they no longer walk in their own strength and power, but in the power of the living Christ. They have overcome the *evil one* by the blood of the Lamb and by the word of their testimony; they do not love their lives, even to death. (See Revelation 12:11.)

This is how we, too, overcome in every area of our lives. As we rejoice in the midst of our fiery trials and speak the promises of God even in our weakness, we will find a new strength and power begin to fill us. As we speak God's faith-filled words against our enemies, we will then see the giants that come against us fall. We must never back down, no matter what we feel or see. Faith is our victory; this is what will lift us up onto the wave of glory that is coming! We have been called to be overcomers, and because Christ overcame for us, we can now be victorious in the power of the Spirit. (See John 16:33.) Because "He who is in you is greater than he who is in the world" (1 John 4:4).

We are surrounded by a great cloud of witnesses who have gone on before us. They are cheering us on in our struggles and temptations. By God's grace we will overcome all that is in the world, even as they did: the lust of the flesh, the lust of the eyes, and the pride of life. (See Hebrews 12:1, 1 John 2:16.)

We are always led in triumph in Christ, and the fragrance of His knowledge is diffused through us wherever we go. We are the "fragrance of Christ" which others will smell as we spend time in the presence of God. (See 2 Corinthians 2:14-16.) Recently, I took a necklace out of a wooden box that also had several fragrant candles in it. As I put the necklace on, I realized that it had taken on the fragrance of the candles because of its *close contact* with them. As we spend time with Jesus, we will smell just like Him, and His sweet aroma will permeate our hearts and lives.

Great spiritual blessings await us as we continue on this narrow path. As we lay everything on the altar of sacrifice, we'll experience abundant fruit and unspeakable joy. Others may look at us and not understand how we can rejoice in our times of suffering, but as they see the manifest glory of His presence emanating from our lives, they, too, will hunger for this peace and joy. It will be worth all the struggle and denial in our lives, to come to this place of glory in Christ. We must never lose heart or grow weary because of the waiting time, for the precious fruit of long-suffering must be fully developed in us. (See Galatians 6:9.)

As we overcome and begin to inherit the blessings of God, we must begin to leave the discussion of the elementary principles of Christ and go on to perfection. We must let go of our past and allow all our wounds to be healed. We have laid a strong foundation of repentance in our lives and of faith toward God; let's now begin to claim and take hold of all the promises of God. (See Hebrews 6:1.)

There's a time to weep, but there is also a time to rejoice. Once the foundation is laid and we have walked in truth and repentance, the Lord would then have us move up onto higher ground. God does not want us to stay where we are, but His desire is that we mature and come to a place of greater usefulness in His kingdom. Even as He told the Israelites that they had "skirted" that mountain long enough, so is the Lord speaking this Word to us. (See Deuteronomy 2:3.) God's kingdom is always moving forward—and so must we. It is easy to get stuck in our past and pain, but as we let go and allow God to take full possession of our lives, we will then find true freedom. Paul tells us to forget those things that are behind and to reach toward those things which are ahead, to "press toward the goal for the prize of the upward call of God in Christ Jesus." (See Philippians 3:12-14.) Satan will try to bind you with your past, but you must continually claim the finished work of the cross. Keep climbing Mount Zion, that spiritual mountain, and don't look back—remember Lot's wife! Repent of your sin, and then believe that the blood of Jesus has the power to free you completely from your past. Press on—no matter what pressure or grief comes your way. This is your hour of freedom—never let go of the rope of faith!

Jesus says that we will have tribulation in this world, but that in Him we can have perfect peace. He tells us to cheer up because He has overcome this world, and that now in Him we can have total and complete victory. (See John 16:33, 17:13-26.) Jesus chose us out of this world, and that is why we are hated. It is for His name's sake that we are persecuted. Out of this persecution, this "fellowship of sufferings," we will know the power of His resurrection. (See Philippians 3:10.) Let's count it all joy, even a privilege to suffer for the Lord, even as the disciples of old did. We will know how to be abased, and how to abound; we will learn to be content in whatever circumstances we find ourselves in. Glory will fill us as we praise Him—whether we are full or hungry—when we abound or are in need. As God's overcomers we will find that we can do all things through Christ who strengthens us. (See Philippians 4:11-13.)

We will consider the sufferings that we go through not worthy to be compared with the glory that shall be revealed in us; it will be like a "light affliction" compared to the "eternal weight of glory" that we will know in Christ. We must never lose heart, for "though our outward man is perishing, yet our inward man is being renewed day by day" (2 Cor. 4: 10, 16-17.) We carry about in our bodies the dying of the Lord Jesus, so that His life may be manifested in our bodies. (See Romans 8:18.) An overcomer is one who knows that it is Christ *in* them who is the hope of glory (See Colossians 1:27.)

Jesus has chosen us to be His overcomers; He has appointed us to go and bear much fruit for Him, and that our fruit would remain. He chose us; we did not choose Him, and we overcome because we have been born of Him. Our *faith* is the victory that overcomes this world—faith that Jesus is the Son of God. (See John 15:16, 1 John 4-5.)

Revelation 21:7 tells us that "He who overcomes shall inherit all things, and I will be his God and he shall be My son." Could there be any greater promise? As we overcome, we will inherit all things as a son or daughter of the Most High God. In this life we will never know our *full* inheritance in Christ, but we can *begin* to walk and experience it *now*. It will be worth any loss, anguish, or crushing pain to know the approval and love of our heavenly Father. Let's count the cost in the light of our eternal reward in heaven, which is far greater than any human tongue could ever tell!

In Hebrews chapter 11, we see that even though some of God's children did not receive His promises immediately, they still saw them from afar and were assured of them. They embraced the promises, even though with their natural eyes they could not see them. (See Hebrews 11:13, 39.) These are God's true overcomer's, for they saw with their *spiritual eyes;* they walked by faith and not by sight. They are now enjoying their eternal reward. Their eyes of faith now see the glory that they hoped and believed in on earth. These are the ones who will be in God's "hall of fame," and they will forever rejoice because they believed, even when they didn't see the promises manifested in their lifetime. These are *true* children of faith, and as they overcame, so are *we* now called to overcome every doubt and fear in our lives. By the grace of God, I pray that someday we will rejoice with these "heroes of faith" as we walk with them on streets of gold!

In the book of Revelation we see what some of the rewards are for overcoming. God says:

- "To him who overcomes I will give to eat from the tree of life, which is in the midst of the Paradise of God" (Rev. 2:7).
- "Be faithful until death, and I will give you the crown of life" (Rev. 2:10).
- "He who overcomes shall not be hurt by the second death" (Rev. 2:11).
- "To him who overcomes I will give some of the hidden manna to eat. And I will give him a white stone, and on the stone a new name written which no one knows except him who receives it" (Rev. 2:17).
- "And he who overcomes, and keeps My works until the end, to him I will give power over the nations— 'he shall rule them with a rod of iron; they shall be dashed to pieces like the potter's vessels' —as I also have received from My Father; and I will give him the morning star" (Rev. 2:26-28).
- "He who overcomes shall be clothed in white garments, and I will not blot out his name from the Book of Life; but I will confess his name before My Father and before His angels" (Rev. 3:5).
- "Because you have kept My command to persevere, I also will keep you from the hour of trial which will come upon the whole world, to test those who dwell on the earth" (Rev. 3:10).
- "He who overcomes, I will make him a pillar in the temple of My God, and he shall go out no more. I will write on him the name of My God and the name of the city of My God. And I will write on him My new name" (Rev. 3:12).
- "To him who overcomes I will grant to sit with Me on My throne, as I also overcame and sat down with My Father on His throne" (Rev. 3:21).

Let us be like Caleb of old, who quieted the people before Moses and said, "Let us go up at once and take possession, for we are well able to overcome it" (Num. 13:30.) In the strength of the Spirit we'll go forth, claiming our land, our inheritance in Christ, for He who is with us is far greater than any enemy that would confront us.

In our victories, we must always remember that it is only through Christ that we overcome! We can do all things through Christ who strengthens us, for it is His power, His ability, His grace, His mercy, and spirit of might *in* us that will overcome every obstacle. On that great Day, when we receive our crowns of victory from His hand, we will cast them at the feet of Jesus and cry, "You are worthy, O Lord, to receive glory and honor and power..." (See Revelation 4:10-11.) Jesus *alone* will be magnified on that day, for we'll know that it was in His power and victory alone that we have overcome. Glory to God!

As we slay the giant of unbelief in our hearts, and overcome in every fiery trial, we will say:

> O Lord, I will praise You; though You were angry with me, Your anger is turned away, and You comfort me. Behold, God is my salvation, I will trust and not be afraid; for Yah, the Lord, is my strength and song; He also has become my salvation...Praise the Lord, call upon His name; declare His deeds among the peoples, make mention that His name is exalted. Sing to the Lord, for He has done excellent things; this is known in all the earth. Cry out and shout, O inhabitant of Zion, for great is the Holy One of Israel in your midst.
>
> -Isaiah 12:1-2, 4-6

> *"Now to Him who is able to keep you from stumbling, and to present you faultless before the presence of His glory with exceeding joy..."*
>
> (Jude 24).

Word from the Lord:

> *"I have called you to be overcomers, My children—to run the race with joy—to walk in obedience to My will and My commands. You must forsake the world and all that it stands for, yes, even your own lives for the sake of My kingdom. Only as you renounce* all *will receive the overcomer's crown. This is not a light word, My people, but it is a true one. Better that you hear and receive this word now and deeply repent, than to stand before Me on Judgment Day and hear My Words of disapproval. No—you cannot earn your salvation—but would you stand before Me*

empty-handed on that Day —or worse yet, see all the works that you have done in the flesh burn up before you? Do you not fear Me, My children, and the judgments that I would speak? My children, to rule and reign with Me throughout eternity—to have My love and approval,—to have a position of honor—is that not worth giving up all for, even this earth's pleasures and fleeting joys?

"Oh children, I will give you all the grace you need to achieve this crown of eternal glory, only yield to Me; obey Me; put down all your fleshy endeavors, and pick up your cross and follow Me—no matter where I would lead you. Be as Abraham—follow his example of abandoning all for the sake of My will and purpose. Be valiant as David, and overcome in My strength all the forces of hell that would come against you; praise and worship Me in the midst of every battle. When you face your Goliath—in My strength and power this giant will come down. Is it lust or fear that binds you? What about unbelief in My promise to never leave you or forsake you? Do you doubt My love and mercy for you in this hour? Do you feel that your needs will not be met by My abundant resources in heaven? What is it that binds you children?

"If you allow Me, I will show you where you are bound, and in My grace I will free you and break every stronghold that binds you. I have called you to be more than conquerors, not one to walk in fear, depression, or defeat. I have called you My warriors, My sons, My daughters, even My beloved bride, but you must put down all unbelief and believe what My Word says concerning who you are in My beloved Son.

"Let Me transform you. Let Me lift you up onto that potter's wheel and spin you, shape you, and form you into that overcomer that I see you are! You need a new image, a new identity, and this can only be found as you lay down your own plans and agenda, and as you lay at My feet every <u>earthly crown</u>—for the sake of picking up your <u>crown of glory</u>—your <u>crown of victory</u>—this <u>overcoming crown</u> that I have planned to place on your head as you stand before Me on Judgment Day.

"The choice is yours, and only you can decide which road you will take. The road you are on is coming to a fork; which direction will you choose? Will you go your own way and suffer loss beyond

words, even to your eternal destruction, or will you choose the path of life, which leads to glory, honor, and praise to My holy name and to your eternal reward in glory? It is time to choose. The hour is late. I wait for your response. Choose life and live, My children!"
(Given to me on September 13, 2011)

CHAPTER 6: COME TO ME AND REST

Come to Me, all who labor and are heavy laden, and I will give you rest. Take My yoke upon you and learn from Me, for I am gentle and lowly in heart, and you will find rest for your souls. For My yoke is easy and My burden is light.

Matthew 11:28-30

There remains therefore a rest for the people of God.

Hebrews 4:9

IN THE PAST FEW months, God has been giving me Scriptures in Matthew 11:28-30—*constantly*—more than any other Scriptures in the Bible. Everywhere I turn these Scriptures come up, and just when I think, "Well, Lord, I guess You've stopped speaking these Scriptures to me," I'll open a devotional, hear in a sermon, or read these Scriptures in a book—*again*!

I do not believe these Scriptures are only for me, though I have needed them greatly in these past months, but they are for this weary and heavy-laden generation that we live in. Never have I seen so many people, not only in this world, but in the Church, so stressed out and overburdened. I believe this generation, more than any other, needs these words of comfort and hope because of the desperate times that we live in. Never has there been a more stressful time to live, or a more wicked generation than the one we are in right now. Many of us have been in heavy labor spiritually, because of the Lord's travail in our souls. There is desperation in our hearts and a longing for His kingdom to come forth in our lives and in this world.

How our hearts long to see our loved ones freed from the clutches of Satan! We desire to see multitudes of souls loosed from their captivity to see their blinded eyes opened!

God is wooing us, drawing us into Himself in this hour, through the tremendous pressures and pains that we have been feeling. We are running to the secret place, longing for His presence, and desiring to hear a word from Him in this season of unrest. Never has there been such discontent and anxiety in the hearts of multitudes of people. Sometimes we wonder if we'll make it until tomorrow: our economy is shaking and the rampant sin and evil around us is accelerating. Many of us stand on His Word and confess His promises daily; we pray and fast, and yet there is a feeling of uneasiness, a fear, a sense of foreboding that we just can't seem to shake! Can anyone relate to this? I say to you in love and truth that in the midst of these very dilemmas that we find ourselves in, God desires to draw us, cleanse us, purify us, and prepare us for the dark days that are ahead.

I believe we are the generation that will enter into His *rest*, that deep place in the heart of our Savior, but it will only happen *if* we run to Him, expose our hearts and fears, and give all of our anxieties to Jesus. He is crying out to us in this hour, and He desires that we come to Him, sup with Him, and allow Him to fill our hearts to overflowing with His presence. Can't you hear Him crying, "Come to Me" in the trials that you are in? Do you think He is impervious to your cries for help? He is not indifferent to our sorrows and pains, even as He wasn't to His children as they wandered in the wilderness. He is calling us to enter into His rest, the place of calm trust and surrender to His will, and into the eye of the storm, where nothing will ever be able to move us again.

Jesus wants us *yoked* with Him in a union so deep, so intimate, that no more doubts and fears will ever be able to disturb us again. This union will make us *one* with Him in desire, passion, purpose, and in His deep heart of rest. As we come to Him and abide in Him, we will find lightness, joy, and love we have only dreamed of. It will be easy to serve the Father, for it will not be our works, but the Lord's ministry being worked out through our lives! There will be no fleshy struggling, trying to bring forth an "Ishmael" ministry (birthed in the flesh), but it will be an "Isaac" ministry (birthed in the Spirit); it will be all of God and nothing of us.

Hebrews 4:3 says that, "…we who have believed do enter that rest…" Only as we take hold of the promises of God and put to death all unbelief in us, will we enter that rest. The children of Israel could not enter in because of unbelief and disobedience. (See Hebrews 3:18-19.)

In the second chapter of Genesis, it tells us that on the seventh day God ended His work which He had done, and He rested. "Then God blessed the seventh day and sanctified it, because in it He rested from all His work which God had created and made" (Gen. 2:3). God made the seventh day a sign between Him and the children of Israel forever, and He commanded that they keep His Sabbaths. God said that the Sabbath is holy, and that those who profane it would be put to death. He said: "Work shall be done for six days, but the seventh day shall be a holy day for you, a Sabbath of rest to the Lord" (Ex. 35:2). I want you to see that God created the seventh day in order to bring us into His rest. These Old Testament truths are significant for us in this very hour.

In 2 Peter 3:8, it says, "But, beloved, do not forget this one thing, that with the Lord one day is as a thousand years, and a thousand years as one day." From Adam until the turn of the century, we have now completed six thousand years or six days, and we are early in the morning on the seventh day. We are now in that seventh day, the Sabbath rest—*spiritually*. Jesus is Lord of the Sabbath, and He made this rest for man, not man for the Sabbath. (See Mark 2:27-28.)

In Genesis 8:4, it reads, "Then the ark rested in the *seventh* month, the seventeenth day of the month, on the mountains of Ararat" (emphasis added). In the flood waters of suffering, many of God's children have been climbing Mount Zion, the spiritual mountain of the Lord. These waters have been lifting them high, and soon they will rest on God's mountain of glory. God has been lifting us to higher ground; we must not look back, but keep climbing until we reach the top of this spiritual mountain. It is here that we will find Christ, the true Ark, and our true Sabbath rest. As the ark rested on that mountain—so will we find deep rest *if* we abide fully in Christ.

Jesus is the Vine and we are the branches. He tells us that if we abide in Him, and He in us, we will bear much fruit. Without this abiding, this resting in Christ's heart, we can do *nothing*, and we will never know true and lasting peace. As we rest and abide in Jesus, we can ask what we desire and it will be done for us, for we will ask nothing apart from His will; we will not ask amiss, because our motives will be pure. Jesus said that if we keep His commandments, we will abide in His love, just as He kept His Father's commandments and abides in His love. (See John 15:5-10.) Without this abiding, without this resting in His love, we will find that we can do nothing. Anything that is done apart from this abiding rest in Christ will burn.

God is calling His overcoming army to enter fully into His heart of rest, so that He can release His glorious plan through them for this generation. God will draw us into a deep union with Him, a deep rest in our souls and bodies, and from this place of rest His power will flow through us to the lost and dying throughout this world. His love will draw us in, and in this love His will shall be accomplished. Remember: *faith works through love—His love!*

God is telling us to let go of our own plans, our own will, and be diligent to enter into this rest, lest we fall according to the same example of disobedience that the children of Israel did. (See Hebrews 4:11.) God has a people in this hour that will cease from their own works; they will do the Father's will alone. All of their fleshy ambition and desires will be put to death! They will be God-pleasers, not man-pleasers. The Spirit is taking hold of them, in order to accomplish His mighty works through them.

The Lord is going to visit His Church once again and burn up all man-made ministries and programs. He will spare no one. Everything that is of the flesh and of the "soulish" nature will burn. Get ready Church; prepare your hearts, for the Lord is on His way! Examine your hearts: Is what you are doing God-birthed, or is it a ministry that you have birthed in the flesh? We must hear what the Spirit is telling us to do—and *do* it! He is calling us to enter His rest by faith, and to implement *His* will and purpose in the earth in this final hour.

As we embrace the will and presence of God, He will go before us and give us rest. (See Exodus 33:14.) Jesus will lead us beside still waters, and we'll find His deep rest as we lie down in green pastures. We "shall not want," for all will be fulfilled in Him. We will "fear no evil," for even when we "walk through the valley of the shadow of death" we'll know that He is with us. (See Psalm 23:1-4.) As we dwell in the secret place of the Most High, we shall abide under the shadow of the Almighty. (See Psalm 91:1.) Now that's rest! That's the place of perfect peace and comfort.

In Psalm 91:4 it says, "He shall cover you with His feathers, and under His wings you shall take refuge." When I was driving home from church one night, I prayed, "Oh Lord, I know you cover us with Your feathers and protect us, but would you show me some feathers to confirm this truth?" I really only prayed this half-heartedly, almost jokingly, because I know the Lord cares for me. The next day my husband and I went for a walk in a park some miles away from our home. As we went down to the lake and walked around the park, we noticed thousands upon thousands of feathers! Never had we seen so many feathers in one place as we did in that park.

The Lord reminded me of the prayer the night before, and I marveled that He would answer this simple prayer so powerfully. Our mighty God is our Protector, and He wants us to rest in His loving arms, with no fear of any evil destroying us. Truly His feathers, His wings, are over our lives!

It is in stillness and quietness that we come to know the Lord's intimate love for us. (See Psalm 46:10.) God needs to bring us to the place where we are *quiet* on the inside. Many times we come before Him weighed down with cares and anxieties, and because of this we cannot hear His still small voice or receive the deep comfort that He has for us. As we quiet our hearts through prayer and praise, we will begin to hear Him, and to *know* Him in the deepest place of our being. We will begin to feed on His love and presence, and our souls will be satisfied as with marrow and fatness. (See Psalm 63:5.) In His heart we find rest; in His love we find comfort.

I remember a time, many years ago, when I was suffering deeply because of the loss of a loved one. No one could comfort me, and in my distress I got down on my knees and simply knelt before the Lord. I couldn't even speak a word. As I waited in His presence, liquid love, which felt like warm oil, began to pour into me and saturate my whole being, until I felt overwhelmed in His presence. This experience was so glorious; I knew that I had entered into the very atmosphere of heaven. As I embraced His presence, I entered deeply into His heart of love, and I knew all was well. God desires that we bring Him every doubt, fear, pain, and heartache. He will meet with us, comfort us, and draw us into the depths of His love.

There are many who refuse to come to the Lord, even in the Church, for fear of exposure. The Pharisee spirit, outward actions that are spiritually bankrupt, will always keep its distance from the true presence of God, for their hearts are not right before the Lord. Jesus said: "You search the scriptures, for in them you think you have eternal life; and these are they which testify of Me, but you are not willing to come to Me that you may have life" (John 5:39). Many scholars and theologians can quote many, many Scriptures, but they refuse to come to Jesus in true repentance. They desire to do their own works and think their own thoughts. They eat from the tree of knowledge of good and evil, but have never been born again by the Spirit of God. They cannot eat from the tree of life, for this Tree is Jesus; He alone is the Way, the Truth, and the Life, and no one comes to the Father apart from Him. They will never enter God's rest apart from Jesus, and unless they come to Him as a child, in humility and trust, they will be separated from Him forever. God desires a heart-to-heart relationship with everyone on the face of this earth, but we must come to Him, ask Him to take our sin, and receive Him into our hearts. We can read the Scriptures, go to church seven days a week, and do many good works, but these things will *never* save us or bring us into His deep rest. We must be willing to surrender our pride and good works and come to Him.

Jeremiah 6:16 tells us to, "Stand in the ways and see, and ask for the old paths, where the good way is, and walk in it; Then you will find rest for your souls." What are the old paths, and what are the good ways? To follow the old paths and the good ways, we must follow the Lord in obedience to His law and His will for our lives. Jesus is the same yesterday, today, and forever, and He has not changed His mind about sin and rebellion. Study the lives of Abraham, Moses, Jeremiah, Job, Isaiah, Joseph, Esther, and all the other saints of old. They walked in paths of holiness and obedience. They revered God; they honored Him. The fear of the Lord governed their hearts and lives in all that they did. As they encountered the Lord, they trembled in His presence, and their hearts were filled with awe. As we follow the examples of these mighty men and women of old, and walk in the same manner that they walked, we will find a deep rest that will begin to permeate our whole being. Holiness and purity must be our passion and our lifestyle if we are to enter into this deep rest.

In Psalm 46:10, it says, "Be still, and know that I am God..." How can we possibly enter into His rest if we are always running and striving in our flesh? Who are we turning to for love and comfort; is it our family and friends that we look to? Only in Jesus, as we run to Him and spend time in His presence as Joshua, Paul, Moses, and many others did, will we ever find that deep peace that we are searching for. A stillness and peace must begin to enter into that deep part of our being if we are ever going to truly come to know Him. It is here that we will begin to hear His voice more clearly and be able to receive the deep love that He desires to give us. Only in stillness and quietness can our souls receive what He has for us. All must die in our flesh, and as we go through our dark night of the soul we will enter fully into His peace. This is the deep work of the cross in our lives. It is *here* that we will begin to enter in and partake of our inheritance in Christ.

When our ways please the Lord, He will make even our enemies to be at peace with us. (See Proverbs 16:7.) As we cross the Jordan (death to self) and enter fully into our promised land—our inheritance in Christ—God will give us rest from all our enemies, and we'll know that our souls are safe in His care. (See Deuteronomy 12:10.) There is a place of quietness and peace that no man—no devil—will ever be able to take from us, and it lies in the depths of the love of our Father's heart. Nothing will move us, nothing will ever shake us again, for we'll find that in returning and rest we shall be saved, and that quietness and confidence will be our strength. (See Isaiah 30:15.)

Deuteronomy 15:1 says that "At the end of every seven years you shall grant a release of debts." You see, we have been fully forgiven of our sin, but our loving Savior wants us to experience rest in our souls and bodies—not only our spirits. As we enter the Sabbath rest of the Lord, we will experience a great release inside of us from fear, unbelief, and even from the burdens that we have carried for so long. All of our striving will cease, and we will rest as a content child in the arms of our loving Father.

"The work of righteousness will be peace, and the effect of righteousness, quietness and assurance forever. My people will dwell in a peaceful habitation, in secure dwellings, and in quiet resting places, though hail comes down on the forest, and the city is brought low in humiliation" (Is. 32:17-19).

God's word to us:

"It is time to enter into your rest. The time of fighting—the time of grief is now over. You are entering a new season of time, and you will show, by the way you live your life, what it is to enter fully into My rest. There will be no more fleshy activity. You will walk in My Spirit and do only those things I tell you to do—not your own will—but Mine. You will say with My Son, 'I delight to do Your will, My God.' Even in suffering and disappointments there will be a rest in your soul, a rest of love and peace, and nothing—no circumstances, no devil, no adversary—will cause you to tremble. All will be love—all will be peace and rest. You will be as a weaned child resting in the arms of her mother. You will now rest in the arms of God, and all will be quiet inside. No more striving—no more looking for approval from man. You will experience only a deep rest in your soul, knowing that I love you and approve of you. Restlessness will be forever gone, for you will know, deep in your heart, a love—an emotional love—that you'll know is from My heart. No more will you doubt My love. No more will you fear rejection; all will be settled deep in your heart.

"I will take you now into your promised land, and you will partake of a feast of all the blessings that I have for you: joy, love, prosperity, ministry doors opening, receiving My favor and man's, an abundance of My presence and glory, total restoration, a harvest of souls, and an intimacy with Me that you've never known.

"Oh children, the joy, love, peace, and laughter will overflow from your hearts and lives now. You see, children, rest means working in the overflow, allowing My Spirit to flow through you as a river. No striving, no fleshy or 'soulish' endeavors. All of Me—none of you! Rest is experiencing what Paul did when he said, 'It is no longer I that live, but Christ who lives in me, and the life I now live, I live by the faith of the Son of God who died and gave Himself for me.' Paul had, at this point in his life, entered into My rest. His thorn no longer bothered him. All was peace; all came forth in love, joy, and rest. He had found that secret of abiding in Me fully, and he no longer feared the past, present, or future. All was laid on the altar of sacrifice. The love in him, My love, was perfected—there was no more fear. This is the place I want to bring My chosen ones into in this hour, says the Lord."

(Given to me on September 8, 2011)

"The Lord preserves the simple; I was brought low, and He saved me. Return to your rest, O my soul, for the Lord has dealt bountifully with you. For You have delivered my soul from death, my eyes from tears, and my feet from falling. I will walk before the Lord in the land of the living"

(Psalm 116:6-9).

RESTORATION AND TOTAL RECOVERY

When the Lord brought back the captivity of Zion, we were like those who dream. Then our mouth was filled with laughter, and our tongue with singing. Then they said among the nations, "The Lord has done great things for them."

The Lord has done great things for us, and we are glad.

Psalm 126:1-3

Now the Lord is the Spirit; and where the Spirit of the Lord is, there is liberty. But we all, with unveiled face, beholding as in a mirror the glory of the Lord, are being transformed into the same image from glory to glory, just as by the Spirit of the Lord.

2 Corinthians 3:17-18

And nothing of theirs was lacking, either small or great, sons or daughters, spoil or anything which they had taken from them; David recovered all.

1 Samuel 30:19

ACCORDING TO THE New College Edition—The American Heritage Dictionary of the English Language, *restoration* means: "the act of putting someone or something back into a prior position, place, or condition. The state of being reinstated, reconstructed, or otherwise restored."

Through our tests and trials, we must let patience have its perfect work, so that we may be perfect and complete, lacking nothing. (See James 1:4.) God's desire is that we lack nothing, but that we would be brought back to His heart, and have restored to us all that we lost in the garden of Eden. In the New Covenant that Christ established for us through His blood, He has won back our position of authority that we had in the garden. His desire is to reinstate us to our former position, and into an even greater one because of what He accomplished on Calvary. We are now seated in heavenly places in Christ Jesus, if we would only believe and receive it by faith (Ephesians 2:5-6).

God's desire is to free us from sin and the bonds that have kept us captive to this earth's sinful pleasures. He wants to give us a new heart, mind, and will, and to completely heal our emotions. The Lord desires that we begin, even now, to enter into our promised land, and take hold of every promise that is in this New Covenant.

God's eternal purpose is coming to pass in a people who have abandoned everything and who embrace their cross and follow Him daily. The Lord's purpose is found in 1 Thessalonians 5:23, which says, "Now may the God of peace Himself sanctify you completely; and may your whole spirit, soul, and body be preserved blameless at the coming of our Lord Jesus Christ." God's deepest desire is to sanctify us fully, in order to bring us back into that place of intimacy with Him that He so longs to have with us.

God is the One who has tested us, who has refined us as silver is refined. We went through fire and through water, but *He* has brought us out to rich fulfillment. (See Psalm 66:10-12.) When we see that *God* has orchestrated our lives—even the painful things that we have needed in order to be purified—we will bless His holy name for taking such pains with us. We will find that our fiery trials have burned off the bands that held us, and have freed us on the inside. As God brings us into His deep, rich fulfillment and oneness in His Spirit of love, we'll find that what we have suffered will pale in comparison to the glory that will be revealed in and to us.

Our purpose and destiny will come forth in a power and glory so great, that we will be overwhelmed as we walk in the divine plan that Christ fore-ordained for us to walk in. "For we are His workmanship, created in Christ Jesus for good works, which God prepared beforehand that we should walk in them" (Eph. 2:10). God will restore to us the years that the swarming locust has eaten, and we shall eat in plenty and be satisfied; we will praise the name of the Lord our God who has dealt so wondrously with us. (See Joel 2:25-26.) The shame of our youth will be forgotten, and we will no longer remember the reproach of our widowhood, for we'll know our Maker as our husband. (See Isaiah 54:4-5.)

Not only does the Father desire that we be born again in our spirit-man, but He also desires to establish His kingdom in and through us, in order for us to bring multitudes to His heart through mighty signs, wonders, and miracles. God has revealed to me that He will flow through His *restored ones* in a power that will make the book of Acts look dull in comparison. These mighty warriors will do the greater works that He talked about in John 14:12.

There is a hidden company in this hour that is about to be released in His full power and glory. They are coming forth from the cave of Adullam, fully trained and fully equipped in the Spirit of God. (See 1 Samuel 22:1-2, 1 Chronicles 12:1.) Through these unknown and unheard-of warriors, God will release and restore a multitude of souls who have been held captive by the enemy through years of suffering and abuse. They are coming out of the wilderness and have renounced the lies of the enemy; they have shattered the stronghold of unbelief in their hearts by the Word of God and through the power and might of His Spirit. They have grown sick and tired of living on the lowlands of doubt, and are even now experiencing restoration in their souls and bodies.

A new joy from the Lord and a stronger faith is consuming their lives. Their hearts have been flooded with a new vision from heaven and they know who they are in Christ. They have seen how the enemy has robbed them of their spiritual inheritance in Christ and of the deep intimacy that they have so longed for with their heavenly Father. They are like the prodigal son who came to his senses and ran back home to his Father's heart. They have received from the Father His robe of righteousness, His ring of authority, and the shoes of the gospel of peace. Their hearts have been torn deeply through godly sorrow, and with unveiled faces they are beholding the face of Jesus—even the glory of the Lord. Daily they are being transformed and renewed in His glorious presence.

They are climbing spiritual Mount Zion—and they refuse to look back. Even now, they can see the very top of this mountain, as their flesh is dying to its former lusts and their souls are being fully renewed in the Spirit. They are beginning to experience the full recovery that God has promised them. Their loved ones are beginning to awaken out of their spiritual slumber; their ministries in Christ are being restored, and true freedom is being released in the core of their being. The image of God, which had been taken from them so ruthlessly, is now being restored. Where they once walked in independence and rebellion apart from the Father, they now are walking with Him in deep communion and intimacy in the cool of the garden in their hearts. Christ has restored *all* to them, and they are daily eating from the tree of life, even the very life of Jesus. The Spirit of God is nourishing their souls through the Word and His presence, and their "inner man" is being strengthened daily.

The world has not yet seen these transformed souls in the full power of the Spirit, but they are beginning to rise. This restoration will be unto the "…measure of the stature of the fullness of Christ," and they will be noted as the mighty ones on the earth. (See Ephesians 4:13.) This restoration is for all who dare to believe the Word of God and His promises to them.

Many are called, but few are chosen, and this is only because many refuse to believe and allow the purifying fires of His love to consume their sin. God chooses us in the furnace of affliction—*if* we are willing to go through the process—the metamorphic change that is necessary to be conformed into His likeness. In the chrysalis, a caterpillar must be willing to endure the horrendous transformation process in order to become a completely different creature. If anyone helps this creature emerge from its chrysalis by even making a small slit in it, it will emerge swollen and deformed, and it will never have the strength that it needs to fly. It is the *struggle* that makes this creature's wings strong and ready for flight, just as our spiritual trials and struggles are meant to make us strong. His power and energy must fill our spiritual wings, in order for us to soar into the heavens with Him, and reach that mountaintop of victory that He would bring us to.

In my pain, I couldn't see that God was refining my character and that I was being transformed into His image in the darkness of my chrysalis. How could I ever have imagined the glorious future that He had planned for me in my dark night? As I began to develop His eyes of faith in the darkness, it was only then that I could begin to see what the Lord had in store for me. Many in the Church are struggling in this very hour, even as I have, but only as they die to their sin will they be able to break out of their chrysalis of unbelief.

In the "first Adam" we lost all of our spiritual blessings because of sin and unbelief, but now in Christ, the "last Adam," we are taking back all that is rightfully ours because of what His cross has accomplished for us. Those who are in Christ have the right to eat from the tree of life freely, for in Him all has been restored back to us as we rightfully claim our position in Christ. In the garden we were robbed, for Satan came to steal, kill, and destroy us, but now in Christ, through the power of the cross, we can be redeemed, healed, and restored back to our former position—the abundant life that He promises us in His Word. (See John 10:10.) In Revelation 1:18, we read that Jesus has the keys of Hades and of death. Christ won back for us the keys that we forfeited in the Garden because of sin, and in His love He is giving back to His true children these keys of power and authority. (See Matthew 16:19.)

Ephesians 1:11, tells us that in Jesus we have obtained an inheritance, but we must receive it and take the Kingdom by force. (See Matthew 11:12.) Even though Christ has won this victory for us, we must take hold of it by faith until we see the full manifestation of His power come forth in our lives. The Holy Spirit will strengthen and help us in this "good fight of faith," for we have been sealed with the Holy Spirit of promise, who is the guarantee of our inheritance until the redemption of the purchased possession. (See verses 13-14.) Christ's sinless life and His perfect sacrifice on Calvary has purchased for us our eternal inheritance; it is ours for the taking, but we must stand firm and contend for the faith and never waver concerning His promises to us. We can even now begin to possess what Christ has purchased for us, and in the eternal ages we will realize the fullness of our inheritance in Christ. All things are possible to them that believe, but we must take hold of these promises in our everyday life.

My prayer is:

> That the God of our Lord Jesus Christ, the Father of glory, may give to you the spirit of wisdom and revelation in the knowledge of Him, the eyes of your understanding being enlightened; that you may know what is the hope of His calling, what are the riches of the glory of His inheritance in the saints, and what is the exceeding greatness of His power toward us who believe, according to the working of His mighty power which He worked in Christ when He raised Him from the dead and seated Him at His right hand in the heavenly places, far above all principality and power and might and dominion, and every name that is named, not only in this age but also in that which is to come.
>
> -Ephesians 1:17-21

Our spiritual eyes need to be fully opened to see who we truly are in Christ. No more must we judge one another according to the *flesh*—but by the *Spirit*. What we need in this hour are divine, heavenly encounters, a true revelation of who Christ is and what He has purchased for us. As the outer shell of our flesh is shattered, we will then be enlightened to see the hope of our calling. We will see that we are *Christ's* inheritance, we are not our own but are here to fulfill His will and calling in our lives. As we are enlightened, His power will explode in us, and we will begin to walk in resurrection power, fulfilling His purposes on this earth.

We are His inheritance—and He is ours. In the covenant that Christ ratified for us through His blood, we realize that all that we have is His—and all that He has is ours—it is all for all. When we take hold of this truth in our hearts it will set us completely free. We'll find that all of our longings and desires will be met in Jesus. *He* is our Promised Land. (See Deuteronomy 18:2.) No more do we need to struggle with sin, for we will see that Christ became sin for us, so that we might "become the righteousness of God in Him." (See 2 Corinthians 5:21.) As we are chastened by the Father we become partakers of His holiness and will bring forth the peaceable fruit of righteousness. (See Hebrews 12:5-11.)

You see, it's all about Christ in us, the hope of glory. It's not about us, our righteousness, our works, or our purity apart from Christ. It is His life, His love, His righteousness in and through us that will bring in this final harvest—not anything that we do in our own strength or power. Let's give "thanks to the Father who has qualified us to be partakers of the inheritance of the saints in the light. He has delivered us from the power of darkness and conveyed us into the kingdom of the Son of His love, in whom we have redemption through His blood, the forgiveness of sins" (Col. 1:12-14). We have been delivered from darkness and now walk in the kingdom of God. We serve King Jesus and do not walk according to the dictates of this world. His kingdom is not a democracy—but a theocracy. There is One Ruler and One Lawgiver—the Lord Jesus Christ. We walk to the beat of a different drum, not the drumbeat of this earth; we listen for the sounds from heaven, even the voice of our God and Father. Our souls burn with the fiery truth of His Word, and we will never be the same.

Those who believe and receive God's truth and allow the trials of life to burn away the outer shell will know this restoration and full recovery of everything that they have been robbed of. They will, even now, begin to bear the image of the heavenly Man. (See 1 Corinthians 15:45-49.) These warriors will be fully renewed in their minds, for the mind of Christ will control their thoughts; they will no longer be bound in the strongholds of their own thinking. The thoughts of Jesus, His plans, and His vision, will fill their minds, and they will fulfill God's will—not their own. To be spiritually minded is life, peace, and rest, and as Christ's mind is fully developed in them, their whole body will experience a deep rest.

This wholeness will bring forth a total recovery of all that Satan has robbed us of. No more will we struggle trying to believe—for this rest will bring all of God's promises to pass. We will see a fulfillment of these promises when we believe from our hearts and not just our minds. Everything must line up inside of us—spirit, soul, and body—for when we are made whole in Christ, we will see with our natural eyes what we have believed for. God's promises in Christ can never fail, for they are "yes and… amen!" (See 2 Corinthians 1: 20.) Doubt and unbelief have robbed us of a multitude of blessings, but especially our intimacy with the Father. Believe and receive that your joy may be full, for this is our destiny—this is our calling! We "…are complete in Him, who is the head of all principality and power" (Col. 2:10). "Beloved, now we are the children of God, and it has not yet been revealed what we shall be, but we know that when He is revealed, we shall be like Him, for we shall see Him as He is" (1 John 3:2).

Even now, with unveiled faces, we can begin to see Him as He is and be conformed into His image. This is not something that we must wait for until we physically die. Paul says in Ephesians 4:13-15, "… till we all come to the unity of the faith and of the knowledge of the Son of God, to a perfect man, to the measure of the stature of the fullness of Christ; that we should no longer be children…but, speaking the truth in love, may grow up in all things into Him who is the head —Christ.."

It is a process, we know, but the Lord wants to bring us into that place of maturity *now*, while our feet still walk on this earthly plane. We must begin to forget the things that are behind, and "press toward the goal for the prize of the upward call of God in Christ Jesus" (Phil. 3:13-14).

I'm sure that even the apostle Paul struggled greatly at times because of his shameful past. He had to overcome the shame, anger, and self-hatred for all that he did against God's children, even though it was done in ignorance. Paul would not allow his past to keep him from the glorious future that Jesus had for him. He embraced his cross through his many torturous trials and sufferings; he was set free and made whole as he refused to doubt the promises that God had made to him. He recovered *all* in Christ and counted all his losses as rubbish, so that he might gain Christ. His desire was to know the love and favor of Jesus—not man.

Through his sufferings and struggles Paul was made whole, and so will we, *if* we continue in faith and refuse to believe the lies of the enemy. This is our choice. Those who have received the Spirit of adoption will realize that they are God's children and joint heirs with Christ, *if* indeed they are willing to suffer with Him. (See Romans 8:15-16.) It is through suffering that the blinders are removed from our eyes and we begin to see in the Spirit who we truly are. As our hearts are torn through godly sorrow, we begin to live behind the veil. I cannot emphasize enough the truth that without the embracing of our cross and death to "self," we will never enter into God's kingdom. The foreskin of our hearts must be cut away in order for the life of Christ to come through our mortal bodies. This is the only path to wholeness and restoration. Out of all the pressure and pain that we suffer, it is then that we will see the purity of Christ come forth in our souls and bodies, and we *will* recover all!

God's faith through love will manifest fully as we step out in obedience. There is nothing greater than having God's love restored to our hearts. As this love is poured into our souls and we begin to know "what is the width and length and depth and height —to know the love of Christ which passes knowledge" and are "filled with all the fullness of God." (See Ephesians 3:18-19.) It is then that we will see the greatest changes in our hearts and lives, and all will be restored back to us. If God's love does not fill our hearts, He cannot entrust us with His riches, for they would only corrupt us. Without God's fiery love in our hearts, we will find that nothing else in this world will ever be able to satisfy us. Apart from His passion in us, we will never enjoy any of life's pleasures, for they hold no lasting enjoyment, but only emptiness.

In this restoration, we will see ourselves as Christ sees us, for "The royal daughter is all glorious within the palace; her clothing is woven with gold. She shall be brought to the king in robes of many colors" (Psalm 45:13-14). God is restoring to His purified ones a robe of many colors. This is the robe that Jacob gave to his son Joseph because of the favor he bestowed on him. His brothers stripped him of this robe out of jealousy, but God restored to Joseph even greater honor and favor after his years of suffering, as he became second only to Pharaoh in all the land of Egypt. So, too, God is giving to His chosen ones, His bride, a robe of many colors, for she has won it in the *crucible of suffering.* All is being restored to her—especially her dignity as the favored bride of Christ! She will be given a new name, just as Joseph's name changed after his trials, and no devil will ever again be able to rob God's child of her place and position in Him. As Joseph was given new garments and a ring of authority, so will Christ's favored child be restored fully to His heart. Those who are willing to go through the process will be clothed with garments of gold. Gold stands for purity, and holiness is the outcome of being restored and made whole. Remember: Holiness is allowing the Lord to live His life through us.

1 Samuel, chapter 30, is a perfect example of total recovery. When David and his men returned to Ziklag, they found that the Amalekites had attacked Ziklag and burned. David's enemies took captive the women and those who were with them. When David and his men saw the destruction, they wept greatly. David was distressed because the people spoke of stoning him, but he strengthened himself in the Lord his God. David did not wallow in doubt and unbelief, but he inquired of the Lord saying, "Shall I pursue this troop? Shall I overtake them?" God answered him saying, "Pursue, for you shall surely overtake them and without fail recover all." (See verse 8.)

As we refuse to wallow in unbelief and fear and instead run to the secret place, listening to what He tells us to do, we will then recover all that has been stolen from us. David pursued the enemy and attacked them, and not one man escaped, except four hundred young men who rode on camels and fled. "So David recovered all that the Amalekites had carried away, and David rescued his two wives. And nothing of theirs was lacking, either small or great, sons or daughters, spoil or anything which they had taken from them; David recovered all. Then David took all the flocks and herds they had driven before those other livestock, and said, 'This is David's spoil.'" (See 1 Samuel 30:1-20.)

What has the enemy robbed you of? Has your marriage gone sour or have your children gone astray? Has the spiritual vision that God has given you died? What about your health—has it deteriorated? Have you lost your reputation or has an addiction destroyed your life? Is your soul dry and barren; do you feel that all the love and passion of God has dried up in your soul? I say to you this day, that if you run to the Lord and cry out from your heart, He *will* hear you, He *will* restore you, and you will once again know joy and laughter. Dare to believe one more time; don't let go of the rope of faith. Stand firm in faith and you will see the Lord restore to you all that has been stolen. It may not be returned in the way that you think it should be, but God *will* make up for every loss in your life.

I remember a time when I felt completely dead to all the promises that God had spoken to me. My heart was dry and barren, and I felt angry and bitter because of my unending trials and pain. I felt abandoned and alone in my grief. As I sat at my kitchen table I noticed a small book on the floor; as I went to pick it up I read the title, "Total Recovery." It was a book written by Benny Hinn that I had purchased some years before. I have no idea how it ended up on my kitchen floor, but I believe that it was placed there by the Lord. It was a personal word from the Lord just for me, because He knew I was discouraged. That evening I went to a church meeting and the message was on total recovery. Was this a coincidence? I don't think so! God comforts us in our afflictions in a myriad of ways, for He loves us so.

I have seen my children released from hard-core drugs and my husband rededicate his life to Jesus. I have also seen my father marvelously saved when he repented and received the Lord into his heart before he passed away. God continues to work in my marriage, and I believe it will be all that God desires it to be as my husband and I both submit to the will of God in our lives. I have seen loved ones and friends released from deception begin walking toward the Lord on a path of healing and restoration. I have seen cancers healed and hardened hearts softened. Though I have not yet seen total recovery in *all* that God has promised me, still, I refuse to doubt; I will not let go of the "rope of faith" until all is restored in my life, family, and this world. I will hold fast my confession of faith without wavering, for He who promised is faithful. (See Hebrews 10:23.)

God will restore you, and you will recover all, *if* you hold fast to your confession of faith and cling to Him tightly. Our God is worthy of our trust! By God's grace we will be able to say:

> He sent from above, He took me; He drew me out of many waters. He delivered me from my strong enemy, from those who hated me...They confronted me in the day of my calamity, but the Lord was my support. He also brought me out into a broad place; He delivered me because He delighted in me... You have also given me the shield of Your salvation; Your right hand has held me up, Your gentleness has made me great. You enlarged my path under me, so my feet did not slip. I have pursued my enemies and overtaken them; neither did I turn back again till they were destroyed. ...they have fallen under my feet. For You have armed me with strength for the battle; You have subdued under me those who rose up against me. You have also given me the necks of my enemies.
>
> -Psalm 18:16-19, 35-40

> "...being confident of this very thing, that He who has begun a good work in you will complete it until the day of Jesus Christ" (Phil. 1:6).

The Lord would say:

> *"Total recovery—total restoration—is being granted to you in this final hour. Wholeness, joy, love, and laughter will be restored to your inner being—a restoration of all that the enemy has robbed you of, yes, even your gifts and calling. For there are gifts and callings that you have been robbed of, but I say: 'No more, My children—no more!' Your identity, even your personality in My Son and who you were created to be in Him, has been taken from you. This is the day, the hour, even the very moment when all will be restored back to you, not as it was prior to the plundering, but in a measure you have not known—in a measure that is supernatural, abundant, and even beyond the human tongue to express! One hundred-fold blessings are coming to you—a full restoration—even all things made new! The destructive powers of Satan have torn down your house— your 'spiritual building,' but*

150

I say to you now, the second temple (our souls and bodies restored and empowered by the Spirit) will be more glorious than the first!" (See 1 Corinthians 6:19 Haggai 2:9.)

"Let it go—don't cling any longer to the old fragments of your life. Rise up out of the ashes of fallen dreams and visions, for what I have for you is new and fresh, and I say: 'These things have not even entered into your hearts and minds, but I will begin to reveal them now by My Spirit.' He is searching out the deep things—the secrets that have long been hidden inside My Being—and will now begin to bring them forth at the end of the age, even now, My children. These are the last moments of history. This is <u>My</u> time now, and I will accomplish My will and purposes in and through you in a measure greater than anything you have seen or could ever imagine!

"Enlarge your hearts—enlarge your understanding in the power of My Spirit. Break through now: all unbelief, all skepticism, and put on your armor of light. Begin to press in now. Go forth in My power and strength. Do not look back. Push in—push on—until all you see, all you feel, is My glorious light and presence.

"It's time to possess. It's time to partake of My divine nature in its fullness. No more doubt, no more fear, no more unbelief, for My glory, faith, and light is about to explode within you. Possess—take hold of all that is yours! You will recover all now—everything that you have been robbed of—in this final hour.

"I am the last Adam, and only in Me will everything be restored—not in your striving, not in your own sweat, but in My presence, love, and power—as you surrender fully, abandon all, and refuse to look back. What's done is done—it's over My children. It's finished! Repent and move on into all that I have for your life. Let go of the last strands of doubt and unbelief, of fear and grief, and move on into My fullness now. I love you—the work is done. Claim it, receive it, and let My cross do its perfect work in separating you fully from your past—the lies, the hindrances, and your mountain of sin.

"Take hold of My promises and believe—I am all that you need in this final hour. Come, and you will be fully restored now! I already hold everything in My hands—it is yours for the taking. I have plundered your adversary, and all will now be restored to you—a hundred-fold in measure. It is so much better than

anything that you have been robbed of—all brand new, all cleansed, and all ready to be used for My glory and honor. Reach out now, My children, and receive everything that I have for you, for not only what you have been robbed of will be restored, but I have new things, things you never believed you'd receive in My Spirit: gifts, joys, and a love beyond measure! Don't miss out in this hour—don't pass by these words thinking, 'This is not for me—it's too late!' Children, I'm right on time, and you are right where I would have you—even in the muck, the mire, and the unbelief. I'm ready, even in your dark place, to restore all to you. I will replace your doubts and fears with faith and love, and say: 'Never again will the enemy plunder your life—never again! I have a new and glorious place for you.'

"*See Me in My chariot reaching out to you, even in your pit, and saying, 'Arise My beloved. Come up into My chariot of power, and ride with Me into the glories that I have prepared for you!' I will turn your ashes into beauty—your losses into great spiritual gain and never again will you doubt My love for you, oh favored child of God!*

"*I love you, My children. Rise! It's time to possess and take all that I have for you. It's time! Come forth and be all that I've called you to be! Release is here! It is now! Take it all! It's for you, My children! I will recompense you for all the years of suffering—for walking in trust and faith when you couldn't see a step in front of you. Now you will see Me! Now you will know and understand more fully the 'whys' that have been in your heart for so long. I love you—completely and eternally! Your King, forever.*"

(Given to me on November 1, 2011)

Chapter 7: The Joshua Generation

Your people shall be volunteers in the day of Your power.

Psalm 110:3

...but the people who know their God shall be strong, and carry out great exploits.

Daniel 11:32

Where are the giant-slayers? Where are those who will stand in faith—no matter what the cost, no matter what it requires to complete the work of God on this earth? I say to you, God is about to reveal to this world a *Joshua Generation* that is fearless, determined, stout-hearted, righteous, uncompromising, bold, and radical in their faith-walk with the Lord! They will not back down before the devil or man, but they will be faithful to speak the truth in love, no matter what the consequences might be, as they wholly obey the Word of the Lord.

They will wear the mantle of Elijah, and will soon be coming forth out of the desert place to preach a message of repentance to a sinful and compromising Church and generation. They will be like John the Baptist, for they will prepare the way for the Lord's soon coming. They will not fear man, but will burn with God's love and holy fear, and as living flames of fire they will go forth and resurrect millions in the power of the Holy Spirit. They will ignite the hearts of a multitude of souls and bring in a harvest that this world has never seen. Through signs, wonders, and miracles, this company of true believers will go forth in the "greater works" of God, declaring the truth of God's righteous standards and holiness. Jesus said, "Most assuredly, I say to you, he who believes in Me, the works that I do he will do also; and *greater works* than these he will do, because I go to My Father" (John 14:12, emphasis added).

They will bring a revolution to the Church that will transform millions of souls and cause the Church to rise up in new power and authority! This army will go forth throughout the world declaring the soon-coming return of Jesus. They are the Lord's witnesses—His true ambassadors. They will declare the coming of His kingdom through God's *power gifts*, as people are healed and delivered. They will be heralds of heaven, declaring Christ's lordship and His victory over death, sin, and the grave. As they declare His resurrection power, blinded eyes will be opened, deafened ears unstopped, and even the dead will be raised to life—both spiritually and physically.

This is a bold, lion-faced company, not unlike the warriors that gathered themselves to David in the cave of Adullam. When David escaped to the cave of Adullam, everyone who was in distress or in debt, and everyone who was discontented, gathered to him, and David became captain over them. You see, there is a generation that is discontent, a company of people who have been in the wilderness crying out to God for years, because of their hunger and thirst for more of Him. They have been robbed and plundered, and they are crying out for the fullness that God has for them. They have been in the wilderness preparing their hearts and lives for this last great move of the Spirit; they have desired to be vessels of honor in order to bring in this final harvest. They have not only experienced a natural robbery of their finances, but a spiritual robbery of their calling and inheritance in Christ, not unlike Joseph when he was robbed of his coat of many colors! They have experienced distress of soul because of their fiery trials and suffering, but they have allowed the Spirit of God to cleanse and purge them of their sin and free them from the enticements of this present age. They have been prepared by the Spirit, and will now come forth out of the wilderness in the power and might of the living God! They have a forerunner's anointing resting upon them, to set multitudes free from their chains and captivity!

They have gone through their dark night of the soul, and have come forth victorious into the light with an anointing that will cause devils to flee and mountains to move! They will *speak* the Word of the Lord and it will be done. No doubt or fear will mar their souls, and they will do only what they see the Father doing. They will be mountain-moving, earth-shaking children of faith who will defy hell as they shatter the gates of hell and free millions upon millions of captives in this final hour! They walk by faith and not by what they see or feel, for they know that not a word that God has spoken to them will fail, but all will come to pass as He has spoken. (See Joshua 21:45.) Their words are power-packed words of faith, for as they speak the words of the Lord, every obstacle, every difficulty will be moved out of the way.

No root of unbelief binds their souls, for their little mustard-seed faith has fully matured. As a black mustard seed in Israel can grow to a twelve foot shrub, so these mighty warriors have fed their souls with the Word of God and have grown strong in faith, and they now walk in the faith of the Son of God.

Nothing will be impossible for this generation. Their outer shell is smashed and the life of Christ has filled them. They have a *different spirit* than the majority of those who call themselves *Christians*. This small group of believers have abandoned all and they follow Christ fully; they will go into the land and take back what the enemy has stolen from them as they stand on the promises of God in faith. (See Numbers 14:24.)

They will stand out in a crowd because their faces will shine with the glory of God, and others will know they are a different breed. The anointing that will rest upon this generation will break strong yokes from those who have been bound for years—it will be a costly, powerful anointing. Their tongues are controlled by the Spirit of God, and they will inherit a blessing, for they do not return evil for evil or reviling for reviling, but they will bless others with their tongues. They refrain their tongues from evil, and their lips from speaking deceit. They turn away from evil and do good; they seek peace and pursue it (See 1 Peter 3:9-12.) All that comes forth from their mouths brings *life* to others, for they speak the truth in love. They rejoice in their sufferings for others, and they fill up in their flesh what is yet needed, for the sake of Christ's body, which is the church (See Colossians 1:24.) Whether through prayer, travail, obedient service, self-denial, or fiery trials, they will do what is necessary to see others set free from sin and bondage. Their hearts are filled with a passionate love for God, for they love God with *all* their heart, with *all* their soul, and with *all* their strength. They are careful to walk in the commands of the Lord, and they teach them to their children when they sit in their homes or walk by the way, when they lie down and when they rise up. (See Deuteronomy 6:5-7.)

When Joshua encountered the Lord as the Commander of the army, he fell on his face to the earth and worshipped before Him; in the same way, so has this Joshua Generation encountered Christ. They have stood on holy ground, bowed to this Captain, and surrendered their lives and their allegiance to Him alone. (See Joshua 5:13-15.) They have seen the Lord face-to-face, just like Moses did, and they are willing not only to go, but also to die for the sake of Jesus and His kingdom. They have counted the cost and have abandoned all in order to see His will come forth on this earth—such is the Joshua Generation that will come forth in this last hour!

This company of warriors is made up not only of men, but also of powerful women of God who have surrendered all and counted the cost. In the kingdom of God there is neither male nor female, for God looks at the willingness of the heart, and not the outward appearance or gender. (See Galatians 3:28.) The Lord has shown me that men and women will minister side by side in the days ahead, and that both will be used as His vessels to bring in this final harvest. Rejoice, women of God, this is your time to rise up and join this powerful army that will sweep across the nations of this world! You will not be overlooked by the Lord because of your gender, for in God's kingdom all are equal in His sight. No longer will the women of God feel substandard, for they will be raised up to fulfill their God-given call and their destiny in Christ.

In the book of Joshua we see that Zelophehad's daughters inherited land among their brothers. (See Joshua 17:3-6.) We also read in Job 42:15, that "In all the land were found no women so beautiful as the daughters of Job; and their father gave them an inheritance among their brothers." God's end-time army will be made up of millions of women who will march with their brothers and bring in this final harvest. God will recruit young and old, male and female, poor and rich, the well-known and those despised by this world, the weak and foolish, even the base things, so that He alone will receive all the glory, honor, and praise for what He is about to do. (See 1 Corinthians 1:27-29.)

Peter and John were uneducated and untrained men, but they were bold, passionate preachers—because they had been with Jesus. (See Acts 4:13.) The Lord is about to raise those who have been spiritually barren and cause them to be fruitful. No matter what nationality, creed or color, the Lord will use all who surrender fully and answer His call in this hour.

As we study some of the characteristics of this Joshua Generation and the blessings that God will bestow on them, I pray that you will examine your hearts and count the cost of being in this end-time army. The cost will be great, but the rewards will be greater than you could ever fathom.

Allow God's life to come forth inside of you; realize that it is Christ in you who will accomplish this work. It is His life, holiness, and power—not yours. It is not in your own strength that this work will be accomplished, but by the power of His Spirit through your yielded vessel. All He wants is your surrender and obedience—Jesus will do all the rest. We must open our hearts and allow the Spirit to put inside of us His own life and virtues, and then He will make us a part of this Joshua Generation. Here are some of the traits and blessings that will be seen in this end-time generation:

They are commissioned by God. "After the death of Moses the servant of the Lord, it came to pass that the Lord spoke to Joshua the son of Nun, Moses' assistant, saying: 'Moses My servant is dead. Now therefore, arise, go over this Jordan, you and all this people, to the land which I am giving to them—the children of Israel. Every place that the sole of your foot will tread upon I have given you, as I said to Moses'" (Josh. 1:1-3). This Joshua Generation has not been commissioned by man—but by God. They walk according to the will of God—*not* man's will. They know who they are in Christ, and they wear His mantle of authority and power.

They are people of faith. "But Joshua the son of Nun and Caleb the son of Jephunneh, who were among those who spied out the land, tore their clothes; and they spoke to all the congregation of the children of Israel, saying: 'The land we passed through to spy out is an exceedingly good land. If the Lord delights in us, then He will bring us into this land and give it to us, a land which flows with milk and honey'" (Num. 14:6-8). Joshua and Caleb looked with eyes of faith, not doubting the promises that God had spoken to Israel. They didn't focus on the giants, but on the bigness of their God.

They have strength, courage, and obedience to God's Word. "Only be strong and very courageous, that you may observe to do according to all the law which Moses My servant commanded you…" (Josh. 1:7). As obedient, stout-hearted servants of God, they will walk into *their* promised land in the strength and power of their God.

Meditate in and speak God's Word. "This Book of the Law shall not depart from your mouth, but you shall meditate in it day and night…" (Josh. 1:8). They are a people who love the Word of God; it is their strength and daily portion.

They are people of strategy. "Now Joshua the son of Nun sent out two men from Acacia Grove to spy secretly, saying, 'Go, view the land, especially Jericho'" (Josh. 2:1). As they listen to the voice of God, He reveals to them His strategy and plan against the adversary. They hear and obey!

They are set apart and sanctified, a people of signs and wonders. "And Joshua said to the people, 'Sanctify yourselves, for tomorrow the Lord will do wonders among you'" (Josh. 3:5). This Joshua Generation is a people set apart to accomplish the purpose of God in this generation. They will walk in powerful signs and wonders that will draw millions into the kingdom of God!

They are a people of trust. "And Joshua said, 'By this you shall know that the living God is among you, and that He will without fail drive out from before you the Canaanites and the Hittites and the Hivites and the Perizzites and the Girgashites and the Amorites and the Jebusites...'" (Josh. 3:10). Their full trust is in the Lord their God alone. Doubt and unbelief have been put to death at the cross; they walk in full faith and assurance that God will accomplish all that He has promised them.

They have come up out of death, into life. "Joshua therefore commanded the priests, saying, 'Come up from the Jordan'" (Josh. 4:17). They have come out of their watery grave, the Jordan River, and have embraced their cross, died to self, and now walk in resurrection power.

The enemy fears them. "So it was, when all the kings of the Amorites ... and all the kings of the Canaanites... heard that the Lord had dried up the waters of the Jordan from before the children of Israel until we had crossed over, that their *heart melted*; and there was *no spirit in them* any longer because of the children of Israel" (Josh. 5:1, emphasis added). The enemy does not fear this Joshua Generation because of *their* own strength and might, but they fear the One who lives inside of them—Jesus!

They have circumcised their hearts. "So Joshua made flint knives for himself, and circumcised the sons of Israel at the hill of the foreskins" (Josh. 5:3). This strong company of believers have allowed the foreskin of their hearts, their sin and iniquity, to be cut away with the sharp sword of the Spirit. They walk in holiness.

They have been made whole. "So it was, when they had finished circumcising all the people, that they stayed in their places in the camp till they were healed" (Josh. 5:8). This army of the Lord has waited on the Lord daily; they have allowed His love and presence to heal them, and they move forward only when they hear the voice of the Lord.

They have been weaned from the world. "Then the Lord said to Joshua, 'This day I have rolled away the reproach of Egypt from you' (Josh. 5:9). This generation has only one desire: to do the will of the Father. They have been stripped of all desire for the things of this world. They live in the world, but they are no longer of it. (See 1 John 2:15-17.)

THEY HAVE COME TO **a place of maturity, and they no longer need to be spoon fed.** "Then the manna ceased on the day after they had eaten the produce of the land; and the children of Israel no longer had manna, but they ate the food of the land of Canaan that year" (Josh. 5:12). They eat and drink of the Word daily and have learned to exercise their spiritual muscles. They are no longer spiritual babes, but eat the *meat* of the Word. They look only to Christ, who alone completes them.

THEY ARE WALL-SMASHERS IN **the Spirit.** "And it happened when the people heard the sound of the trumpet, and the people shouted with a great shout, that the wall fell down flat" (Josh. 6:20). This powerful group of intercessors has allowed the Spirit to tear down every wall in their hearts, and now in God's anointing power they go forth to break the strongholds and chains that hold God's children captive.

They are a humble and repentant people. "Then Joshua tore his clothes, and fell to the earth on his face before the ark of the Lord until evening, he and the elders of Israel; and they put dust on their heads" (Josh. 7:6). This end-time group walks in daily repentance, for they know they need continual washing from the defilements that they encounter in the world every day. Their one desire is to have clean hands and a pure heart before the Lord.

THEY CONFRONT THEIR OWN **sin and the sins of others.** "Get up, sanctify the people, and say, 'Sanctify yourselves for tomorrow, because thus says the Lord God of Israel: *There is an accursed thing in your midst, O Israel; you cannot stand before your enemies until you take away the accursed thing* *from among you*" (Josh. 7:13). They are bold to speak the truth in love in order to see others set free.

They are fearless, mighty men of valor. "So Joshua ascended from Gilgal, he and all the people of war with him, and all the mighty men of valor. And the Lord said to Joshua, 'Do not fear them, for I have delivered them into your hand; not a man of them shall stand before you'" (Josh. 10:7-8). These warriors of the Lord fear no devil, no man. They face every giant and every mountain that would stand in their way. God has made them strong for the sake of possessing their inheritance.

They know that God fights their battles. "So the Lord routed them before Israel, killed them with a great slaughter at Gibeon, chased them along the road that goes to Beth Horon, and struck them down as far as Azekah and Makkedah" (Josh. 10:10). God fights for those who have surrendered all for Him and His kingdom; they never lose a battle.

They are people of authority; they speak the Word of God and it is done. "Then Joshua spoke to the Lord in the day when the Lord delivered up the Amorites before the children of Israel, and he said in the sight of Israel: 'Sun, stand still over Gibeon; and Moon, in the valley of Aijalon.' So the sun stood still, and the moon stopped, till the people had revenge upon their enemies... And there has been no day like that, before it or after it, that the Lord heeded the voice of a man..." (Josh. 10:12-14). These warriors hold the keys to the kingdom.

They are ruled by their spiritual senses. "But these five kings had fled and hidden themselves in a cave at Makkedah...So it was, when they brought out those kings to Joshua, that Joshua called for all the men of Israel, and said to the captains of the men of war who went with him, 'Come near, put your feet on the necks of these kings.' And they drew near and put their feet on their necks...And afterward Joshua struck them and killed them, and hanged them on five trees..." (Joshua 10:16, 24, 26). This elite group that God is raising has learned to live in the Spirit realm—they see, hear, touch, smell, and taste in the Spirit. Their natural senses no longer *rule* their lives, for these five kings have been put to death by the power of the cross.

They will recover all that the enemy has stolen. "So Joshua *conquered all* the land…he left nothing remaining, but utterly destroyed all that breathed, as the Lord God of Israel commanded" (Josh. 10:40). No one will prevent this army from recovering all that Satan has robbed them of, for they are lion-faced warriors who will stop at nothing to receive all that God has for them. They will receive their full inheritance in the Lord, for they believe the Word of the Lord.

The fruit of long-suffering will mark their lives. "Joshua made war a *long time* with all those kings" (Josh. 11:18, emphasis added). The fruit of the Spirit will exude from their lives, especially the fruit of long-suffering. Many of them have suffered for years in silence as they embraced their cross and overcame the sin and temptations that the enemy relentlessly bombarded against them. Their fruit is ripening, and we are about to see this righteous generation come forth in power.

They are giant-slayers. "And at that time Joshua came and cut off the Anakim from the mountains…Joshua utterly destroyed them with their cities" (Josh. 11:21). These children of might and power destroy every giant that gets in their way; they are true children of faith!

They have entered the rest of God. "So Joshua took the whole land… and Joshua gave it as an inheritance to Israel… Then the land rested from war." (See Joshua 11:23.) The works that this generation will do will be the works of God and not their own, for they have ceased striving and have entered into the rest of God fully. God will make even their enemies to be at peace with them.

They follow the Lord with their whole heart. "…but I wholly followed the Lord my God" (Josh. 14:8). This elite group holds nothing back from the Lord; they have abandoned themselves fully to the will of the Lord— no matter what it costs them.

They have perseverance, stamina, and are bold and courageous. "Now therefore, give me this mountain of which the Lord spoke in that day; for you heard in that day how the Anakim were there, and that the cities were great and fortified. It may be that the Lord will be with me, and I shall be able to drive them out as the Lord said" (Josh. 14:12). With the heart of a bear, these Kingdom-minded people will climb spiritual Mount Zion until they reach the top—until every giant has fallen to the ground under their feet. They will not fear, but in boldness they will confront their enemies, and tear down every wall of resistance.

They are a people of expansion. "But the children of Joseph said, 'The mountain country is not enough for us'...And Joshua spoke to the house of Joseph...saying, 'You are a great people and have great power; you shall not have only one lot, but the mountain country shall be yours. Although it is wooded, you shall cut it down, and its farthest extent shall be yours; for you shall drive out the Canaanites, though they have iron chariots and are strong'" (Josh. 17:16-17). These are a people who will "enlarge the place" of their tent, who will "stretch out the curtains" of their dwellings; they will "lengthen their cords," and strengthen their stakes. They will expand to the right and to the left, and their descendants will inherit the nations, and make the desolate cities inhabited (See Isaiah 54:2-3.) These conquerors in Christ will not be content seeing just their own loved ones saved, but they will burn with passion to enlarge the kingdom of God with a multitude of souls, for they long to see the nations of this world love and serve their King. They will bring in the lost, lame, blind, and bound, until they see the kingdom of their Lord expand, even to the ends of the earth.

They love the *ways* of the Lord and not just His *acts*. "But take careful heed to do the commandment and the law which Moses the servant of the Lord commanded you, to love the Lord your God, to walk in all His *ways*, to keep His commandments, to hold fast to Him" (Josh. 22:5, emphasis added). These lovers of God want to know Christ intimately; they long to know His heart and ways, to be close to Him, and to obey Him.

They will plunder the enemy. "...and spoke to them, saying, 'Return with much riches to your tents, with very much livestock, with silver, with gold, with bronze, with iron, and with very much clothing. Divide the spoil of your enemies with your brethren'" (Josh. 22:8). Not only will God provide for this end-time army with monetary wealth, but God will use them to free millions of captive souls from the clutches of the enemy. They will have sufficient finances to go forth and do the will of the Father. The overflow will be so great that they will freely share this wealth with their brothers and sisters. There will be no greed and selfishness in the hearts of these victorious warriors.

They have chosen the Lord above all else; they have cast down their idols. "'But as for me and my house, we will serve the Lord.' So the people answered and said: 'Far be it from us that we should forsake the Lord to serve other gods'" (Josh. 24:15-16). These surrendered saints have forsaken the idolatry of this world and also the idols in their own hearts that have bound them for so long. They have made a choice to go the entire way with the Lord; they have counted the cost, and now they belong wholly to the Lord.

They are worshipping warriors. "Now Joshua built an altar to the Lord God of Israel in Mount Ebal… And they offered on it burnt offerings to the Lord, and sacrificed peace offerings" (Josh. 8:30-31). These lovers of Christ have made themselves to be living sacrifices unto their King. On the altar of their hearts they worship and praise the One they love every moment of every day. In all they say and do, they glorify their King. All their words bring glory and praise to their Lord, and their greatest delight is to worship Him in spirit and in truth. There is a song of praise on their lips, even in the night season, for their Lord is with them, and they know, without a shadow of a doubt, that He will never leave them nor forsake them. Jesus is the lover of their souls, and their delight is in Him alone. They have given their all to Him on the altar of sacrifice.

They are hungry for the presence of the Lord. "So the Lord spoke to Moses face to face, as a man speaks to his friend. And he would return to the camp, but his servant Joshua the son of Nun, a young man, did not depart from the tabernacle" (Ex. 33:11). Hunger for God marked even the early years of Joshua. He was a man who craved the presence of the Lord. This Joshua Generation is marked with a strong desire for God's manifest glory, for nothing else will satisfy their hungry souls.

They are strong leaders in the Lord. "But command Joshua, and encourage him and strengthen him; for he shall go over before this people, and he shall cause them to inherit the land which you will see" (Deut. 3:28). These warriors have strong leadership qualities, and as they are fully developed in the Spirit, we will see them lead multitudes into the kingdom of God. They will teach and train them, and lead them into all that God has for them. They are dynamic children of faith who will encourage others to rise up in faith, to conquer devils, and to receive their full inheritance in Christ.

Because these revolutionary leaders have been radically changed on the inside by the Lord, they are now able to bring this change into the hearts of a multitude of souls. God has released them from the fear of man and now they fear only God. In this radical change they will be able to pave the way for the coming of the Lord. Their lives are filled with the living Christ and their lives of holiness and purity will bring conviction to the masses. The life of Christ will explode in them, and the life that they live will be in the faith of the Lord Jesus Christ.

No doubt, no deadly unbelief will mar their lives, for they have been through the fire and have been radically changed on the mountaintop with Jesus. They are doers of the Word, for they not only believe God's Word, but they live out all of the Lord's commands. Their foundation is strong, for all the cracks and weak areas in their lives have been filled with the Lord's love and presence. The kingdom of God is within them, and they bow their knee only to Jesus. (See Luke 17:21.) They walk in wholeness and power, and the faith inside of them works mightily through love. Their speech and preaching are not with persuasive words of human wisdom, but in the demonstration of the Spirit and of power. They are determined not to know anything among God's people except Jesus Christ and Him crucified. (See 1 Corinthian 2:2, 4.) "For the kingdom of God is not in word but in power" (1 Cor. 4:20). They will be like their forerunner, John the Baptist, and they will preach a gospel of repentance. There will be many signs, wonders, miracles, healings, and deliverances that will follow their preaching.

I believe the Lord will send these passionate forerunners to the Church first, to ignite a fire in many, many souls. There will be a strong force of repentance that will sweep across thousands of churches, bringing in a wave of glory such as this world has never seen. This new wave of God will bring to repentance a multitude of souls that have sat in pews for years and will cause many to abandon everything for the sake of God's kingdom. When they see the state of their lukewarm hearts; many will be awakened to the truth and embrace their cross for the very first time. Their hearts will burn with a passionate love for the Lord.

Many in the Church have fallen asleep spiritually, and some are just downright dead. Revival must first come to the Church of Jesus Christ, and this revolutionary, passionate, Joshua Generation will be used to wake up God's sleeping Church. As the Church begins to rise up with new wings of faith and trust, this *Remnant* will be used to teach and train God's children in the ways of the Lord. The Remnant will be commissioned to go forth into the world and reap the final harvest before the Lord's coming. We will see, as we study this end-time Remnant, that it is not necessary for the Lord to have an overwhelmingly large army to bring in this harvest; only those who are willing to abandon all will be part of this group and the first wave of glory that is about to come forth upon this world. Prepare your hearts, saints of the Most High; it's time to give your all if you are to be prepared to ride this glory wave with Jesus. His Word to us in this hour is: "Get Ready!" The time of His appearing is sooner than we think.

Word from the Lord:

> "This Joshua Generation will not strive in the flesh, for they will be full of My might and power, and no man, no devil, will bring them down. Walls around cities, states, and even nations will come down now. They will shout the shout of faith, and these walls will come down, for there will be no unbelief in their hearts. They will believe Me for the impossible, and nothing will be denied them. This generation is a pure generation, a generation who walks fully in My Spirit—in full obedience to My will. Self-will has been fully eradicated from their lives, and they will walk in a power and might that man has never seen. Perfect trust—perfect obedience—will be seen in this company of true believers.
>
> "This new breed will take nations by force—they will push back the powers of hell with a shout of praise and victory. This is the generation that will do, in its fullness, the greater works that I spoke about. Greater works have been done in the past, but these greater works will cause past works to seem as <u>nothing</u> in the light of what I am about to do.
>
> "Call forth this Joshua Generation, for they will take down the enemy. Claim every promise in My Word, and come forth fully into all the glory that I have promised this generation. Call them forth! Blow the trumpet! For the time is <u>now</u> that I will send forth My troops into the places of darkness—places that even the angels fear to tread! This is a fearless company of believers that will see only Me—not the enemy, not the giants, not the mountains of difficulties—for they will see only the mighty power and glory of the Lord their God. Call forth this company, this Remnant, this elect group of revolutionaries. My hand is upon them and they shall now rise up—out of unbelief, out of the ash heap— and I will fully restore them and they will shout so loudly that the whole

world will hear them! The dead shall rise, the broken hearts will be healed, and those in captivity will rise and shake off their chains at the sound of My voice in them.

"Prepare to go forth, oh army of the Lord! Put on your breastplate of righteousness—your belt of truth—and speak My Words in power and might. Cut back the lies of the enemy with the sword of My Word—speak in the authority and power of My Word. Gird yourselves, My people. Keep on the helmet of salvation. Keep your heart and mind stayed on Me. Above all—keep before you and around you the shield of faith. Quench all the fiery darts of the enemy. No longer believe the lies of the enemy! All unbelief must go from your heart and mind in this hour—every bit of it! No more will this armor come on and off—sleep in it, live in it—and I say to you that never again will you fail or fall, for I will be your covering by day and that pillar of fire by night!

"Rejoice—all is ready! I have saved the best wine for this last Joshua Generation. Go forth now! All is prepared! Walk in it! For every place the sole of your foot goes—I will give to you. This is your inheritance in Me. Take hold of it now! It is yours!" -Jesus (Given to me on September 8, 2011)

THE REMNANT

"In that day," says the Lord, "I will assemble the lame, I will gather the outcast and those whom I have afflicted; I will make the lame a remnant, and the outcast a strong nation; so the Lord will reign over them in Mount Zion from now on, even forever."

Micah 4:6

Then the remnant of Jacob shall be in the midst of many peoples, like dew from the Lord, like showers on the grass, that tarry for no man nor wait for the sons of men. And the remnant of Jacob shall be among the Gentiles, in the midst of many peoples, like a lion among the beasts of the forest, like a young lion among flocks of sheep, who, if he passes through, both treads down and tears in pieces, and none can deliver. Your hand shall be lifted against your adversaries, and all your enemies shall be cut off.

Micah 5:7-9

*You are My battle-ax and weapons of war: for with you I will
break the nations in pieces; with you I will destroy kingdoms*
Jeremiah 51:20

OUR GOD IS COMING in a way that very few are expecting Him to. He is
saying:

> Do not remember the former things, nor consider the things
> of old. Behold, I will do a *new* thing, *now* it shall spring
> forth; shall you not know it? I will even make a road in the
> wilderness and rivers in the desert…to give drink to My people,
> My chosen. This people I have formed for Myself; they shall
> declare My praise.
> -Isaiah 43:18-19, 21, emphasis added

Who are these people that will see this *new* thing that God is going
to do; who will declare His praise? These called and chosen vessels are
God's end-time Remnant. They will go forth and declare the glories of
His Majesty to the farthest corners of this earth.

According to The American Heritage Dictionary, a *remnant* is: "1.
something left over; a remainder. 2. A leftover piece of fabric, as one
remaining after the rest of the bolt has been sold. 3. A surviving trace or
vestige, as of a former condition. 4. A small remaining group of people.
Remaining; leftover."

There is a Remnant, a small group of people, that God has set apart
for this season and time, that He is about to send forth across this nation
and the nations of this world. These true prophets of the Lord are not
"religious" people, but powerful preachers of righteousness who will speak
the truth about the narrow gate that the Lord has asked us to enter, "…for
wide is the gate and broad is the way that leads to destruction, and there
are many who go in by it. Because narrow is the gate and difficult is the
way which leads to life, and there are few who find it" (Matt. 7:13-14).
They will not lighten the truth of God's holy Word, for they know that
only the knowledge of truth will set the captives free. They have humbled
themselves as children to walk with Jesus; their pride has been crushed,
and they are fully abandoned to the Father's will. They have gone through
the narrow gate and have released their baggage to Jesus, and now they go
forth on the path that He has prepared for them.

The Lord told Abraham to "Get out of your country, from your family and from your father's house, to a land that I will show you." (See Genesis 12:1.) Abraham was called to abandon everything for the call of God on his life, and in this hour Jesus is calling this Remnant to a radical commitment to Him and to abandon all. This Remnant has one focus, one purpose in this life: to follow the Lord and fulfill His will on this planet. They will never again lean on the staff of Egypt (the things of this world again), for they depend on the Lord alone—the Holy One of Israel. Though there are many that call themselves "Christians," only a small few will return fully to the Lord and walk with Him in total abandonment. (See Isaiah 10:20-22.)

When Elijah thought that he was the only prophet left in Israel, the Lord said, "'I have reserved for Myself seven thousand men who have not bowed the knee to Baal. Even so then, at this present time there is a remnant according to the election of grace'" (Rom. 11:4-5). God has reserved for Himself, in our present generation, those who will not bow their knee to the enemy, and He will use them to bring in this final harvest. They are pressing forward into the presence of God in a fervor and intensity that has scarcely ever been seen. In the process of letting go of their past, they are taking hold of what Christ has for their lives. This humble company of believers knows that they have not arrived, nor attained all that Christ has for them, but they are forgetting their past blunders, failures, and hideous sins as they reach forward to the things which are ahead. Their goal is the prize of the upward call of God in Jesus. (See Philippians 3:12-14.)

As they keep God's Word, their earnest desire is to be perfected in His love, for they know that as great as the gifts of the Lord are in their lives, without His love burning in their souls, they have nothing. (See 1 John 2:5-6.) Their desire is to do everything in love—with clean hands and a pure heart. Faith must work through love if it is to be effective in their lives and in the lives of those that they touch. Without God's love—they know they are nothing. Jesus must be their life and their love, or all that they do is in vain. This Remnant will be called "the lovers of God," because all that they do will be for the glory of God; they will be hidden behind the cross of the Lord Jesus. First Corinthians chapter 13, is the mirror that they look into daily, for they know that without Jesus' love dwelling in them deeply and powerfully, they can do nothing of lasting value. The pursuit of the love of God is their highest goal as they walk in the spiritual gifts that God gives them. As God's fruit is developed in their lives and is ripened, it is then that others will be able to partake of Christ's life in them.

Not only are they lovers of God, but these mighty men and women of God are valiant warriors. They have been called with "a holy calling," not according to their works, but according to the "purpose and grace" which has been given to them in Christ Jesus before time began. (See 2 Timothy1:9.) The works that come forth in this hour will be the "works of God"—not the "works of man." These ambassadors of Christ walk in the supernatural realm, for they have overcome the adversary, and their feet are on the necks of the five kings that have controlled their lives for so long. No more do they allow their natural senses to control them or rule their lives. They walk in their spiritual senses, for these have been fully developed in them. They see and discern in the Spirit, for their spiritual perception has been fine-tuned by the Spirit of God. They have "ears to hear what the Spirit of God is saying" to them daily; they follow His direction, and obey Him implicitly. Daily you will find them feasting at the table of the Lord, tasting of His goodness and drinking the wine of His love. These are God's true overcomers. These are the faith-walkers, the hearers and doers of the Word, that live by the faith of the Son of God. They hold fast the confession of their hope without wavering. (See Hebrews 10:23.) They are true "apostles of faith" and, like Paul, at the end of their journey they will be able to say: "I have fought the good fight, I have finished the race, I have kept the faith" (2 Tim. 4:7).

In this season, for "such a time as this," we will see these leaders, generals, prophets, apostles, and called out and chosen ones begin to rise. They have the holy and anointed words of God in their mouths, and God will use these words to root out, to pull down and destroy, and to build and plant. These powerful prophetic words will do a work that will bring a change of heart to multitudes of people. As peace is proclaimed, and God's salvation is revealed to the ends of the earth, these glad tidings of good things will release a joy and comfort to His people—and a glory this world has never seen. (See Isaiah 52:7-10.)

As truth is spoken, the lies of the enemy will be exposed, and many captives will be released from their prisons of unbelief. The words that they speak will be living and powerful, sharper than any two-edged sword, piercing even to the division of the soul and spirit. This is the hour of "examination," for *all* will be laid bare and naked before the Lord, even the very thoughts and intents of our hearts. (See Hebrews 4:12-13.) The high praises of God will be in their mouths, and a two-edged sword will be in their hand. This two-edged sword will accomplish a dual work in the hearts of God's people. One edge will expose and uproot deep roots of sin in the hearts of God's people, and the other will build up and bring wholeness. One edge of this sword will bring death to self and the other will bring life and freedom in the Spirit. Out of repentance and mourning will come forth the joy and life of Jesus—in a measure that most in the Church have not yet experienced. This "shaking" will bring many in the Church to a place of deep conviction and repentance, for they have not lived their lives in obedience and submission to the will of the Father.

God is about to shake His Church in this late hour, for the Word says, "'Yet once more I will shake not only the earth, but also heaven.' Now this, 'Yet once more,' indicates the removal of those things that are being shaken, as of things that are made, that the things which cannot be shaken may remain" (Heb. 12:26-27). After this shaking only those who trust the Lord implicitly will be found standing.

Second Thessalonians 2:3 says, "Let no one deceive you by any means; for that Day will not come unless the falling away comes first, and the man of sin is revealed, the son of perdition." The Day—which represents God's end-time judgment—will not come until this great falling away. As God sends forth His warriors, speaking the whole counsel of His Word, many will turn a deaf ear to the cries from the heart of Christ. As His servants preach a strong message of repentance and warn of the judgment to come, many will harden their hearts and refuse to give up their idols. Even as God's fire begins to burn seven times hotter, many in churches around the world will still refuse to turn from their wicked ways. Millions will begin to fall away, for they will refuse to embrace the message of the cross.

This end-time group of warriors will be used as God's battle-ax to thresh His people, for they will be "a new threshing sledge with sharp teeth" (See Isaiah 41:15-16.) They shall winnow God's people, and the wind of the Spirit will blow away all the sin and chaff from those who repent. This "shaking" will be like the shaking of an olive tree—like the gleaning of grapes when the vintage is done—and those who are left, who come forth out of this fire that is seven times hotter, will be part of this Gideon Army.

There is a separation going on, even in the Church of Jesus Christ, between those who are going the whole way with the Lord and those who are in a place of compromise. In the book of Genesis, we read about the strife that developed between Abraham and Lot. When their possessions were so great that they could not dwell together, Abraham said to Lot:

Is not the whole land before you? Please separate from me. If you take the left, then I will go to the right; or if you go to the right, then I will go to the left. And Lot lifted his eyes and saw all the plain of Jordan, that it was well watered everywhere… Then Lot chose for himself all the plain of Jordan, and Lot journeyed east. And they separated from each other. Abraham dwelt in the land of Canaan, and Lot dwelt in the cities of the plain and pitched his tent even as far as Sodom.

-Genesis 13:9-12

You see, Lot lived in his "soulish" nature, by what he saw and felt, but Abraham desired his inheritance in Christ—no matter what it looked like in the natural. Abraham knew that God desired what was best for him; he did not doubt His love for him. Lot walked according to the desires and dictates of his flesh, but Abraham walked in obedience to the will of the Spirit. This separation had to come between them, even as the separation had to come between Ishmael, the "son of a bondwoman," and Isaac, the "child of promise." Ishmael was born according to the *flesh*, but Isaac was born through *promise*. One gives birth to bondage, the other to freedom. The bondwoman and her son had to be cast out, for he could not be heir with the son of the free woman. The two could not abide together. (See Galatians 4:22-27, 30.) The flesh can never inherit what the Spirit of God wants to give us, for the flesh wars against the Spirit—and the Spirit against the flesh. (See Galatians 5:17.) It's like oil and water—they just won't mix. Ishmael represents our flesh—and Isaac the Spirit. In order for the fullness of the Spirit to come forth in us—*the flesh must die.*

As we continue to study Lot's life, we read about some of the horrible consequences because of his life of compromise. When the men of Sodom came to Lot's house in order to "know" the two angels who were lodging with him, Lot said, "See now, I have two daughters who have not known a man; please, let me bring them out to you, and you may do to them as you wish; only do nothing to these men, since this is the reason they have come under the shadow of my roof" (Gen. 19:8). When the angels told him that the Lord would destroy the city, they urged Lot to hurry and get out of the city, but he lingered, and the angels had to take hold of his hand, his wife's hand, and the hands of his two daughters, and they brought him out and set him outside the city (vv. 14-16). The angels then told him to escape to the mountains lest he be destroyed, but Lot was afraid to do what he was told, and he asked if he could flee to a "little" city called Zoar. He said,

"See now, this city is near enough to flee to, and it is a little one; please let me escape there (is it not a little one?) and my soul shall live" (v. 20). The angels warned them not to look back, "But his wife looked back behind him, and she became a pillar of salt" (v. 26). "Then Lot went up out of Zoar and dwelt in the mountains, and his two daughters were with him; for he was afraid to dwell in Zoar. And he and his two daughters dwelt in a cave" (v. 30). Both of Lot's daughters made their father drink wine, and because they wanted to preserve their lineage, they both became pregnant by him. (See vv. 31-38.) Out of this incest with their father, the Moabites and the Ammonites came forth from their wombs. They became ungodly nations, and brought many troubles to Israel for many years to come.

The first horrible sin we see here is that Lot was willing to give up his own children to those who would horribly abuse them. Where there should have been a godly covering over them from a protective father, instead they were left open to demonic attack because of fear and compromise. The "spirit of the world" had entered Lot's heart and it would lead him down a very painful path of loss and suffering. His seed had become corrupt because of compromise and unrepentant sin, and it was only by the grace of God and His covenant promises to Abraham that Lot was saved. Because Abraham lived an uncompromised life of obedience, not only was he blessed, but so were those who were under God's covenant care.

Next, we see that Lot and his family *lingered* when the angels told them to hurry and escape to the mountains. When there is worldly compromise in a person, the person's heart is divided—one foot is in the world, and the other is with God. This never works. God's Remnant knows that it is *all* or *nothing* with the Lord, and they have decided with faithful Abraham to go all the way.

Next, we see that Lot had fear and confusion in his life; he was a double-minded man. He was afraid to go to the mountains and wanted to flee to a "little city." He wanted just a little bit of sin in his life, just like so many in the Church in this hour. Many think that just a little sin, just a little compromise is okay—it *never* is! All sin must be confessed as the Holy Spirit brings conviction. God's Word tells us that a little leaven (sin), leavens the whole lump. (See Galatians 5:9.)

Just like Lot's wife turned back after being warned not to, many in the Church are still looking back at the pleasures of this world, for they have not completely given up their hearts to Jesus. This is where many fail; this is where I failed for years. We must lay all on the altar of sacrifice, even as Abraham did, if we desire to be totally set free. Lot was fearful even in the little city he had chosen, and he ended up going to the mountains that he had tried to avoid. Mountains can represent great troubles, and that's what he found in the "cave of sin" that he entered. It was here that the full-blown sin of compromise brought forth a harvest of destruction that would last for many generations to come.

There is no "little sin," and this "righteous Remnant" knows that all sin must be burned up, for if it is not, it will eventually bring forth a harvest of death to all the promises of God in their lives. Not only did Lot lose his family because of his initial decision to live by his own wants and desires, but he lost his seed. His descendants, the Moabites and Ammonites, lived a life of compromise and idolatry that would eventually cause the hand of God to move in judgment against them. (See 2 Chronicles 20:22-23.)

God's "heavenly plumb line" is descending, and a strong line of demarcation is being drawn between the uncompromisingly righteous and those who embrace compromise. There is no middle ground; we are either for the Lord or against Him; we will either submit fully to His lordship in our lives or we will go the way of the world—there is no in-between. This *Remnant* will bring forth out of their "spiritual loins" a pure generation of true believers who will abandon all for the Lord Jesus.

They will be given authority to trample on serpents and scorpions and over all the power of the enemy, and nothing will by any means hurt them. (See Luke 10:19.) This is the "greater works" generation that will trample down the enemy and tear down the gates of hell. (See John 14:12.) Out of their hearts will flow rivers of living water. In the fullness of the Spirit multitudes will be freed, healed, and ushered into the Lord's glorious kingdom, for God has given them power and authority over all demons. They will go forth preaching the kingdom of heaven, and will heal the sick, cleanse the lepers, raise the dead, and cast out demons. They will go into the entire world and preach the gospel to every creature. (See John 7:37-38, Luke 9:1-2, Matthew 10:8, Mark 16:15.)

Jesus is the "Child of Promise," and God desires that He be fully formed in us. We must die in order for His life to come forth in us, and this Remnant is willing to die so that others can live. They desire to be separated from all that is unholy and ungodly in order for the life of Christ to be manifested fully in them. They are kingdom-minded people, and their passion is to see God's will manifested on this earth as it is in heaven.

You may wonder what the Joshua Generation and the Remnant have to do with the subject of unbelief; I say they have everything to do with it. If we do not deal a death blow to the root of unbelief and doubt in our hearts and lives, we will never be a vital part of this generation of overcomers—this Remnant—that God is about to raise up so soon. We do not want to miss this first "glory wave" that is coming from heaven. If we do not prepare—if we do not allow the Spirit of God to remove this deadly root of unbelief in our souls—we will miss this wave of glory, and may even be found sitting on the sidelines, only watching the glorious works of God being performed through the lives of others. Unbelief will cause us to lose our inheritance and the joy of being used to bring in this final harvest.

Unless we are cleansed from the sin of unbelief, we will never be conformed into the image of Christ on this earth, for we will doubt God's holy Word in the midst of our trials, and reject the very cross that we are called to embrace, not push away. We'll see our trials as the work of the enemy and not as the spiritual work that God is trying to accomplish in our lives. Our discernment will be dull, because our spiritual senses have not been developed in the dark fiery trials that were meant to refine us—not destroy us. We will not be chosen in our "furnace of affliction," because we have refused to submit to this work and surrender our rebellion and idolatry to Jesus. How can He choose us if we refuse to let go and give up our lives fully to Him?

We must repent with godly sorrow or we will be disqualified from this end-time army that God is about to raise in the earth. Hardness of heart and not believing and obeying God's holy commands will disqualify us. If we listen and believe the lies of the enemy as Eve did, we will forever live in our "lower senses" and never climb Mount Zion; we will forever live in the "lowlands" of unbelief and fear. Only in the crucible of suffering, as we embrace our cross daily, will we be changed into the image and likeness of Jesus and come into our promised land, the very heart and promises of our Savior in this hour. As we take the land in our hearts (those areas of darkness and compromise), subdue every enemy and the sin which so easily ensnares us, and claim our whole beings for the Lord Jesus, it is then that we will come into the freedom and liberty of the Spirit. Every place that the sole of our foot treads upon God will give us because we walk in obedience to His will and do only those things that are pleasing to Him. We'll draw near to the Father with a true heart in full assurance of faith, for our hearts have been washed with the water of the Word and are clean from an evil conscience. (See Hebrews 10:22.)

GOD'S GIDEON ARMY

GOD HAS A COMPANY of believers that He has set apart for this hour. They have been redeemed from every lawless deed, and have been purified by His refining fire. They are a passionate people, zealous for good works. (See Titus 2:14.) The trials they have gone through have at times seemed brutal, but this was necessary in order to bring them to the place that God has for them.

In the book of Judges we read that the Angel of the Lord came and sat under a tree while Gideon threshed wheat in the winepress in order to hide from the Midianites. The Angel of the Lord appeared to him and said, "The Lord is with you, you mighty man of valor." (See Judges 6:11-12.) In himself, Gideon was a weak and fearful man, hiding out from the enemy, and yet the Lord saw past his weaknesses. God's desire was to raise Gideon up in His own strength and power and make him a valiant warrior. It wasn't Gideon's strength that caused the Lord to choose him—it was his weakness. God was not looking for one who was self-sufficient, but for one who knew his weaknesses and failures. So many times we look at our own weaknesses and inadequacies and feel that God could never use us. We look at our lack of ability and gifting and feel that God could never choose us. We take our eyes off of the Lord and His power and strength, and see ourselves only as grasshoppers compared to the strength of our enemies. Only as we focus on Jesus and on His strength and power in us, can we overcome every doubt and fear. We question the Lord, as Gideon did when he said, "...if the Lord is with us, why then has all this happened to us? And where are all His miracles which our fathers told us about, saying, 'Did not the Lord bring us up from Egypt?' But now the Lord has forsaken us and delivered us into the hands of the Midianites" (v. 13).

When our emotional pain overwhelms us because of the circumstances we find ourselves in, we moan and complain that the Lord must have left us, or that He is angry with us. We allow our circumstances to dictate to us, and we believe the lie that God must have left us, instead of believing and standing on the truth of His Word that says that He will never leave us or forsake us. We allow our emotions to rule us, our "soulish" realm, instead of God's Spirit within us. We believe the lie that the enemy has the upper hand in our lives and not the Lord. This is where we fail so many times, even as God's people did in the wilderness. It is right here, in the midst of the fiery trial, that we must overcome our emotions and allow the Spirit to heal our deep wounds and pull up every root of unbelief in our souls.

We see that God did not coddle Gideon in his unbelief and fear, but said, "...Go in this might of yours, and you shall save Israel from the hand of the Midianites. Have I not sent you?" (v. 14). This is how the Lord will deal with us in this late hour, for we must rise above our doubts and insecurities and respond to the call that He has placed on our lives. No more excuses; we must die fully to ourselves as we take up our cross and follow Jesus wherever He may lead us. There is no more time to coddle our emotions. We will find that as we lay down our lives for Jesus and His kingdom, our emotions will be healed, and we will be made whole in this hour. We must die in order to truly live; there is no other way. There is a time to weep over our past and the deep losses that we have suffered, but we must not pitch a tent and live there for the rest of our lives. As we focus on the call that God has placed upon our lives, we will find that self-pity will leave, and we will rise up into that new glory that He has reserved just for us.

Gideon made many excuses, just like we all have, saying that his clan was the *weakest* in Manasseh, and that he was the least in his family's house (v. 15). Gideon did not realize that it was for these very reasons that God laid His hand on him—so that He alone would receive all the glory for the victory over the Midianites. God assured Gideon that He would be with him, just as the Lord assures us that He is with us through all the storms of life. Even after all of this assurance, Gideon still wanted a sign from the Lord, and the Lord granted it to his servant (vv. 17, 37-40). God is so patient and merciful toward us, for He will give us numerous signs of His presence as He strengthens and assures us of the calling that is upon our lives. He is a merciful and loving Father, who understands all of our weaknesses and fears; He is willing to draw us close and assure us of His great love for us, but we must come to Him and not run away in fear. God desires to consume us fully—our souls and bodies—even our very lives. If we are willing to allow His fire to burn up all that is unholy in us, we will then see Him face to face, just as Gideon did (vv. 19-23). When we say "Yes" to the Lord, He will give us peace and remove our fears, but we must be willing to surrender all.

As Gideon was willing to renounce and destroy the idols of his father's house, so must we renounce all ancestral iniquities, strongholds, and curses from our past (vv. 25-32). If we are willing to let go of every sin and allow the Spirit to purify every unholy motive that lies hidden within our hearts, only then will we experience total victory over our enemies, and we will run into our destiny unhindered. Many will come against us because of our uncompromised stand with the Lord, but God will stand with us and give us all the strength that we need to stand against the enemy of our souls. We will take the "land" (all of our hearts and lives), and we will give ourselves over to the Lord—fully.

After Gideon renounced the sin and darkness in his life, he was then ready to advance with his army. In Judges 7:2-3, we see that the army was too big, and God did not want Israel to take the glory that belonged to Him, saying, "My own hand has saved me." So whoever was afraid was told to leave, and 22,000 of the people left, with 10,000 remaining. The Lord told Gideon that there were still too many people, and that they were to go down to the water; it was here that they would be tested (v. 4). I see that the Lord is doing this very same thing in the hearts and lives of His end-time warriors. Many are being tested and are drinking the waters of affliction; God is looking deep inside many hearts to see if they are willing to obey Him and abandon all—no matter what the cost. The Lord is asking us to obey Him, even when it looks foolish, even when others do not understand and may even mock us. He is asking for implicit obedience in this hour, and there are only a "few," a Remnant, that will truly go all the way with the Lord (vv. 5-6).

After the army was tested at the water there were only *300* men left, and with these the Lord saved Israel from their enemies. With their trumpets and pitchers in their hands, they went forth in the might of the Lord. God was with them; it was God's power and ability in them that won the victory over the enemy that day. As they blew the trumpets and broke their pitchers, the Lord set every man's sword against his companion throughout the whole camp (vv. 20-22). God will put His Word in the mouths of the *Remnant* in this hour. They will cry out as a trumpet and speak the *whole truth* of God, not just parts of it, into our barren land, and life will spring forth in the hearts of multitudes. As the outer shell of their hearts are smashed, even as those pitchers were, the glory of God is going to pour through them and the enemy will scatter in confusion. Multitudes of chained souls will be freed in this hour and be brought into the kingdom of God. What an hour this will be, for when this Gideon Army rises, no one will be able to stop the glory that will come forth from their vessels. It will be the light and life of Jesus flowing through them, and God will receive *all* the glory!

Walking Behind the Veil

...that you may be filled with all the fullness of God.

Ephesians 3:19

There is a company of revolutionary leaders that will soon rise up in the power of the Lord. They will walk "behind the veil," in the "Shekinah" glory of God—the very manifest presence of God. God's glorious presence will be made manifest in their lives, and other's will see and feel God's power and holiness coming forth from them. They have boldly entered into "the Holiest," by the blood of Jesus. (See Hebrews 10:19.) This is the place of power, glory, miracles, and the holiness of God—that place where all will see Christ in you.

We have seen that when they built the tabernacle, there was the "outer court," the "Holy place," and the "Holy of Holies." What the Lord recently showed me corresponds with what happened in Gideon's army when it dwindled down to only 300 men. The "outer court" represents the original 32,000 that joined this army. This would represent the Body of Christ that has come to a place of repentance and acceptance of Jesus as their Savior. The "outer court" contained the altar and the laver. The altar would represent the cross of Jesus, for we have been saved through the blood of the Lamb, and the laver represents the Word of God, the washing of the water through the Word. (See Ephesians 5:26.) The laver was as a mirror (made of brass) in order to show us our sin—you could actually see your own reflection in it —and as a judge, the Word will expose our sin. This would represent the first test. Will we in *fear* cover our sin, or will we allow the light of His presence to expose it, in order to wash it away. In Gideon's army, this first test eliminated all who were afraid and fearful, and 22,000 left. The 10,000 that remained represent those who went on with the Lord into the "Holy Place."

The first item in the Holy Place is the *showbread*; it was ground and placed in the fire. This represents those who have entered this place and have been made *broken bread* in the hands of the Lord so that He might feed the multitudes through them. (See Matthew 15:36.) They have gone through purifying fires and their wills have been fully surrendered to Christ. As they continue to submit to this fire, they are continually renewed in their spirit-man and are made "vessels of honor" for the Master's use. Their wills have been crushed, and now their only desire is to do the Father's will.

The next item in the Holy Place is the *seven-branched lamp,* which represents the Holy Spirit in the life of the believer. He illumines our inner beings so that we can understand the Word of God through the renewing of our minds. (See Romans 12:2.) The lampstand was fashioned from beaten gold. As our Father scourges us in His loving discipline, we find that the "blows that hurt cleanse away evil, as do stripes the inner depths of the heart" (Prov. 20:30).

The next item in this place is the golden *altar of incense.* This is where our emotions are yielded and surrendered to the Lord as we pray and worship before His holy throne. Our hearts are penetrated by the Holy Spirit as He comes into our wounds through worship. As our hearts open to the Lord, He then brings His healing love—the "balm of Gilead." This is where His fire purifies us fully as He prepares to take us into the "Holy of Holies." The Remnant has surrendered their minds, wills, and emotions fully to the Lord in the "Holy Place," and God is ready to bring them into the "fullness of the stature of Christ," where the "soulish" man will no longer rule, but Christ *in* them will have full sway and control of their lives. Only 300 of the 10,000 in the "Holy Place" were willing to go all the way with the Lord and enter into the very "Holy of Holies."

The small, but powerful army that God is raising up in this hour will enter into the Holiest Place through the blood of Jesus and by the grace of God. It was a place of glory—the place of God's manifest presence. As we have seen, the "Holy Place" is that place of total surrender, where everything is laid on the altar of sacrifice before Him. All who desire to move on into the "Holy of Holies" must first go through this place of death. No flesh can stand in the presence of God, but there is a Remnant that is entering "behind the veil" in this very hour, a company of believer's that are willing to be fully identified with His cross. This small army will stand in the very glory and manifest presence of God! They will walk in a power and might that this world has not yet seen, for God will fill them to overflowing with His presence and power. They have journeyed from their natural senses to their spiritual senses, and no devil in hell will be able to stand against them; no man will destroy them in this final hour! This world has yet to see what God can do through a small band of totally committed, radical, and uncompromisingly dedicated people. This is how God is working in this hour, and only those who submit 100 percent of their lives to Him will be part of this end-time army.

Does this seem drastic to you? It is not, for God needs to use drastic measures to prepare an army that is strong enough in Him to stand against an enemy whose sole purpose is to kill, steal, and destroy! He needs those who are free from fear and doubt, and who will stand in full assurance of faith against a vicious enemy. He needs faithful warriors who will not back down or faint, but in holy boldness confront every evil, and who will speak the truth in love. God alone will receive all the glory and honor, for this work will not be accomplished through human wisdom and ingenuity, but through humble and broken vessels who know they can do nothing apart from His grace.

I want to give one more example of this end-time Remnant from Mark 4:20, which says, "But these are the ones sown on good ground, those who hear the word, accept it, and bear fruit: some thirtyfold, some sixty, and some a hundred." Here again we see this principle: The thirtyfold group would be those who come to the Lord for salvation and live in the outer courts; the sixtyfold group live in the Holy Place, and the third group is those who bring forth a hundredfold harvest of fruit in their lives, for they have given 100 percent—their whole lives—to the Lord. They have entered into the very Holy of Holies. Jesus' promise to them is found in Mark 10:29-30, which says, "...Assuredly, I say to you, there is no one who has left house or brothers or sisters or father or mother or wife or children or lands, for My sake and the gospel's, who shall not receive a hundredfold now in this time—houses and brothers and sisters and mothers and children and lands, with persecutions—and in the age to come, eternal life." There will be great persecutions, but compared to the glory of His presence, they will be light afflictions.

The one boast, the one aim of this elite group, will be to lift up the cross of Jesus to this lost and dying world. (See Galatians 6:14.) They preach Christ crucified to all who will listen—young or old, rich or poor, and every race, creed, nation, tongue and tribe. (See 1 Corinthians 2:23.) Nothing will keep this army from moving forward; they laugh at what man says is impossible.

When Sarah was 90 years old and Abraham 100, she birthed their son Isaac, the long-awaited son that God had promised them. This was the child of promise that they had believed for, and at the set time that God had promised, he came forth Sarah's dead womb. Through the long delay of waiting, Abraham became strong in faith, "...he did not consider his own body, already dead (since he was about a hundred years old), and the deadness of Sarah's womb. He did not waver at the promise of God through unbelief, but was strengthened in faith, giving glory to God, and being fully convinced that what He had promised He was also able to perform" (Rom. 4:19-21). May we, as Abraham, be fully convinced that God will keep His promises to us in this hour! I pray that God, by His grace, will strengthen and perfect our faith.

Recently the Lord gave my sister-in-law a powerful dream about the end-time War-Horses that He is about to reveal to the Church and to this world. In this dream, Denise, who is a part of the group of people that come to my house for Bible study and prayer, stood in front of a large window (meaning revelation), and as she looked out she saw a white horse, enormous in size, standing in majestic power. As a man and woman approached this horse, the man reached out his hand to touch him, and as he did, the horse immediately reared its front legs and kicked the man in his stomach so hard that he literally flew through the air away from the horse. In the dream, when my sister-in-law saw this, she knew that we had to pray immediately for this man who was kicked.

I prayed for revelation about this dream, and the Lord led me to 2 Samuel 6:2-7, which tells us about David bringing the ark of God back to the City of David on a new cart. When they came to Nachon's threshing floor, Uzza put out his hand to the ark of God and took hold of it, for the oxen stumbled. "Then the anger of the Lord was aroused against Uzza, and God struck him there for his error; and he died there by the ark of God (v. 7). As I pondered on this verse, the Lord led me to 1 Chronicles 15:13, which says, "For because you did not do it the first time, the Lord our God broke out against us, because we did not consult Him about the proper order" (emphasis added).

You see, there is a proper order in the way that we are to do things in the kingdom of God. The Levites were to bare the ark on their shoulders as Moses commanded, not put it on a new cart as the Philistines did (v. 15). God showed me that this final work that will be accomplished on this earth will be His work and *not* ours. It will be accomplished through those who have ceased from their own works and have entered into His rest fully. This work will be completed by those who have entered behind the veil; they will not be the works of the flesh.

The white horse represented the end-time move of the Spirit of God. As the "Holy Ark" could not be touched by the flesh of man, neither will this end-time move of the Spirit be controlled or touched by man's own reasoning or ability. Those who attempt to stop this move of God will be violently pushed out of the way by the Spirit of God. No man—no devil—will stop this end-time work of the Spirit! The White Horse also represents the Lord who judges and makes war; He is the mighty War-

Horse of heaven. (See Revelation 19:11-16.) It also represents those who the Lord will fill with His power and glory and use to bring in this last revival and outpouring that is coming to the earth.

In the back side of the desert, many in this Remnant have waited for years in faith, believing to finally see the promises of God come forth in their lives. In God's perfect timing they will experience the birth of their "Isaac" (meaning laughter), when God brings forth the fullness of these promises in their lives. They will experience a joy beyond measure that will overflow through their lives as they take hold of all that has been promised to them. They have grown strong in their faith through the delays, and now they are fully convinced that their heavenly Father loves them and that He is their faithful God. Their faith has been perfected in the fires of delay, and no doubt whatsoever mars their souls and lives. This is the faith of the Remnant, a perfect faith, a perfect love that will radiate through their lives in this final hour. These mighty warriors have given *all* to their Creator, and there is nothing that can compare to the blessings that He will bestow on them. We must not look at the deadness of our circumstances or feelings, but move forward in full assurance of faith and take all the "land" that He has promised us. Our God is faithful!

CONCLUSION

MY PRAYER FOR US is that we will be part of this Gideon Army, this Joshua Generation, and that by the grace of God we will walk in mighty signs, wonders, and miracles, such as this world has never seen. I pray that the very atmosphere around us be changed as we walk in His glory. As "vessels of honor," may we be used to bring in a multitude of souls—for the glory of His name.

This is a time of great acceleration in the Spirit; we will see these things come to pass quickly now. We must earnestly prepare our hearts and lives if we are to be a part of this end-time *move* of the Spirit of God. We must repent of our idolatrous ways and ask the Lord to purify our hearts in the deepest places within us. The very motives of our hearts must be exposed and purified, for only then will we be ready. If we prepare our hearts, we will find that when the fires of judgment come, they will not touch us, for all the darkness in our lives will have been already burned up!

I pray these Scriptures will encourage you as you press on to be part of His chosen *Remnant*; for not only are they meant for the physical nation of Israel, but they are also meant for us.

But I will leave within you the meek and humble. The remnant of Israel will trust in the name of the Lord. They will do no wrong; they will tell no lies. A deceitful tongue will not be found in their mouths. They will eat and lie down and no one will make them afraid. Sing, Daughter Zion; shout aloud, Israel! Be glad and rejoice with all your heart, Daughter Jerusalem! The Lord has taken away your punishment, he has turned back your enemy. The Lord, the King of Israel, is with you; never again will you fear any harm. On that day they will say to Jerusalem, "Do not fear, Zion; do not let your hands hang limp. The LORD YOUR GOD IS WITH YOU, THE MIGHTY WARRIOR WHO SAVES. HE WILL TAKE GREAT DELIGHT IN YOU; IN HIS LOVE HE WILL NO LONGER REBUKE YOU, BUT WILL REJOICE OVER YOU WITH SINGING... AT THAT TIME I WILL DEAL WITH ALL WHO OPPRESSED YOU. I WILL RESCUE THE LAME; I WILL GATHER THE EXILES. I WILL GIVE THEM PRAISE AND HONOR IN EVERY LAND WHERE THEY HAVE SUFFERED SHAME. AT THAT TIME I WILL GATHER YOU; AT THAT TIME I WILL BRING YOU HOME. I WILL GIVE YOU HONOR AND PRAISE AMONG ALL THE PEOPLES OF THE EARTH WHEN I RESTORE YOUR FORTUNES before your very eyes," says the Lord.

Zephaniah 3:12-17, 19-20 (NIV)

Word from the Lord:

"Rejoice, oh children of Zion—this is My hour—your hour of victory! I have already won the victory so long ago, but now, so many years later, there is going to be a glory coming into your nation and to many nations in this hour—this glory will explode in the hearts of My children and will release millions upon millions of captives!

"Rejoice—for all the blood, sweat, and tears of the martyrs through the ages will now bring forth this harvest that you are about to see, walk in, and experience! It is a glorious day to be alive, My children, for never has there been, nor will there ever be again, the outpouring that is about to be poured out over the nations!

"Multitudes of angels are gathering in strategic places. They are getting places ready— getting people ready—for the last great outpouring. If I would show you, or try to explain to you

the magnitude of the outpouring, you would not be able to take it in! But know this, My children, it is so much bigger—so much greater than you could ever fathom! You do not want to miss it children! You do not want to negate the place and position that I have for you in this final ingathering of souls. Don't miss it! Ready your hearts! Abandon all for My sake and for My kingdom! Seek Me above all, and care not what others say or do against you. Believe Me, it will not matter, for you will be so caught up in My glory, that nothing will disturb you—nothing evil will penetrate your hearts—for you will be full of My glory!

"It's time for release—a release of all that is in your hearts and lives that is not of Me. Release is here! Take hold of it! Let go of all your past now and begin to receive what I have for you in the glory realm—miracles beyond words—even creative ones that you never even dared to dream, will I work through your hands, through your yielded vessels. Blinded eyes opened and deafened ears hearing, a glory cloud of signs and wonders so glorious that the human tongue will not be able to express it! Signs in the heavens—signs on the earth— even heavenly angelic visitations daily! What you have experienced up to now is nothing compared to what is coming! Prepare your hearts for visitations—My angels—even My own Presence coming to meet with you in the night season!

"Open wide your mouth and declare My praises—declare the truth of who I am—the truth of My cross—and the truth of My glorious resurrection power.

"Rise up into a new level now—a new place in Me—and do not be timid. Fear and timidity will be swallowed up in My glory. No more groveling in the dust and the ashes of your past. Rise up, strong and mighty warriors, and put on My strength, even as Gideon did! I give you My Spirit of power and might so that you will be able to accomplish My will now. No more defeat! No more dragging your feet! Begin to run—begin to possess now! The finish line is right before you. Stretch out your arm and break through that spiritual ribbon, that finish line, and rise up into that glory cloud—My chariot of fire!

"This is not the time to be slack or to be passive in the Spirit. This race is for the swift, the bold, and the stout-hearted—not for the fearful and timid! See yourself, My children, as the warriors in Me that you are meant to be. Be part of the Remnant, the small Gideon Army that I have called you to be. There must be no more delay! Come forth out of the fire and out of the troubled waters that you have been in, and put on the warrior cloak of victory! It is for you—for YOU! Receive it—believe it, My children—and come out of the dark now and run in the light of My glory! I love you—now and forever! -Your God
(Given to me on November 3, 2011)

Remember: Keep your focus on Jesus, for He alone is "...the author and finisher of our faith." For "He who calls you is faithful, who also will do it." (See Hebrews 12:2, 1 Thessalonians 5:24.)

If you desire to be freed from the unbelief that has shackled your life for so long and to be a part of this Remnant, this Joshua Generation, then pray this prayer with me:

"Father, I ask that You set me free from all unbelief—through the power of the cross and through the shed blood of Your Son. My earnest desire is to be a part of this Remnant, this end-time army that will go across this nation and the nations of this world. I am willing to pay the cost and to lay down my life as a living sacrifice for You. Free me from myself—all selfishness and all self-pity—and make me into the warrior that You have called me to be. I'm willing to be broken, and I surrender my will fully to You, Father. Take my life and do with me as You desire, and may my earnest, daily prayer be: Father, not my will but Yours be done.

"I trust You, Jesus, and I will no longer doubt the love that You have revealed to me through the cross. It cost You everything to free me from this insidious sin of unbelief and from all the sin in my life. It tore Your heart to shreds, and I will no longer take lightly the agonizing suffering You went through to redeem, not only my spirit, but my soul and body. I surrender fully to Your work in my life, Holy Spirit. Forgive me for doubting that You are ...able to do exceedingly abundantly above all that we ask or think, according to the power that works in us. All things are possible with You, Father. Make me into that child of faith that You have called me to be. Lead me now and guide me into the fullness that you have for my life, so that Your purposes through me will be accomplished in this hour. In the name of Jesus I pray these things. Amen."

ABOUT THE AUTHOR

THERESA REYNA WAS BORN and raised in Milwaukee, Wisconsin, and currently lives in Cudahy, Wisconsin, with her husband Ron. She has three grown children—April, Sarah, and James. She also has five grandchildren—Alicia, Amber, Nathaniel, Annabel, and the youngest, Savannah Rose. They are the joy of her life—after Jesus, of course!

Theresa was born again in 1976 and has walked with the Lord through many trying times and fiery trials in preparation for the call and vision He has placed on her life. In 2006, the Lord led her to Midwest Bible College through New Song Church in Greenfield, Wisconsin. She has a Master's degree in Biblical Studies and was ordained by Son Rise Ministries in November of 2009.

Theresa has ministered in various places in the past years, preaching and teaching the Word of God, and she loves to dance prophetically before the Lord. A small group of loved ones and friends meet at her house for weekly Bible study and prayer.

Her passion is to see others set free by the Word of God and by the power of the Spirit. God has granted her a forerunner's anointing to call the Body of Christ to repentance and into the freedom of the Spirit of God. Her passion is for missions, and there is a strong call on her life to go to China and the nations of this world.

This is Theresa's first book.

ACKNOWLEDGEMENTS

THERE ARE SO MANY that I would like to thank for the love and support that they have shown me through the years.

Thank you Ron for the love and support you have given me as I spent countless hours at the computer putting this book together. We've been through thick and thin; God knew what He was doing when He put us together 40 years ago.

My beloved children, April, Sarah, and James, you saw the call on my life even when I struggled deeply through many trials and dark days of suffering. Our tough times together have strengthened us and prepared us for the days ahead.

For those who stood with me through my "dark night"—words cannot express the love that I feel for you. Sharon, Patty, Denise, Ken, Alanna, Tanya, Sasha, Delbert, Sherri, Joanne, Linda, Pastors John and Rene, Eva, Guy and Renee, and to all who have prayed and given me support—I love you! Delbert, you'll never know how your words of encouragement uplifted and strengthened me through the years—I bless you.

Thanks Pastor Roy for teaching and preaching the message of holiness and repentance. It is not a popular message, but the knowledge of God's truth will set many captives free. The best is yet to come.

Julie, thanks so much for your labor of love in the editing of this book. It wasn't by chance that the Lord brought us together to complete this work for the glory of His name.

Jesus, You are my Joy, my Peace, my Inspiration, my Comfort, my All in All. *All* glory goes to You alone. You are my passion and my delight— now and forever.

THE JOSHUA GENERATION

There's a generation coming forth – in purity and power,
In passionate love they seek the Lord – in this glorious, final hour.
They've repented of their deepest sins – all their idols are cast down,
And they walk with their dear Savior – in a pure, white, spotless gown.
They're single-minded in their walk – their home is up above,
God has freed them from all bitterness – and they walk in perfect love.
This is the Joshua Generation – they're running the great race,
Their eyes are fixed on Christ alone – as they gaze upon His face.
They're as bold as a strong lion – and yet gentle as a lamb,
They bow only to Christ's Lordship – and do not fear the face of man.
They lift their hearts in worship – and look only to their King,
And they speak His truth in boldness – and to Him alone they sing.
The Lord, so strong and mighty – has won all of their battles,
They walk in overcoming power – as hell's gates now shake and rattle!
The King of glory has come in – and consumed their inner being,
And as they walk in full obedience – it's <u>His</u> vision they are seeing!
This Joshua Generation – they live high on God's Holy Hill,
They've seen the Lord transfigured – and they do only <u>His</u> good will.
Their desire is to please the Lord – and not the heart of man,
They've counted the cost to serve the King
– and in Him alone they stand.
They are a people who are separate
– they love not the things of this world,
Daily they cut down their enemies – as Christ's mighty sword they hurl!
In freedom, they now walk in power – under a wide and open heaven,
For all their sins have been removed – along with <u>all</u> of the leaven.

On Mount Zion up above they stand
– and receive the Lord's great blessing,
They've pushed through all the darkness
– and into glory they are pressing!
They rule over their oppressors – and have taken from them great spoil,
They're anointed by a mighty God – and are smeared with His holy oil.
God will bring them forth in strength and power
– into their "promised land,"
A holy, undefiled nation – for in His righteousness they stand.
They know deep rest from all their sorrow
– from bondage and from fear,
For their precious Lord and Savior – has wiped away their every tear.
Will you join this great army – and walk in Christ's passion and zeal,
And make that full commitment
– as before the Lord you humbly kneel?
If you confess all of your sin and shame
– and your weakness that's so great,
You'll be used by your Lord and Master
– to rescue souls from Satan's fate!
God asks, "Will you open up your heart
– and surrender to Me your all?
And lay down your life completely – to answer My great call?"

COME TO ME

(Matthew 11:28-30)

"Come to Me, My dear children – in your heavy labor,
And you will find rest – in My deep love and favor.
You have labored so long – and have birthed many souls,
Now it's time to find rest – and see that I am your goal.
For these things have been working – to bring you to Me,
To experience My glory – and to set you now free.
Lay your head on My shoulder – and rest in My arms,
As I draw you so close – and keep you safe from all harm.
You have struggled and battled – with an enemy so strong,
But you'll find full release – before very long!
You've labored and sought Me - with strong, earnest desire,
And now I'm coming, My beloved – to consume you with fire!
You've grown weary and weak – walked through waters so deep,
And have climbed a high mountain – so wide and so steep.
You have been heavy laden – with sorrow and grief,
But here in My Presence – you will find sweet relief.
Take My yoke now upon you – for it is easy and light,
And rest from your struggle – and your long, fearsome fight!
Learn of Me and receive – for I am lowly in heart,
Take hold of My peace – and know we never will part.
In quietness and trust – you will find a deep rest,
For I'll flood you with glory – yes, I'll give you My best!
Sweet peace and deep rest – is what I have now in store,
For I'll mend your heart fully – and repair what's been torn.

So come, don't delay – you'll find My grace is sufficient,
And I'll send you forth quickly – to accomplish <u>My</u> mission.
In ease and in joy – you will run near and far,
Like a bird out of prison – never more to be barred!"

SPIRITUAL REVOLUTION

"There's a revolution that is coming - to My Church in this
final hour,
An explosion of My Spirit – that will release My awesome
power!
Many in the Church are dissatisfied – and are looking for so
much more,
And soon My prophetic leaders will rise - and go forth with
My mighty roar!
This revolution will be painful and bloody – for some will
resist this great change,
For there's pride and rebellion in their hearts – but they
struggle against Me in vain!
For My Kingdom will come forth in power – in the Holy
Sprit's great might,
And I say to you now, My dear children – it will not be
without a great fight!
Like a dam that is full and about to burst – it is coming
forth now so strong,
Many of My children have prayed for this hour – and have
waited for O' so long
For you see, this is a new season – and My foundation must
be laid -
Of holiness and repentance – full heart surrender must now
be made!
Prophetic leaders have been prepared – in their dark and
hidden caves,

They will now come forth out of the desert – and with Me
will ride the waves!
I have called these *children of destiny* – and their mantles are
now ready,
And in the Spirit and power of Elijah – they'll walk with Me
firm and steady.
They'll release My power and glory – into the nations that
are so dark,
As new and sharpened instruments – they will never miss
the mark!
This Elijah Company will be strong – In miracles, signs, and
wonders,
They'll take much spoil from the enemy – precious souls as
their great plunder!
They will outrun the "chariot of Ahab" – as Elijah did so
long ago,
Overcoming this world in the power of My Spirit – and
defeating every foe!
Nations will be turned around – in this great and awesome
transformation,
Governments will bow to Me – and to My Kingdom's full
formation!
Many nations will tremble before Me – and the devil's
kingdom will now shake,
As the gates of Hell are torn down fully – and captive souls
My children take!
In the Spirit and power of Elijah – they'll call fire down
from heaven –
And remove from My Church completely – all the sin and
all the leaven!
They've been fully trained in the desert – for many, many
years,
But now I will commission them – and wipe away all of
their tears!
No longer will they look with shame - at their own stature,
small and weak,
For I'll fill them with My Holy Spirit – to do mighty
spiritual feats!

They'll prepare the way for My soon coming – with a new
and heavenly sound,
And through strong prayer and intercession – they will as
Joshua, take new ground!
They are simple, ordinary people – who have hungered and
sought Me for years –
In brokenness and deep repentance – and yes, with many,
many tears,
They've given their lives completely to Me – and have
counted the cost so great,
Won't you be part of this *Company* – and bring in the lost
before it's too late?"

TOTAL RECOVERY

"You have been robbed, My dear child – your identity has been taken,
But now in your deepest heart – My new life will fully awaken.
I'll restore what I've promised – and you'll rejoice with great wonder,
As I give you My best gifts – along with the enemies spoils and plunder.
No more will you tremble – with intimidation and with fear -
Before men or strongest devil – for you'll know that I'm near.
You will stand firm in My power – and tear down the gates of Hell.
And you'll hear Me say clearly - "Child, in this hour, all is well."
I'll lift you up into My loving arms – and bring you into glory,
So you can go throughout this world – and tell My Redemption story.
For so long you've sat in darkness – in gloom and deepest shame,
But now I'll restore you fully - and give to you a glorious, new name!
Your season of winter is over, child – and the ice in your heart will melt,
And in My mercy and compassion – My deep love will now be felt!
The calling and vision I've given – has in you, child, all but died,
But now in My resurrection power – you'll see that I've not lied!
All My promises will come to pass – for in Me they are, "Yes and
Amen,"
And as My mouthpiece and ambassador – it is YOU that I will send!
You'll go to nations far away – and cross many waters so deep.
And a multitude of souls will come to Me - a great harvest you will reap!
A new strength and power you will find – I'll restore you to full health,
I'll open up My heavenly storehouse – and you'll know My spiritual
wealth!
With My passion restored in your deep heart – inflamed with My holy
fire -

You will walk and never faint, dear one - and in Me you will never tire!
Sing and rejoice, Oh barren one, for the fullness of time has come,
For what is birthed inside you now – is Jesus Christ, God's Son!
This is the day of restoration – I'll fill your mouth with laughter,
And with Me, your heavenly Prince and King - you'll live happily ever
after!"

The Dark Night Of The Soul

In darkest of night – when all seems so lost,
It is then that we find – how much it will cost –
To follow our Lord – and to go *all the way* --
As we embrace our cross daily – and go into the fray.
You see, there's a cross – we are called to embrace,
As we follow His will – and run in this race.
When the waves are so high – we can rest in His arms,
And we'll find He's our Shelter – and are safe from all harm.
When the enemy of our souls – comes in like a flood,
It is then that we'll see – the power of His blood!
The storm brings great fear – and chains try to bind,
But now in His Spirit – it is Christ we will find.
There's lightning and rain – and sounds of great thunder,
But in the storm we will find – our chains torn asunder!
We're free in Your love – Your Word tells us so,
The power of Your blood – has defeated every foe.
With our eyes on You, Lord – and not on the waves,
We can walk on the water – and know You will save.
"Come out of the boat" – I hear the Lord say,
For the night is now past – this is a new day!
Take My hand, dearest child – and I'll give you My peace,
And you'll find that your soul – is now fully released.
Hells gates have been shattered – by your deep cries of pain,
And in the midst of your sorrow – I've washed away every stain.
Your dark night is over – I've made you so strong,
You'll see now My grace – as I right every wrong.

It's not in the good times – that My glory is shown,
But deep in the pit – that My presence is known.
Embrace every cross – that I send in My love,
Keep your focus on Me – and look always above.
My light that's within you – will never grow dim,
You'll see Me now clearly – for I've conquered your sin!
Look not at the darkness – but finish the race,
For soon in My glory – you'll gaze on My face!"

Made in the USA
Columbia, SC
10 November 2019